KENTUCKY COLONIZATION IN TEXAS

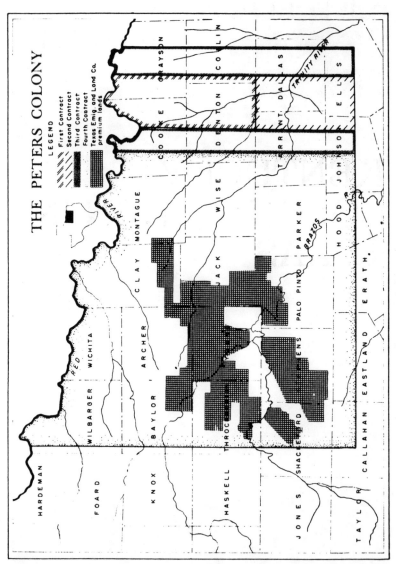

The Peters Colony of Texas

KENTUCKY COLONIZATION IN TEXAS

A History of the Peters Colony

BY SEYMOUR V. CONNOR

CLEARFIELD COMPANY

Reprinted for
Clearfield Company, Inc. by
Genealogical Publishing Co., Inc.
Baltimore, Maryland
1994

Originally published in *The Register*
of the Kentucky Historical Society
(January 1953 - October 1954).
Excerpted and reprinted in book form by
Genealogical Publishing Co., Inc.
Baltimore, 1983.
Library of Congress Catalogue Card Number 83-80997
International Standard Book Number 0-8063-1032-4
Made in the United States of America

NOTE

This work originally appeared in eight consecutive installments in *The Register of the Kentucky Historical Society* between January 1953 and October 1954. With the permission of the Kentucky Historical Society and the author, Seymour V. Connor, the eight articles have been gathered together and reproduced in this present form.

Readers might note that an expanded version of this work was published by The Texas State Historical Association in 1959 under the title *The Peters Colony of Texas*. Since this later publication contained very few revisions or additions of genealogical substance, we have chosen to reprint the more concise *Register* version.

Genealogical Publishing Company

KENTUCKY COLONIZATION IN TEXAS

A HISTORY OF THE PETERS COLONY
SEYMOUR V. CONNOR

Part I

The Colonization Law and Its Originators

In the year 1841 a number of small business men from Louisville, Kentucky, chanced to interfere in the affairs of the Republic of Texas in a way which may well have altered the destiny of that state and consequently, as small things sometimes do, changed the course of American history. These Kentuckians were unpretentious men, of small means, and had they known its ultimate consequences they might never have dared to begin an action which was certainly to have a marked effect on Texas history if it was not to shape the course of empire. For the Kentuckians were to be responsible for determining a Texas land and immigration policy at a critical time in the history of the Republic.

Land and immigration in Texas were closely associated. From 1836, when Texas won her independence from Mexico, until 1845, when she finally became a state in the Federal Union, Texans struggled constantly to maintain their Republic against the ravages of Mexican armies, Indian depredations, political hanky-panky, and, worst of all, bankruptcy and economic collapse. The salvation of the Republic, as all Texans knew, was an increase in population. Immigrants would bring in new money, buy land, man the army and navy, pay taxes, fight Indians, stimulate trade and commerce, push back the frontier, and in countless other ways support the new Republic. To private citizens in Texas an increase in population also meant an increase in land values and consequently an increase in private fortunes, for then, even more than today, land was the basic feature of Texas economy.

So in their legislative assemblies Texans, as individuals, were rent between the public necessity of attracting immigrants by offers of free government land and the private desire to put a fixed price on government land in order to uphold the value of privately owned land. The Texan heritage was that of the American

1

frontier, where since 1820 the minimum price on government land had been $1.25 per acre; but the Texans themselves had known the powerful inducement of free land. Most of them had come to Texas to receive the free *league and labor* (4,605.5 acres) which the Mexican government had generously offered to settlers under the old *empresario* system. For five years Texans postponed establishing a permanent land policy, clinging to the intention of eventually putting a price on the public land, but during that time passing a number of temporary laws granting free land to settlers in the Republic. In the winter of 1840-1841, the darkest period in the history of the Republic, circumstances demanded a more progressive land policy. Various bills were presented to the Texas Congress suggesting the establishment of empresario colonies to induce migration, after the earlier practice of the Mexican government. One bill in particular found favor with many, including the astute Sam Houston who had then finished his first term as president of the Republic and was serving as a representative from San Augustine. The bill was known as the Franco-Texienne Bill, and it incurred the wrath of a good many Anglo-Americans in Texas because it proposed the establishment of a colony of French soldiers on the Texas frontier. The debate over this bill was fierce in Congress and fiery in the editorial columns of Texas's few newspapers. One editor rebuked Houston and the bill's supporters as follows:

> And in this grand scheme of conquest where would Texas be found? The puny fraction of a French colony! And what would be the reward for all this sacrifice of territory and perhaps of nationality? Protection from the incursions of a handful of naked, half-starved, unarmed savages, who in less than two years will be scattered to the four winds by the hosts of hardy pioneers that are pressing into their hunting grounds.[2]

The "host of hardy pioneers" was editorial phantasy, yet it was such a dream of a host of Anglo-American settlers, combined with the popular distaste for foreigners, that brought about the defeat of the Franco-Texienne project.[3] Congress dropped the French proposal partially because of the strong opposition to it and partially because the timely introduction of an alternate plan offered a scheme far more likely to please the public. This new plan seems to have reached Congress initially in the form of a petition or memorial signed by twenty men who declared their interest in colonizing some unoccupied portion of the Republic.[4]

These petitioners were the originators of the Peters colony; of the twenty whose names were affixed to the well-timed memorial, eleven were residents of London, England, and nine of Louisville, Kentucky. The Englishmen were Daniel S. Carroll, Alexander McRea, Rowland Gibson, Robert Espie, William Oldmixon, Daniel Spillman, Robert Hume, John Salmon, William Byrne, Henry Richards, and Robert Stringer. The Americans were W. S. Peters, John Bansamere

(Bansamen?), William Scott, Phineas J. Johnson, Timothy Cragg, and Samuel Browning.[5]

Virtually no information at all has been found to clarify the origin of the petition to congress. Apparently the men who signed it were not prominent and whatever documents they may have preserved in connection with the petition have not come to light. What little is known about the men is presented in the next few paragraphs. The origin of the petition itself is entirely a matter of speculation. Of the Englishmen who signed, nothing is known except that they were probably residents of London. The eleven Londoners actually are relatively unimportant to the history of the Peters colony. Never active in the colony's early affairs, in December, 1842, this group transferred its interest in the colony to a second group of Englishmen whose story will be developed later in this work.[6] Only one of these Englishmen, Daniel J. Carroll, is known to have visited Texas.[7] Carroll apparently made several trips to the United States and to Texas, and may have been in Texas when the original law was passed, though this is strictly conjectural.

Of the Americans, little more is known. No information about either William Scott or John Bansamere has yet been found; indeed, the actual spelling of Bansamere's name is in doubt. Phineas J. Johnson was located in the Federal census of 1830 in Jefferson County, Kentucky.[8] He appeared as a resident of Louisville, between 40 and 50 years of age; he had six children and owned no slaves. Unfortunately the census of 1830 contains no other vital information, such as occupation, value of real estate, etc. The Kentucky census for 1840 was not available to the writer; however, a city directory of Louisville for the year 1843[9] does not list Phineas J. Johnson. From the tenor of the reference to the petition in the *House Journal* of the Texas Congress,[10] it might possibly be inferred that Phineas Johnson was one of the men who presented the memorial to congress directly. Johnson did make one or more trips to the colony on business, but he never became a resident of Texas.

Timothy Cragg was not listed in Louisville on the Census for 1830, but he was listed in the Louisville directory in 1843. At that time he was residing on the west side of 4th Street, between Main and Market Streets, and was a member of the firm of T. P. and T. Cragg, located at the same address.[11] According to the firm's advertising card in the same directory, "T. P. & T. Cragg still continues to manufacture Pianofortes, which they warrant of the best materials, workmanship, tone, and durability. Purchasers are respectively invited to call and examine before they buy, as we will sell low for cash. Pianofortes for hire. Tuning and repairing done with neatness and dispatch."[12]

Two other items have been found concerning Timothy Cragg. One of these is the statement that he died in 1841;[13] the other is the following brief statement from a musical history:

> Timothy Cragg and his brother, Thomas P. Cragg, associated themselves together under the firm name of T. P. and T. Cragg about the year 1835 or 1836. They entered into the manufacture and sale of pionafortes, and made good and sweet-toned pianos until about 1850 . . .[14]

Samuel Browning, a son-in-law of W. S. Peters, [15] was neither listed in Louisville on the census for 1830 nor in the directory for 1843. Browning was in Texas in August, 1841, when he signed the first contract for the Louisville petitioners, and probably he came earlier to present the petition of the twenty men to congress. Apparently he resided in Austin for about a year and moved in the winter of 1841 or the following spring to the colony area, where he died in 1844.[16]

The Peters family seem to be the most important persons signing the petition, yet very little is known of them either. W. S. Peters was the father of W. C., H. J., and John.[17] William Smalling Peters was an Englishman by birth, and although he lived in the United States for a number of years, he never became naturalized. One of the executives of the Louisville company which later colonized the Peters grant wrote:

> I have just learned that old man Wm. S. Peters who's now in London and the original contractor with the Government of Texas, together with his son Henry J. Peters and [mss. unreadable] others of the family who are interested in the stock of our company, are all aliens. They were born in Great Britain and have never taken an oath of allegiance to the United States altho they are all residents of this country.[18]

W. S. Peters is known to have returned to England in the summer of 1847,[19] and he may have made other trips to Europe. It seems probable that he was the organizing force behind the petition to congress, since his name headed the list of the twenty grantees, since the colony almost immediately became known as "Peters' Colony," and since he could have enlisted the English petitioners through his contacts in England. It has been suggested that he visited Texas as early as 1823, though this is uncertain.[20] In the *Dallas News*, on March 1, 1941, there appeared a picture of a man presumed to be W. S. Peters.[21]

The greatest part of the information found on the Peters family is connected with William C. Peters, who was the most prominent member of the family.[22] William Cumming Peters was born in Woodbury, Devonshire, England on March 10, 1805. He came to America with his parents about 1820 and taught music in Pittsburgh from 1825 to 1828. In 1829 he moved to Louisville, Kentucky, where he may have opened a music store.[23] Apparently he returned very soon to Pittsburgh, for on December 8, 1830, he inserted the following advertisement in a Pittsburgh paper:

A few months later Peters announced that he would play a public concert:

Mr. Peters will give a concert on Wednesday evening next, the 16th inst. [February] at Mr. Band's Concert Hall, on Penn Street. Tickets may be obtained in the principal Book Stores.

The qualifications of this gentleman as a musician are already too well known and admired to require comment from us.

Mr. Burns is engaged to perform some Solos on the Kent bugle, which alone would be a treat of no ordinary value.[25]

By the close of 1831, Peters had gone into business with W. D. Smith and John Mellor, selling sheet music and musical instruments.[26] Apparently he continued giving music lessons, and sometime about this period (or perhaps earlier) was engaged as a music teacher by the family of Stephen Collins Foster, who lived in Pittsburgh during the songwriter's youth[27]

During the eighteen-thirties (probably 1832) Peters moved again to Louisville, opening a music store and continuing to give music lessons, and in 1839 he opened a branch store in Cincinnati.[28] He is listed in the Louisville directory for 1843 as the proprietor of a music store on the south side of Main Street between 3rd and 4th Streets, with a residence on the East side of 1st Street between Chestnut and Prather Streets.[29] Cincinnati directories give the following addresses for the Peters firm in that city:

1864—Peters & Company . . . South side of Fourth Street between Main and Sycamore.
1849—Peters, Field & Co . . . 12th and Walnut Streets.
1851—William C. Peters & Son . . . Melodian Bldg., cor. Fourth and Walnut.[30]

It was during this period that Peters was associated with the colonization venture in Texas. At the time the petition was presented to congress, William C. Peters was still relatively unknown; he later gained more fame both as a composer and as a publisher of music. By 1846 Peters, Field and Company were established as music publishers in Cincinnati, and in that year this firm published Stephen Foster's melody "There's a Good Time Coming." A year later Peters copyrighted Foster's "Lou'siana Belle" and "What Must a Fairy's Dream Be?" During 1848 Peters published a longer list of Foster's songs: "Uncle Ned," "Stay Summer Breath," "Susanna Don't You Cry,"[31] "Away Down South," and "Santa Anna's Retreat from Buena Vista." In the years that followed Peters published only an occasional song for Foster, since the songwriter had made business arrangements with a New York publisher, but the melodies of 1848 proved to be for Peters, a commercial bonanza. It has been said that Peters made $10,000 from the sale of "O, Susanna," alone, and it seems generally to be thought that Peters dealt unfairly with Stephen Foster. That the latter was not the case, Foster's biographers, from his brother to the present time, have been careful to show, but nevertheless the tradition of the unscrupulous publisher perserveres. In point of fact it seems that an unexpected payment, which Peters made to Foster for "O, Susanna," and "Uncle Ned," turned Stephen Foster into a commercial songwriter. Foster had given those songs, as well as the earlier ones, to Peters as a gift, no doubt as a friendly gesture to his old friend and music teacher. Foster wrote in connection with "O, Susanna" and "Uncle Ned": "Imagine my delight in receiving one hundred dollars in cash! . . . the two fifty dollars bills I received for it had the effect of starting me on my vocation of song-writer."[32] The spectacular and unexpected success of Foster's songs, especially "O, Susanna," was probably viewed in good spirit by both Foster and Peters as a lucky business gamble. The notion that Foster was anything but grateful to Peters is unfounded. In 1849 Foster wrote to a critic:

> I hasten to acknowledge the receipt of your favor of the 21st. . . I gave manuscript copies of each of the songs "Lou'siana Belle"–"Uncle Ned"–"O, Susanna," to several persons before I gave them to Mr. Peters for publication. Mr. Peters has my receipt for each of the songs."[33]

The songs of Foster that Peters published were extremely popular, and probably made a substantial profit. Peters, however, was not the only early publisher of Foster's music; dozens of pirated editions have been found. That Peters made some money in this venture can be gathered from the fact that in 1849 he expanded his business, opening a branch in Baltimore. The following year Peters began the publication of a monthly musical magazine which ran for twelve issues. It was called *The Baltimore Olio and American Musical Gazette,* and has been described as a "monthly parlor companion designed for ladies and devoted chiefly to music, the arts, and musical intelligence generally."[34] The twelfth and last issue of the magazine contained a statement that the *Olio* was being discontinued, not because of lack of support, but because of the difficulty of securing music plates in Baltimore and because Peters' health was poor.[35] Peters returned to Cincinnati and died there suddenly of heart disease on April 20, 1866.[36]

In addition to his business ventures, Peters had been active as a leader of choirs and concerts, and composed a number of pieces of music, both religious and secular. His most significant religious writing was a mass for the Roman Catholic Church. He also compiled *Peters Catholic Harmonist* (1848), and *Catholic Harp* (1862). Among his secular compositions were "Citizens Guards March" (1841); "Sweet Memories of Thee" (1839); and "Kind, Kind and Gentle is She" (1840). He edited a revised and enlarged edition of Burrowes Piano

Forte Primer (1849, again revised in 1869), and compiled several other additional pieces, including the Eclectic Piano Instructor (1855).[37]

Henry J. Peters, William C. Peters' brother, also was a musician of some ability. Henry J. was younger than William; he was listed in the Louisville directory for 1843 as a "Professor of Music," at William's store,[38] and he seems to have succeeded to the proprietorship of the store about 1847. About that time he took Benedict J. Webb into partnership with him,[39] and in 1850 Peters and Webb reorganized as Peters, Cragg and Company, amalgamating with T. P. and T. Cragg mentioned earlier. This firm manufactured and sold pianos and retailed other musical instruments and sheet music.[40] According to the best of the somewhat sketchy information available, Thomas P. Cragg withdrew from the firm in 1860, but the firm continued to manufacture pianos as the Peters, Webb Company. "Their trade grew and spread over a large portion of the South, with important agencies at Nashville, Memphis, Vicksburg, New Orleans, Mobile, and Galveston, as well as St. Louis . . . and they continued to make exceedingly fine-toned pianos."[41] About 1877 Peters and Webb closed out their stock and dissolved their firm.

About that same time, Henry J. Peters moved with his family to some of the land in Texas that had accrued to him as his share of the colonization venture. The family, consisting of Henry J. and his wife Mary A. Peters; two sons, Harry and Carl; and a daughter, Adele (Peters) Benedict and her children, Harry Yandell (later president of the University of Texas) and Carl Peters Benedict, settled in Young County, Texas. According to tombstones in the Oak Grove Cemetery in Graham, Mary A. Peters died July 5, 1877, at 59 years of age, and Henry died the following year, August 28, 1878, at 62 years of age.[42]

Much less is known about the third son of W. S. Peters. His name was John Peters, and he was a signer of the original petition to congress. There was a John Peters listed in the Louisville directory of 1843 as a shoemaker, and after the Civil War a John Peters began publishing music in New York.

In the above paragraphs the present writer has put down virtually everything that he has been able to learn about the original petitioners. The information is entirely too meager. Nothing was found to indicate by whom or in what way the petition was originated. That its timeliness at the Fifth Congress of the Republic of Texas was simply conincidental is hard to believe, yet there is nothing to show otherwise. That the type of people whose names were on the petition could be capable of instigating the colonization venture and could have the initiative to draw up the petition is also hard to believe, but again there is nothing yet found to indicate otherwise. The only conclusion to be drawn from the available evidence is that W. S. Peters was chiefly responsible for the promotion of the colony.

7

The memorial, signed by the petitioners who have been discussed above, was presented to congress prior to January 14, 1841. The earliest mention of it was made on that date in the *House Journal* which stated:

> The committee on the state of the Republic to which was referred the memorial of Johnson, Browning and others, asking permission to introduce emigrants within the Republic. . . reported by a bill to that effect.[43]

The bill passed through the customary parliamentary channels, perhaps receiving some special attention from congress because of its timeliness, and after having been several times changed and amended finally emerged from the senate on February 1, 1841,[44] It became law when signed by Acting President David G. Burnet on February 4, 1841.[45] Essentially the law was an imitation of the Mexican empresario law. It empowered the president of the Republic to enter into an empresario contract with the twenty petitioners and provided an elaborate legal basis for that contract. The twenty petitioners were specifically named in the law, and the privileges outlined were exclusively theirs, although later laws extended the privileges to other empresarios.[46] Thus the action initiated by Peters in 1841 soon became the fundamental basis of Texas land and immigration policy during the time of the Republic and resulted in the settlement of a large colony of Germans around Fredericksberg and New Braunfels and a smaller colony of Swiss and French around Castroville. According to the law, colonists who were heads of families would after three years receive up to 640 acres and single men up to 320 acres if a "good and comfortable cabin" were built on the place and at least fifteen acres of the tract were fenced and cuiltivated. Sections 8 and 9 of the law anticipated that the empresarios would demand a portion of the 640-acre and 320-acre tracts as recompense for their services to individual colonists, by prohibiting the contractors from taking more than half of a colonist's grant.

The law of February 4, 1841, gave legal foundation to a shift in Texas land policy and a shift from unpromoted migration on an individual basis to migration promoted in a manner similar to Mexico's earlier policy. The law also gave legal foundation to the establishment of the Peters colony and the consequent development of the Dallas-Denton-Grayson County region by the empresarios. There is no question that the area would have, sooner or later, been settled; it is a moot question, much debated in its day, whether the empresarios were a help or a hindrance to the area's development.

Part II

Organization of the Texas Emigration and Land Company

Although the law of February 4, 1841, did not establish the colony, it did authorize the president of the Republic to enter into an empresario contract with those persons named in the law, and it set fourth in fairly minute detail the provisions which such a contract might include. Hence, prior to the settlement of the colony, the twenty empresarios had to organize themselves, sign a contract with the government, and make plans for carrying out the contract. As it turned out, a contract was made before the empresarios had any sort of organization, and settlement was begun before any plans for it were made. It is the purpose of this chapter to relate the history of the early business relations of the empresarios; later chapters will deal with the actual settlement of the colony.

It is curious that despite the timeliness of their original memorial or request in January 1841 and the immediate consideration given it by congress, the empresarios delayed almost seven months before first contracting with the government under the provisions of a law which had been passed at their behest. This delay was caused by the lack of organization among the petitioners, and the Louisville group finally tired of waiting on their English partners. Samuel Browning, one of the Kentuckians, came to Austin in August 1841, and with Samuel A. Roberts, the acting secretary of state for the Republic, drew up a contract under the provisions of the law.[1] On August 30, 1841, Mirabueau B. Lamar signed the contract for the Republic and Samuel Browning signed for himself and for Henry J. Peters and Phineas J. Johnson, who had taken it upon themselves to act for the twenty petitioners.[2]

The terms of this first contract closely followed the law. The contractors, by the action of Browning, agreed to "introduce or cause to be introduced" into Texas a colony of six hundred families within three years. All of the colonists were to be free white inhabitants of a foreign country and were to reside within the limits of the colony. Of course in terms of Texas law at this time, the United States was a foreign country, and the term "free white" was not interpreted to exclude slaves of the colonists. The colony was to be located as shown on the map, on the Red River in north central Texas. The Republic of Texas agreed to grant 640 acres of land to each family settled by the empresarios and 320 acres to each single man over seventeen. The grantees would receive a full and absolute title to this land provided they "shall have built a good and Comfortable Cabin upon it, and shall keep in Cultivation under good fence, at least fifteen acres on this tract." This the Republic promised to settlers; to the contractors the Republic promised as "compensation for their Services and in recompense of their labor and expense, attendant on the introduction and settlement of the families introduced by them," a premium of ten sections of land for every hundred families and five sections for every hundred single men. The premium lands were to be selected within the limits of the colony and no premium was to be granted for fractional portions of a hundred settlers. The Republic further agreed to give each individual settlement within the colony a section of land to be used to aid the settlers "in the erection of buildings for religious public worship." It

9

was further agreed that the empresarios would introduce at least two hundred of the six hundred families within a year, four hundred within two years, and the remainder within the third year. If these time limits were not fulfilled the contractors were to forfeit their rights. A final clause provided that the emigrants introduced be of good moral character. First and last the contract was fairly detailed and explicit. The responsibilities and obligations of both parties were clearly defined and an attempt was made to settle matters of definition, which might later cause misinterpretation.[8]

It soon became evident that the contract was not satisfactory as a basis for colonization. Whether or not Browning returned to Kentucky to consult the Louisville group is not known. It is probable that he did, since Johnson and Peters seemed to have some knowledge of the need for amending the first contract.[4] In any event, the necessity of changing the contract was clear to both parties, and on November 9, 1841, a second contract was made by Browning and Lamar. This second contract explains why the first contract was a failure; there was not enough unappropriated land in the colony limits. In other words, a relatively large amount of land had already been located and patented within the proposed colony. Browning feared that difficulties would arise if the empresarios attempted to settle six hundred families in the area.

Browning pleaded for an extension of the contract, and as his argument was not without merit, the new contract was made. It read in part as follows:

> Whereas. . . there is not sufficient vacant and unappropriated land in the limits designated in the said contract for the settlement of the families which the parties of the second part [the empresarios] have contracted to introduce; and whereas the said parties of the second part have expressed their willingness to contract for the introduction of two hundred families in addition to the six hundred already contracted for. . .
>
> It is therefore mutually agreed . . . that the limits of [the colony] shall be so enlarged and extended as to embrace, over and above the tract of land already designated and described in the [first] contract, the following limits, viz: commencing on the boundary line of Robertson and Fannin counties at the south east corner of the tract before designated, thence due South forty miles; thence due West twenty two miles; thence due North to the boundary line of Fannin county; thence East along said line to the place of beginning.[6]

In addition the contract of November 9 further provided that sixty-six additional families (one-third of the additional two hundred) would be introduced within a year from the contract date and that the contractors would survey within eighteen months all the land in the colony area needed for the settlement of the eight hundred families.

When the news of the second contract reached Louisville, the empresarios formed an association to promote its fulfillment. The Louisville men, Johnson, Browning, the Peters family, Timothy Cragg, John Bansamere, and William Scott, felt that they had been deserted by the English constituency. Hence, to aid them in fulfilling the contracts, and in a sense to supplant the eleven Englishmen, the Louisville group associated with them in the venture seven additional residents of Louisville; namely, B. Hensley, Henry Bolton, Guerdon Gates, Sceptre Ayres, Edward B. Ely, Jacob Elliot, and Thomas Cragg, a brother of Timothy Cragg.[6]

On November 20, 1841, in Louisville, the nine original contractors and the seven new associates organized the Texas Agricultural, Commercial and Manufacturing Company. This company was not chartered, either by the legislature of Kentucky or the congress of Texas, nor was its organization noted in the Louisville newspapers. Apparently the sixteen men simply made an agreement among themselves to support the project. Their agreement may not even have been committed to writing, though from the preciseness of the date later assigned to the event, it probably was a written agreement.[7]

Some time thereafter (the exact date is undocumented) the Texas Agricultural, Commercial and Manufacturing Company elected Henry J. Peters, Samuel Browning, and Phineas J. Johnson as "trustees." This triumvirate, which had already engineered the first two contracts, now prepared to supervise the settlement of the colony. As will be noted in a later chapter, Peters and Johnson made several trips to Texas, while Browning himself moved to the colony. To fulfill the surveying clause of the second contract, an old Texan, Horace Burnham, was employed as "general agent for the company.[8]

Within a few months the company realized that they would have to have an extension of time. Considerable difficulty was encountered in bringing into and maintaining the required number of colonists on the frontier of Texas, and the task of surveying the area loomed larger and larger. On June 22, 1842, six months after the formation of the Texas Agricultural, Commercial and Manufacturing Company, Horace Burnham delivered to the president of the Republic a letter from the trustees of the company requesting an extension of time. On July 21 the trustees wrote a second letter repeating the plea, but before it was received Sam Houston, on behalf of the Republic and Horace Burnham on behalf of "W. S. Peters and others" had made a third contract extending the time requirements and the boundaries of the colony in return for certain concessions by the company.[9]

This third contract, dated July 26, 1842, recited briefly in its opening paragraphs the history of the grant and stated that the new contract was being made because the empresarios had prayed for an extension of time. A six-month extension therefore was granted for the introduction of the first third of the colonists, though the overall three-year time limit was not extended, and no time restriction was placed on the surveying of the colony. The earlier contracts were further modified by (1) an extension of the boundaries of the colony, and (2) a reservation of each alternate section of land for the Republic.[10] The territorial extension added a ten-mile wide strip along the western boundary and a twelve-mile wide strip along the eastern boundary, as shown on the map. The reservation by the Republic of each alternate section of land within the colony increased the burden of surveying on the empresarios, but was shrewd bargaining by Sam Houston for the Republic. The contract stated in this regard:

> The Republic of Texas hereby expressly reserves (except as is hereinafter excepted) each alternate section of six hundred and forty acres of land, to be surveyed at the expense of the said W. S. Peters and others, his associates, throughout the territory that shall be located and settled by the colonists introduced under the contracts aforesaid, bearing date August 30, 1841, and November 9, 1841, and this agreement altering and modifying the same.[11]

Houston's idea in reserving the alternate sections is clear; as the colony settled up, the alternate sections of land would become more valuable to the Republic. These alternate sections would also be open to the laying of land certificates after the contract expired, thus tending to quiet some opposition that was being pressed by the holders of unlocated land certificates. Furthermore the expense of surveying would be borne by the empresarios and would add to the potential value of the land. This concession made by the empresarios for an extension of time and partly compensated for by an extension of territory caused the contractors, as can readily be imagined, increased difficulties of administration. Incoming colonists would have to be kept off the reserved sections and certificate holders, pressing into the colony before the contract expired, were certain to cause disturbances. The empresarios won a minor privilege in this bargain: The alternate section scheme was not to apply to a region fifteen miles square in the heart of the colony; instead the company was to locate for the Republic an equal number of sections "as nearly as may be of the same average value in other portions of the territory" designated in the various contracts.[12]

The third contract was the last made separately by the Louisville constituency. The Americans had signed three contracts with the government, had organized a colonization company, and had actually begun settlement without hearing from their English partners. The English interest was written off by the Americans, if not as a liability, at least as a frozen asset. These eleven Englishmen took no part in the first three contracts and were inactive in promoting colonization. The first indication that the English interest was not completely extinct was the transfer of their collective rights to another group.

This transfer was engineered by Daniel J. Carroll, a member of the original English group, and was effected by a contract, signed in London on October 3, 1842, in which the original English constituents assigned whatever interest they might have under the law of February 4, 1841, to Daniel J. Carroll, Sherman Converse, Thomas Jones Mawe, Martin Stukely, Edward Tuke, and Charles

Fenton Mercer.[13] Stukely, Tuke, and Mawe were apparently well-intentioned as they later seem to have separated themselves from the intrigues of the others. Carroll was an opportunist and Sherman Converse proved to be a promoter of no inconsiderable ability. Charles Fenton Mercer, whose name was the most respectable of the group, was a down-at-the-heels Virginia aristocrat, who had been a member of Congress of the United States and a public figure in Virginia during the Jackson regime. Under the press of financial distress, possibly occasioned by the panic of 1837, Mercer had moved to Tallahassee, Florida, and opened a bank on English capital.[14] Though he seems to have a good reputation historically, his connection with the Peters colony is rather nefarious. Mercer, Converse, and Carroll apparently each tried separately to gain control of the colony. Of the three, Carroll was the least clever and Mercer the most successful.

The exact arrangements these men made among themselves is not clear, though it is fairly obvious that each one had some sort of scheme in mind when the group obtained, on October 3, 1842, the original English interest. What is clear is the fact that Sherman Converse went to Kentucky claiming to be an agent for the new English "owners," that Mercer later went to Texas to handle affairs on his own, and that Carroll went to New York and tried to sell the entire colony to men long interested in Texas land speculation, the Swartwout brothers.

The same day that the transfer of interest was effected, October 3, 1842, Sherman Converse obtained an open letter of introduction from Ashbel Smith who was then the Texan minister in England.[15] Shortly thereafter Converse sailed for the United States, arriving in Louisville late in November. There he made himself acquainted with the members of the Texas Agricultural, Commercial and Manufacturing Company and soon won their confidence. Evidently he spoke grandly of the wealth and enthusiasm of the new English constituency and outlined for the more timid Louisville minds a magnificent prospect for the colony in Texas. Apparently spell-bound, the Louisville men on December 3, 1842, turned over to Converse their entire interest in the colony! Converse promised in return that he would go to Texas and secure an enlargement and extension of the grant; that he would organize in London a great corporation on the basis of this enlarged grant, a corporation of one hundred thousand pounds or more capital stock; and that he would in due time send each of the members of the now-defunct Texas Agricultural, Commercial and Manufacturing Company who had so generously put their trust in him a share in the proposed corporation.[16]

In Texas Converse met Daniel J. Carroll,[17] and by some devious means charmed a sufficient number of Texas congressmen to secure a fantastic enlargement of the old Peters grant. His methods went unrecorded in the congressional journals or private correspondence, and his presence was unheralded by the local newspapers, but the success of his efforts is the measurement of his peculiar ability. On January 16, 1842, both houses of congress concurred in passing a joint resolution making important and in a sense unbelievable concessions to the Peters colony contractors, whoever they were, for by this time congress was not quite sure with whom it was dealing.

The joint resolution provided that the president of the Republic (at this time Sam Houston, serving his second term—was he caught in the web of promises spun by Converse?) could make such modifications of the Peters contracts "as he deems for the benefit of the Republic." Congress authorized Houston (1) to extend the time limit for five years from July 1, 1843; (2) to "prescribe the limits of the grant on which they can settle any number not exceeding ten thousand families;" (3) to give title to the settlers' sections of land, not to the settlers, but to the contractors, who were to be permitted to convey to each settler any part of his section not less than 160 arces; and (4) to sell to the contractors the alternate sections, reserved according to the contract of July 26, 1842, at the remarkably low price of twelve dollars for each 640-acre section.[18]

The whole resolution was a preposterous and flagrant violation of common sense, of the Republic's trust in congress, and of the general trend of the Texas land policy. The concessions made to the contractors were ones which the Louisville storekeepers and musicians would never have dared to ask for. On January 20, four days after the passage of the joint resolution, Converse signed a new contract in his own name and as agent for the five other men in the London group. No mention was made of the share of the Louisville storekeepers in the colony that they had originally established. The new contract embodied all the features of the joint resolution of January 16 and added over ten million acres to the colony as indicated on the map. Essentially the colony was extended westward, from the eastern boundary fixed by the contract of July 26, 1842, for a distance of one hundred and sixty miles.[19] Though in dispute for some time, this contract became the permanent basis for the colonization of the Peters colony.

Converse did not remain in Texas to gloat over his success. Within a few days he began a return trip to London, with Carroll apparently in tow.[20] News of the January 20 contract probably accompanied Converse to London in official correspondence. On the day the contract was made, actually the day before it was signed, Anson Jones, Secretary of State, wrote the following note to Ashbel Smith in London:

> A contract has been this day concluded between the President and Messrs. S. Converse, D. J. Carrol, Charles Fenton Mercer, Thomas Jones Mawe, and Martin Stukely to introduce a number of emigrants into Texas not exceeding ten thousand. For this purpose the president has granted them a territory on Red River fronting on the stream 164 miles, and including upward of 16,000 square miles. As these gentlemen

appear to be acting in good faith in carrying out their proposed scheme you will give them every proper facility in your power to enable them to effect the same. The colonizing of the country with industrious and respectable emigrants from Europe is an object which the President strongly desires to promote, while every attempt at speculation or imposition by persons who may be disposed to effect this object by entering into contracts for colonization (should any such exist or arise) cannot be too promptly exposed and arrested, by our agents abroad.[21]

In London Converse's activities were noticed by persons interested in Texas, and it was a simple matter for him to convey the impression that he was in control of the colonization venture. Within a few months after his arrival his position seemed generally accepted. A note of inquiry from William Henry Daingerfield, Texan *Charge* at the Hague, to Ashbel Smith, then at Paris, evidence the common acceptance of Converse as the empresario. He asked: "How comes on the company at London at which Mr. Converse was the head and front?"[22]

The news of the contract secured by Converse was received in London a good deal more coolly than many Texans had imagined. A letter from Lachlan Rate, Consul General for Texas in Great Britain, betrayed the lack of substance to Converse's promises and was the first indication of a sensible reaction to the flamboyant promoter. Rate wrote as follows:

With reference to my dispatch No. 4 of the 15th ult. I have now the honor to inform you that I have received a visit from Mr. Converse one of the Gentlemen whose names are mentioned in the Grant alluded to in your letter of the 20th of January.

Mr. Converse has made me acquainted with the details of his plan and as I have before said I shall be happy to give any advice and assistance in my power in furthering the views of the parties interested so long as their operations are marked by good faith towards the Government and managed with that prudence which is absolutely necessary in order to give any hope of a satisfactory result. I have not been able to give very close attention to the subject but I am inclined to think that Mr. Converse may meet with some difficulty in procuring a Capitalist willing to embark in the undertaking.[23]

Converse did meet with difficulty and six months later, on January 4, 1844, one of the more conservative partners in the venture, Thomas J. Mawe, who was apparently an acquaintance of Ashbel Smith's, wrote to Smith requesting him to use his influence in extending the time for beginning the execution of the contract.[24]

While Sherman Converse unsuccessfully tried in London to establish the grand empresario company that he had talked of in Texas as an accomplished fact, the Louisville storekeepers grew uneasy. No doubt they read the following notice (or others similar) which appeared in a Texas paper shortly after Converse secured the contract of January 20, 1843:

The contract of Messrs. Peters, Johnson, Browning and others, for the Colony west of Fannin, has been declared forfeited, and another contract with the government has been entered into, by Dr. Sherman Converse, of New York, Dr. D. J. Carroll, of Maryland, Charles Fenton Mercer, Esqr., of Virginia, Messrs. Thos. J. Maw and M. Stukely of England. The line is to run from the mouth of Mineral Creek, due South 100 miles; thence due West 164 miles; thence due North to Red River, which is to be the northern boundary. These lines, we are told, will include the Big and Little Cross Timbers, as well as the former colony of Messrs. Peters, Browning & Co. The colonists of the first company may be reinstated if they wish, and 250 families annually, are to be introduced by the new contractors, for the term of five years, and as many more as they please, not exceeding 10,000. The new company state their capital at 100,000 sterling. The contractors have returned to their homes to commence operations, with the exception of Dr. Carroll, who will reside in Fannin and the Colony. Mr. Mercer was for many years a respected member of the Congress of the United States; Dr. Converse has, we think, been a book publisher in New York City. The others we know nothing of.[25]

The newspaper announcement that their colony had been forfeited was alarming, and as the memory of Sherman Converse's visit in Louisville dimmed, the fact became more apparent to the Americans that they had been duped. Nothing was heard from London or from Sherman Converse, nor was there any news of the promised one hundred thousand pound corporation. Charles Fenton Mercer finally wrote them that he was going to Texas as the agent for the colonization venture. The members of the defunct Texas Agricultural, Commercial and Manufacturing Company held an indignation meeting.

On December 21, 1843, they reformed the company and passed a set of resolutions, which were published as a broadside, denouncing Converse and his associates. They declared that Converse and his friends had forfeited their interest in the colony, and that the contract of January 20, 1843, secured by Converse, devolved onto the reformed Texas Agricultural, Commercial and Manufacturing Company.[26] They then determined to send E. B. Ely, secretary of the company and an auctioneer in Louisville, to Texas to intercept Mercer and to protect their interests in the Texas capitol. Ely wrote to the Texas government asking that Mercer be ignored or delayed until he arrived as the true agent of the Peters colony.[27]

From this point the situation became complicated, and the scant amount of information available makes the developments even more difficult to trace. Mercer, however, was on his way to Texas, and it seems apparent that he planned to put himself at the head of the venture by securing a further extension of time in his own name. In the meantime, upon hearing that the Kentuckians had repudiated him and the bogus London corporation, Sherman Converse hurried to Louisville to try to retrieve his lost advantages. The Kentuckians welcomed him as the prodigal returned. They called a meeting of the recently reorganized Texas Agricultural, Commercial and Manufacturing

Company, and Converse convinced the entire group that they had done him a grave injustice. His tongue was so skillful and his manner so ingratiating that the Kentuckians contritely began adopting measures which Converse suggested "to correct the mischief they had done."[28]

They hastily repudiated their recent denunciation of Converse and handed back to him entire control of the venture. Converse then wrote the government of the Republic of Texas requesting that it ignore whatever business Mercer and Ely, separately or in collusion, might suggest in connection with the grant. He sent another Kentuckian, Jacob Elliott of Louisville to intercept Major Ely and inform him of the new developments in Louisville. He then wrote Anson Jones, Texan secretary of state, that Mercer's business should be confined to securing an act of incorporation for Converse's mythical London company, which Converse had begun to refer to as the "Texas Emigration and Land Company."[29]

But with victory in his grasp at Louisville, Converse was to have the prize snatched from him in Texas; he had not accurately judged the abilities of Charles Fenton Mercer. Only the barest outline of what took place in Texas can be reconstructed. Whether Elliott, the second Louisville emissary, caught up with Ely, the first, is not known; nor is it known whether either or both of them met with Mercer. It is known that Mercer was very busy on his own account.. Much must have happened at Washington-on-the-Brazos during January 1844 while the Eighth Congress was in session, but the historian can record only that a bill was introduced and passed to nullify the law of February 4, 1841, its subsequent amendments, and the joint resolution of January 16, 1843. Thus congress endeavored to stop all colonization contracts. The bill went through both houses but was vetoed by President Sam Houston, who immediately signed a contract with Charles Fenton Mercer, in Mercer's name alone, authorizing him to establish an empresario colony adjacent to the Peters colony. On the following day, January 30, congress passed over Houston's veto the bill to repeal all laws authorizing the president to form colonization contracts.[30]

As the situation stood, Mercer had secured from Houston through a legal trick (Houston's veto) and expressly against the wishes of congress a contract for himself "and such associates as he shall choose."[31] His old associates, especially his "friends" of Converse's Texas Emigration and Land Company, were not included in the new contract. It is not necessary here to trace the later history of Mercer's colonization venture, except to note that it was generally unsuccessful; the circumstances of the original grant together with the character Mercer had in Texas as an "abolitionist", a "speculator", and a "monopolist" all mitigated against the colony. Mercer soon organized a company, "The Texas Association," selling shares for five hundred dollars each. In the years that followed, the Texas Association and the Mercer colony were plagued by litigation, and eventually the colony and the claims of the company to premium lands were forfeited.[32]

The Mercer contract of January 29, 1844, left in doubt the status of the Peters colonization project and the control of the colony under the fourth, or Converse contract, of January 20, 1843. By the provisions of that contract, it was necessary on penalty of forfeiting the contract that two hundred and fifty colonists be settled by July 1, 1844. The forfeiture clause of the contract was strengthened by the law of January 30, 1844, which repealed all laws permitting the president to make new empresario contracts and cancelled all contracts not complied with. Hence, it was obvious to all concerned that if anyone was to have any rights under the contract, the settlement stipulations had to be fulfilled. The Louisville group decided to save the contract first, and argue about its control later. Both "Major" Ely and "Colonel" Elliott were in Texas, having been sent as special emissaries to the Republic, and Samuel Browning was residing in the colony area. These three undertook to promote sufficient migration to establish the contract. They faced a number of problems which are discussed in the following section of this work. One of the most puzzling of these was the fact that the company had sent more than enough settlers to Texas to fulfill the contract stipulations, but these people were not living in the colony area. Ely visited the colony, and finding only one hundred and sixty families living within its limits, advertised urging persons who had come to Texas to settle in the colony to move immediately within its boundaries. He stated optimistically: "The company *have not* and *will not* incur a forfeiture—all statements of that character are erroneous."[33] By July 1, 1848, there were 197 families and 184 single men residing in the colony.[34]

In Louisville, the colony affairs moved slowly. Converse again deserted the Louisville group, apparently because his old cohart, Mercer, had double-crossed him by getting a separate contract. As the responsibility and expense involved in the establishment and maintenance of the colony became apparent, and as the Texas venture assumed the aspect of a long time business enterprise, there was a reorientation in the views of the Louisville storekeepers. The Texas project looked bigger than they could handle alone, and during the summer of 1844 they interested a number of other Louisville business men in the venture. On October 15, 1844, a new company was organized and articles of association were drawn up in which the past history of the colony and of the Texas Agricultural, Commercial and Manufacturing Company was briefly reviewed, the terms of the various contracts set forth, the name "Texas Emigration and Land Company" adopted, officers elected, and the reasons for the formation of the new company explained.[35] The newly formed Texas Emigration and Land Company maintained (1) that the Converse group had

18

failed to make good their part of the contract of December 3, 1842; (2) that the responsibility for the fulfillment of the contract of January 20, 1843, had been assumed by the old Texas Agricultural, Commercial and Manufacturing Company; (3) that even after the repudiation of the contract of December 3, 1842, the old association had been induced to readmit the Converse element and still the English had failed to participate in establishing the colony; (4) that the Converse faction (Mawe, Tuke, Stukely, Mercer, Carroll, and Converse) therefore had forfeited all rights they may have had under any of the contracts; and (5) "that the contract of January 20, 1843, now stands as if it had been made between Texas and the original association." The Texas Emigration and Land Company therewith assumed all the rights and obligations under the laws of Texas and the four contracts with the Republic.[36]

Finally, the new company agreed that its capital stock should be fixed at $500,000 to be divided into two thousand shares at $250 each; that these shares might be sold by the trustees of the company as they saw fit; that five hundred shares would be distributed free among the original members of the association; that five hundred additional shares would be proportionately distributed among the stockholders of the Texas Agricultural, Commercial and Manufacturing Company; that William C. Peters, Willis Stewart, and John J. Smith would act as trustees for the company and be given full powers except they could not borrow more than $20,000 for the company; and that the trustees were to apply to the government of Texas for an annulment of the contract of December 3, 1842, and an act of incorporation for the Texas Emigration and Land Company.[37]

Thirty-six names were signed to the articles of association, including eight of the original grantees and three of the six men who had been associated with the Texas Agricultural, Commercial and Manufacturing Company.[38] The original members of the Texas Emigration and Land Company are listed below:

OLD MEMBERS OF THE TEX. AGRIC., COMM. & MFG. CO.

Original Grantees:

John C. Bansamere
Emma Browning (for Sam'l Browning)
Thomas S. Cragg (who inherited Timothy Cragg's interest)
Henry J. Peters
John Peters
William C. Peters
William S. Peters
William Scott

Others:

B. Hensley
G. Gates
Scepter Ayres

NEW MEMBERS OF THE TEX. EMIG. & LAND CO.

P. S. Barber
Thomas Coleman
W. E. Culver
John C. Cragg
George B. Didlake
Moses Dickson
D. M. Dowell
John C. Evans
Carroll Kendrick
Rodman Lewis
Warwick Lynn
R. G. McGinis
F. Massol

John M. Monahan
William Pettet
J. B. Redd
Minor W. Redd
A. P. Starbird
James Stewart
Willis Stewart
Thomas S. Sturgeon
Ira Vail
A. B. Van Winkle
M. D. Walker
Prentice Wersinnger

Willis Stewart was the most influential member of the new company. It was Stewart who guided the colony's destiny for the next decade, who furnished most of the necessary capital, and who was chiefly responsible for keeping the company on a stable business keel. He was not, however, an unimaginative business drudge; he was rather an enterprising capitalist who was interested in investing in any venture that offered a fair chance for a profit. He operated, in partnership with John Owen, a general merchandise store in Louisville, lent money on mortgage, was interested in the Louisville and Elizabethtown Turnpike Road Company, the Louisville and Nashville Railroad, and was a director and for a time president of the Kentucky and Louisville Mutual Insurance Company.[39]

Stewart was born about 1799 in Kentucky; he married Patsy Oldham Taylor about 1825, and they had thirteen children. Willis Stewart was listed on the United States Census for 1830 as the head of a family and the owner of eight negro slaves. He first became interested in Texas lands in 1836 when with his brothers Isaac and James Stewart he purchased a share in some land near Nacogdoches. He seems to have lost the money he invested there but not the desire to speculate in Texas.[41] His leadership of the new company was largely responsible for what success was to be obtained in Texas.

With the reorganization in Louisville, control of the colony was claimed by the Texas Emigration and Land Company, which repudiated a second time the agreement of December 3, 1842, and all other agreements with Sherman Converse. The Louisville men had secured the contract by settling 381 colonists in the grant by July 1, 1844; the company now undertook to establish its claim to the contract by securing releases from the old Converse-Mercer group. Mercer was persuaded to sign a document renouncing any rights he might have in the Peters colony or in the Texas Emigration and Land Company.[42] A similar agreement was effected with Sherman Converse,[43] but with Daniel J. Carroll agreement was impossible.

Carroll seemed convinced that he held a major interest in the colony, and he tried in devious ways, not to establish his position legally, but to sell his "share" to a speculator. Carroll argued that he had been one of the original grantees, that he had been the assignee of the shares of the eleven original English grantees and that he was the true representative of all but the American interest, which, by some unfathomable arithmetic, amounted according to Carroll to only one-fifteenth of the venture. Carroll ended up in New York in 1845 in contact with the Swartwout brothers who had long been interested in Texas.[44] On December 12, 1845, Robert Swartwout made a memorandum noting that he had talked with Daniel J. Carroll who was growing impatient about the Texas contract. Carroll, according to Swartwout, was anxious to connect some "monied man in the Association . . . with which we may also accommodate him."[45] Swartwout made the following note to one of his associates:

> Suppose we conclude an agreement with Dr. Carrol for two thirds of his contract in Texas. We may be disposed to sell 500,000 acres of that land at 20 cents an acre, and which would amount to 100,000$ payable as follows: 25,000 in cash and the balance in one two and three years without interest, and to insure the fulfillment of our engagement—we pledge 20,000 acres of our Texas property, giving the parties their option at the expiration of one year, to take the 20,000 acres for the advance made in full, or to cancel that part of the contract and hold on to the greater part, to wit 500,000 acres at 20 cents an acre.[46]

This was a fancy scheme for financing the venture, apparently typical of the Swartwouts. In brief Swartwout planned, if he bought Carroll's interest, to sell five hundred thousand acres to which he had no title at all, but which might be obtained by fulfilling the contract. For the sale of this land he did not own he would get $25,000 as a cash down payment and would put up as security twenty thousand acres to which his title may have been equally nebulous. Either way he could not lose; if he forfeited his pledged 20,000 acres it would be at a price of $1.25 per acre, at least twice as much as any Texas land was selling for at the time.

Apparently Swartwout desired more specific information about the venture than he trusted Carroll to furnish him. On December 28 he wrote to an associate asking him to have a "full talk with Texas people in regard to Carroll's contract."[47] Swartwout discussed the project with Branch T. Archer, then visiting in New York. On January 24, 1846, as he was leaving New York, Archer wrote Swartwout telling him he had talked with Carroll, and promising that he would make a full investigation of "our business" when he returned to Texas.[48]

It was eventually decided by Swartwout that Carroll was the actual owner in his own right of one and one-half shares out of the twenty shares belonging to the original grantees, the half share having devolved upon Carroll by the death of one of the Londoners. Swartwout assumed that this entitled Carroll to a corresponding share in the grant operated by the Texas Emigration and Land Company, and that it was roughly equivalent to more than three hundred thousand acres of land. On October 20, 1846, Swartwout gambled that the validity of Carroll's rights could be legally proved, and he purchased Carroll's "share and a half" for twenty thousand dollars. A cautious man, Swartwout stipulated in the contract of sale that the twenty thousand dollars would be paid out of the first proceeds of the sale of scrip which Swartwout proposed to issue against the prospective three hundred thousand acres.[49]

Swartwout's next step was to try to establish Carroll's claim to a part of the grant of the Texas Emigration and Land Company. His attorney opened a correspondence with Willis Stewart and received a very emphatic reply to his inquiry, which is quoted in full:

Louisville, Ky:
November 10, 1846

John W. Leavitt, Esq.

Sir. Yours of the 5th Inst. received this morning. The Texas Emigration and Land Company located in this place are the assignees of the English Company who contributed nothing toward carrying on the Enterprise. Dr. Dan Joseph Carroll never paid one cent and forfeits all rights if he ever had any under the contract of the English company. This company have carried out the contracts as far as they have been carried, with their own means, and that too often they were notified by those representing the English interest that they had abandoned the enterprise. This they have done at great expense and trouble, and when but for the execution of this company, the whole contract would have been forfeited.

This company can make no arrangements with Dr. Carroll and it gives us pleasure to repeat that by abandonment and assignment this company are now the exclusive owners of what was once considered the English interest. This company are not disposed under any circumstances to relinquish its management. The prospects ahead are of the most cheering kind and when we say to you and for the information of our friend Mr. W. C. Fellows that James Guthrie, Levi Tyler, Robert Tyler, Governor Whitcomb of India. and Judge Douglas the distinguished representative in Congress from Illinois are all interested. Some idea may be formed of what we consider its importance. The only difficulty we have to encounter is the want of a sufficient amount of means to carry it out to the extent of its capacity.

(PS) Should any further information be desired in relation to our enterprise we shall with much pleasure communicate it to you.[50]

It is interesting to note that later in writing to his own attorney, Stewart characterized Carroll as follows:

As for Mr. Dan Joseph Carroll, he has never been considered a member of our company. He has never complied with a single condition on which he was to have obtained an interest, and we suppose does not consider himself as having any. Certain it is that he is not a resident of Texas; we heard of him not a great while since as a drunken loafer about the streets of New York, and he never was a resident of Texas although he may at one time have been there.[51]

Swartwout's attorney furnished him a legal opinion on Carroll's rights, and consequently of Swartwout's as the assignee of Carroll. The opinion, in part, follows:

The Constitutionality of the Law and the validity of the Contract have never been doubted, but universally recognized throughout the Territory of Texas—the present Circuit Judge of the U. S. for the State of Texas, Judge Watrous, recently appointed by the President is now in the City and has given a full and explicit opinion verbally on the subject.

Reference is also made to the . . . fact that there has been a full compliance with the terms and conditions of the contract. . .

And to the above add the continued and undisturbed action of the American Parties in their strenuous exertions to push forward the contract to its full and final accomplishment.[52]

This seems to have ended the discussions between Carroll and Swartwout, and ended Swartwout's interest in the colony. Whether Carroll offered to sell his doubtful rights to anyone else is not known, and since nothing has been found further to link Carroll with either Texas or the colony, it may be presumed that he abandoned the project.

Thus were the rights of Mercer, Converse, and Carroll disposed of by the company. Of the six London assignees of the original English grantees, Mawe, Stukely, and Tuke remained. It seems that the Louisville company dealt with them in the same way as with Converse and Mercer, obtaining from them a relinquishment of their rights. Though the actual releases have not been located, a letter from Stewart, quoted below, makes it clear that such arrangements had been made.

When Mr. Johnson was here in the Spring he advised us to furnish copies of the several compromises entered into with Messrs. Mawe, Tuke, Stukely, Mercer and Converse, who constituted all the party named under the fourth and last contract with Texas except Dan Joseph Carroll, Esq. He has failed to comply with all and every one of the conditions on which he was to have an interest in our enterprise.[53]

This letter supplies a final answer to the question of the status of the contract. Mercer, Converse, Mawe, Stukely, Tuke and Carroll were disassociated from the venture; the control of the colony, its affairs and its settlement, was vested exclusively in the Texas Emigration and Land Company of Louisville.

FOOTNOTES FOR *PART I*

¹This brief background discussion of Texas land policy is based on a study now in progress by the author. Some of his conclusions have appeared in a paper he read at the 1952 meeting of the Texas State Historical Association and in an article entitled "Land Speculation," to be published in the *Southwest Review*.

²The *Telegraph and Texas Register*, July 21, 1841. Discussions of the Franco-Texienne Bill may be found in Walter Prescott Webb, *The Great Plains*, Boston (1931), 181-182; William C. Binkley, *The Expansionist Movement in Texas*, Berkley (1925), 53-55; and Bernice B. Denton, "Count Alphonso de Saligny and the Franco- Texienne Bill," *Southwestern Historical Quarterly* (hereafter cited as *SWHQ*), XLV, 136-146. The proposal itself may be found in Texas Congress, *House Journal*, Fifth Congress, First session, 473-480, 484ff.

³Tex. Cong., *Senate Journal*, 5 Cong., 1 sess., 187. Mayfield, James S. to Alphonso de Saligny, March 29, 1841, in George P. Garrison (ed.), *Diplomatic Correspondence of the Republic of Texas*, Part III, 1315. See also *Telegraph and Texas Register*, February 17, 1841; Garrison, *Diplomatic Correspondence*, III, 1008, note *a*; and Saligny to Anson Jones, January 16, 1842, in *ibid.*, 1353-1354. The following year Saligny unsuccessfully tried to reawaken interest in the Franco-Texienne proposal through Henri Castro who had just arrived in Texas.

⁴The whole origin of this colonization plan has not come to light. The first mention of the memorial occurs in the *House Journal* on January 14, 1841 (p. 508): "The committee on the state of the Republic to which was referred the memorial of Johnson, Browning and others, asking permission to introduce emigrants within the Republic . . . reported by a bill to that effect." The present writer was unable to find earlier in the the *Journal* a reference to the introduction of the memorial and further was unable to find the memorial itself in the file of memorials to congress in the state archives. Although it has not been located, its contents may easily be inferred from the text of the law of February 4, 1841.

⁵This information, though substantiated elsewhere, is based chiefly upon the "Articles of Association of the Texas Emigration and Land Company," originally drawn up on October 15, 1844, a true copy of which, notarized September 11, 1847, was found in Envelope I, William G. Hale Papers, archives of the University of Texas. (This collection is hereafter cited as Hale Papers.) Scott's residence was later given as Blairsville, Pennsylvania, and W. S. Peters' as Pittsburgh. W. C. Peters moved to Cincinnati, John Peters to New York, and Browning to Texas.

⁶"Articles of Association," October 15, 1844, Hale Papers.

⁷The writer is not completely convinced that Carroll was English.

⁸Line 17, p. 83, Microfilm roll 38, Federal Census of Kentucky, 1830.

⁹G. Collins, *The Louisville Directory for the year* 1843-1844.

¹⁰". . . Memorial of Johnson, Browning, and others . . ."Tex. Cong., *House Journal*, 5 Cong. 1 sess., 508.

¹¹Collins, *Louisville Directory*, 32.

¹²*Ibid.*, appendix, vii.

¹³"Articles of Association," October 15, 1844, Hale Papers.

¹⁴Mildred J. Hill, "History of Music in Louisville," in J. Stoddard Johnson (ed.), *Memorial History of Louisville from its first settlement to the year* 1896, n.d., II, 95.

¹⁵James Curry to Ashbel Smith, June 1, 1856, Ashbel Smith Papers, Envelope 1856, Archives, University of Texas.

¹⁶Obituary notice, *Northern Standard*, July 3, 1844. Browning seems to have received mail through Fort Towson and gave his address as the "forks of the Trinity," *Northern Standard*, April 3, 1844.

"One of Peters daughters married Browning; another may have married William Scott.

"Willis Stewart to William G. Hale, April 15, 1848, Hale Papers. Naturalization papers of Henry J. Peters are in the possession of Mrs. Carl Peters Benedict of Graham, Texas, and Fort Sumner, New Mexico.

"Stewart to Hale, September 20, 1847, Hale Papers, no. 146. Also a certificate dated March 22, 1848, in Devonshire, England, in Peters colony scrapbook, archives, University of Texas, and Curry to Smith, June 1, 1856, Smith Papers.

"Refer to the discussion of W. C. Peters that follows.

"Dallas News, March 1, 1941. The present writer has been unable to authenticate the picture.

"This information has largely been brought to light by the extensive research that has been done on the career of Stephen C. Foster, the American songwriter, with whom Peters was occasionally associated. Foster's principal biographer, John Tasker Howard, prepared a sketch of the life of William Cumming Peters for the Dictionary of American Biography. In this biographical sketch incidentally there is no mention of the Peters colony or of the Peters family's connection with Texas history. Nor in any of the other Foster material dealing with Peters has there been any connection. The identification of Peters the music publisher as Peters the colonizer was made in an interesting way: the writer had nearly given up hope of ever locating any information on Peters when one day while idly turning the pages of a musical history of Louisville, he discovered the names of W. C. Peters and Henry J. Peters, music publishers, linked together with the names of Thomas and Timothy Cragg. The Craggs were for a time in partnership with the Peters in the music business. Both of these Craggs were connected with the Peters colony. Later developvent have substantiated this identification.

"[John Tasker Howard], "William Cumming Peters," in Dumas Malone (ed.), Dictionary of American Biography, XIV, 512. Howard states that between 1820 and 1823 the Peters family "lived for a short time in Texas." The present writer has checked Howard's bibliography and has corresponded with Mr. Howard (in 1951 curator of Early American Music at the New York Public Library), but has been unable to authenticate the Texas visit beyond a similar statement in James Grant Wilson and John Fiske (eds.), Appleton's Cyclopedia of American Biography, IV, 744. A search has been made of the standard archival sources but no indication has been found that any Peters were living in Texas in the years suggested. Because of the unsettled and isolated conditions of Texas at this period, the present writer thinks it unlikely that a family of English musicians were here that early.

"Evelyn Foster Morneweck, Chronicles of Stephen Foster's Family (two volumes), Pittsburgh (1944), I, 81.

"Ibid. 82.

"Ibid., 81, 82. Peters was not listed in Louisville in the census for 1830.

"Morrison Foster, My Brother Stephen, Indianapolis (1932), 36.

"D. A. B.; John Tasker Howard, Stephen Foster, America's Troubadour, New York (1934), 124; Morneweck, Chronicles, I, 298.

"Collins, Louisville Directory, 117.

"Howard, Stephen Foster, 136.

"Later famous as "O, Susanna."

" Howard, Stephen Foster, 138, quoting J. P. Nevin, "Stephen Foster and Negro Minstrelsy," The Atlantic Monthly, November, 1867.

"Stephen C. Foster to William E. Millet, May 25, 1849, in Morneweck, Chronicles, I, 357.

"Willard R. Jillson, "In Memory of Stephen Collins Foster, 1826-1864," The Register of the Kentucky State Historical Society, XXXVIII (April, 1940), 101. Mr. Fletcher Hogdes, Jr.,

Curator of the Foster Hall Collection at the University of Pittsburgh, graciously loaned the writer the only complete file of Peters' *Olio.*

[15]*D. A. B.,* XIV, 512.

[16]*Cincinnati Commercial,* April 21, 1866. His obituary notice also appeared in the *Cincinnati Daily Gazette,* April 21 and April 23, 1866.

[17]*D. A. B.,* XIV, 512.

[18]Collins, *Louisville Directory,* 1843-1844, 117

[19]J. Stoddard Johnston, "Benedict J. Webb, Kentucky Historian," *The Filson Club Quarterly,* VI April, 1932), 206.

[40]Hill, "History of Music in Louisville," 95.

[41]*Ibid.,* 97.

[42]As far as the present writer knows, the descendants of this family are the only members of the Peters family living in Texas. Accounts of their arrival in Texas are somewhat conflicting. "In 1868 Captain Benedict married Adele Peters, granddaughter of one of the founders of the Peters Colony, who was born in 1847 . . . Just one year before Young County was reorganized he moved his family to Texas . . ." (Carrie J. Crouch, *Young County History and Biography.*) "In 1877 H. J. Peters, son of the colonizer, set out from Kentucky to settle on Peters Company land . . . In the wagons with H. J. Peters and his wife and two sons came his daughter, Mrs. Adele Peters Benedict, and her two sons, Harry Yandell, born in 1869, and Carl Peters, born in 1874 . . . The Peters family, the Benedicts continuing to live with them, located on a half section of land fronting the Clear Fork of the Brazos River . . ." (J. Frank Dobie, "Introduction," in Carl P. Benedict, *A Tenderfoot Kid on Gyp Water,* xiii) House No. 23, Family No. 25, Federal Census for 1880, Young County, Texas, Precinct 2, page 3 lists Mrs. Benedict with her sons H. Y. and Carl P. and her brothers Harry and Carl Peters at the same residence. Joseph Benedict, the husband of Adele (Peters) Benedict, was listed separately on the census (Dwelling 217, family 226) as a divorced person. Also buried in the cemetery plot at Graham with Henry J. and Mary A. Peters were Adele P. Benedict (1845-November 13, 1894), Carl Peters (December 3, 1858-March 10, 1902), and Rachel Bailey (whose tombstone had no dates) who according to the census of 1880 was a widowed aunt of Adele Benedict, born in Nassau in 1814.

[43]Tex. Cong., *House Journal,* 5 Cong., I sess., 508.

[44]The details of the bill's tortuous but fairly rapid passage through congress are omitted here, but can be traced in the following: Tex. Cong. *House Journal,* 5 Cong., 1 sess., 508, 521, 543; *Senate Journal,* 151, 156, 162, 171, 177, 181. An attempt to block the bill was made by Benjamin Fort Smith of Montgomery, who on January 18 introduced a bill vaguely similar except that the original petitioners were not mentioned by names and the empresario provision, so intrinisic in the plan, was omitted. This bill was sent to the Committee on Public Lands and then tabled. See also File 1960, File Box 21, Fifth Congress, in the archives of the Texas State Library. As an indication of congress's attitude toward the question it might be worth while to note the contents of this proposed bill. Ben Fort Smith and his supporters, while opposed to the proposition before the House, yet desired to use the public lands to attract settlers. Their substitute plan was to close all Texas north and west of the military road leading from the Nueces to Red River to the laying of existent land certificates, and to open that same area to pre-emption homesteading. Two year's residence and the cultivation of five acres in the restricted area was to entitle a settler with a family to six hundred and forty acres (to include his improvements) and a single man to three hundred and twenty.

[45]H. P. N. Gammel (comp.), *The Laws of Texas,* 1822-1897 (10 vols; Austin, 1898), II, 554-556, 663. The law as it stands in Gammel is dated January 4, 1841, but this erroneous

date is corrected in the *errata* on page 663. The incorrect date, however, has led to a number of subsequent errors in standard histories of Texas.

⁴⁰The first of these, dated February 5, 1842, authorized the president of the Republic to contract with other individuals or companies on the same terms as he had with the Peters group. Gammel, *Laws of Texas*, II, 785.

FOOTNOTES FOR *PART II*

¹Copy of contract between Browning, *et al* and Mirabeau B. Lamar, August 30, 1841, Colony Contracts file, General Land Office.

²Power of Attorney, October 18, 1841, Colony Contracts file, G. L. O. This power of attorney from Johnson and Peters to Browning is dated after the first contract. It may be assumed that a similar power of attorney had been executed previously.

³Contract, August 30, 1841.

⁴Power of attorney to Samuel Browning, October 18, 1841.

⁵Contract, November 9, 1841, Colony Contracts file, G. L. O.

⁶Articles of Association, October 15, 1844.

⁷*Ibid.* This document explains the formation of the earlier company and assigns the date November 20, 1841 to the event.

⁸The information in this paragraph has been inferred from later events. As noted above, no documents have been found bearing directly on the subject. Horace Burnham had entered Texas as a member of the Robertson colony and apparently had been employed as a surveyor in Nacogdoches County before becoming the agent of the Louisville people.

⁹Joseph Waples to W. S. Peters, H. J. Peters and associates, August 18, 1842, acknowledging receipt of both letters, Colonization Papers, Archives, T.S.L.

¹⁰Contract between Sam Houston and Horace Burnham, July 26, 1842, Colony Contracts file, G.L.O.

¹¹*Ibid.*

¹²*Ibid.*

¹³Copy of a contract between the Texas Emigration and Land Company and Charles Fenton Mercer (undated fragment), p. 134 of a scrapbook in Rare Books Collection, Louisville Public Library. A microfilm copy is in the archives, T.S.L.

¹⁴Nancy Eagleton, "The Mercer Colony in Texas, 1844-1883," *SWHQ*, XXXIX and XL (1936). For further details of Mercer's life see the *D. A. B.*

¹⁵Garrison, *Diplomatic Correspondence*, II, 1025.

¹⁶The document itself has not been located; however, it can be reconstructed from descriptions of its terms in the following sources: Articles of Association, October 15, 1844; copy of contract between Mercer and T. E. & L., no date; broadside, "To All Whom it May Concern," December 21, 1843.

¹⁷Carroll's part is not clear. He had apparently preceeded Converse to Texas.

¹⁸Gammel, *Laws of Texas*, II, 851-852.

¹⁹Contract between Sam Houston and Sherman Converse, January 20, 1843, Records of the president's office, archives, Texas State Library.

²⁰Converse to Anson Jones, February 1, 1843, in file "State Dept. Colonization Papers, 1845-1873," archives, T.S.L.

²¹Jones to Smith, January 19, 1843, Garrison, *Diplomatic Correspondence*, I, 1083.

²²Daingerfield to Smith, November 8, 1843, *ibid.*, 1476.

²³Lachlan Rate to Anson Jones, May 18, 1843, Colonization Papers, 1843-45, archives, Texas State Library.

[21]T. J. Mawe to Ashbel Smith, January 4, 1844, *ibid.*

[25]*Northern Standard*, February 4, 1843.

[26]Broadside, Louisville, Ky., 1843: To All Whom it May Concern.

[27]Ely to Jones, December 21, 1843, Colonization Papers, 1843-45, archives, Texas State Library.

[28]Sherman Converse to Anson Jones, January 18, 1844, Domestic Correspondence 1844, archives, Texas State Library.

[29]*Ibid.*

[30]Gammel, *Laws of Texas*, II, 958.

[31]Contract between Sam Houston and Charles Fenton Mercer, January 29, 1844, State Dept. Colonization Papers, 1843-45, archives, Texas State Library.

[32]A. J. Peeler and T. J. Maxey, *History and Statement of the Mercer Colony Case* is the best reference for Mercer colony history. The unsatisfactory work by Nancy Ethie Eagleton, "The Mercer Colony in Texas, 1844-1883," has already been cited.

[33]*Northern Standard*, March 2, 1844, and issues following.

[34]Ralph H. Barksdale to Anson Jones, December 7, 1844, "List of Emigrants that arrived in Peters Colony prior to July 1, 1844," Colonization Papers, 1843-45, archives, T. S. L.

[35]Articles of association, October 15, 1844.

[36]*Ibid.* Their interpretation and assumption of control seems never to have been seriously challenged.

[37]*Ibid.* Neither of these last two was obtained.

[38]Phineas J. Johnson had moved to Arkansas; Emma Browning signed in the place of Samuel Browning who had died in Texas; Jacob Elliott had sold his share; and E. B. Ely's heirs were issued script in lieu of stock. Why Henry Bolton did not sign is not known.

[39]Based on a personal interview with Walter Preston Stewart, grandson of Willis Stewart, in Dallas, September 14, 1949, and an advertisements in the *Louisville Daily Journal* for the period, January 1840 to December 1845. Doubtless Stewart was interested in enterprises other than those mentioned.

[40]Interview with W. P. Stewart, September 14, 1949.

[41]On February 15, 1836, George Hancock, Henry Shivers, Carter Beeman and several others contracted to purchase from Frost Thorn, a well-known speculator in Texas lands, two eleven-league tracts near Nacogdoches. Title to the land was made from Thorn to Hancock alone, as agent for the others. The Stewart brothers bought the interest of Carter Beeman in the two grants, and in July 1836 executed four notes of $1650.00 each payable to Hancock on November 1, 1836, 1837, 1838, and 1839 respectively, in all with interest, amounting to a total of $5,542.00. The Stewarts paid these notes, but in the meantime the title to the eleven-league grants, which Thorn had sold, was repudiated, and Thorn substituted other lands believed to be of the same value. The Stewart's share in the compromise was to have been three leagues, but apparently they never received any land. Stewart may have been slow to enter the second speculation in Texas when first approached by the Peters group, but once associated with them, he became a leader in the venture. Stewart was still trying to recover the Nacogdoches land as late as 1854, but he died in 1856 (after a trip to Texas) and there is no evidence that he or his heirs received a title to it. (George Hancock to William G. Hale, February 15, 1854, Hale Papers.)

[42]Only an undated fragment of a copy of this agreement is available, page 154 of a scrapbook in the Rare Books Collection, Louisville Public Library.

[43]*Ibid.* The copy of the contract states that it was made between the Texas Emigration and Land Company and Sherman Converse and Charles Fenton Mercer. Sherman Converse's

name has been lined off the manuscript. Stewart later stated that such a release had been made by Converse. (Stewart to Hale, August 14, 1847, Hale Papers.)

⁴⁴Robert and Samuel Swartwout had become interested in Texas land as investors in the Galveston Bay and Texas Land Company. The Swartwouts did not have a clean reputation. Samuel had received the appointment of Collector of Customs at the port of New York during Jackson's administration and had absconded to England with a large sum of money. In Texas the Swartwout land deals were also tainted with dishonesty and fraud. In the archives of the Texas State Library there is a file labelled "Carroll's Contracts, 1820 to 1846, and 1848 to 1873." It contains a number of unsigned, undated, unidentified, and largely unrelated documents, a few of which are germane to the problem. The present investigator identified most of these items as the work of Robert Swartwout by a comparison of handwriting and tried to arrange them in order. The following paragraphs in this study are based on these documents.

⁴⁵Unsigned memorandum dated December 12, 1845, Carroll's Contracts, archives, T. S. L.

⁴⁶Undated, unsigned fragment, Carroll's Contracts, T. S. L.

⁴⁷Unidentified letter dated December 28, 1845; also another unsigned, undated fragment in Carroll's Contracts, T. S. L.

⁴⁸Branch T. Archer to General Robert Swartwout, January 24, 1846, Carroll's Contracts, T. S. L.

⁴⁹Various legal instruments signed by D. C. Carroll and George T. Catlin (for Robert Swartwout), all dated October 20, 1846, State Dept. Colonization Papers, 1846-1873, archives, T. S. L.

⁵⁰Willis Stewart to John W. Leavitt, November 10, 1846, State Dept., Colonization Papers, 1846-1873, archives, T. S. L.

⁵¹Stewart to Hale, October 23, 1847, Hale Papers.

⁵²Carroll's contracts. There are no identifying marks on this document, which is rather lengthy, but is obviously a legal opinion and clearly was prepared for Swartwout.

⁵³Stewart to Hale, August 14, 1847, Hale Papers, no. 139.

(To be Continued)

KENTUCKY COLONIZATION IN TEXAS

A HISTORY OF THE PETERS COLONY

SEYMOUR V. CONNOR

Part III

The Settlement of the Colony

The Peters grant embraced an extensive area in north Texas, but in general settlement was confined to the eastern portion of the grant, which was essentially the drainage area of the upper Trinity River and its tributaries in the present counties of Collin, Cooke, Dallas, Denton, Ellis, Grayson, and Tarrant. Physiographically this region was then characterized by open, rolling plains, covered by deep grasses, with small stands of timber along waterways, and was identified by an ususual feature—the Cross Timbers. The Cross Timbers, as mentioned in contemporary accounts, usually referred to what was actually the eastern Cross Timbers. This was a band of scrub oak, mostly post oak, extending in a fairly uniform width of about ten to twenty miles south from Red River to about present Hill County.

At the time when the region was just "opening up," as the phrase went, there were two principal Indian groups in the vicinity: the Wacos on Village Creek in present Tarrant County, and the Shawnees in and around present Grayson and Cooke counties. Newspaper accounts and pioneer reminiscenses refer also to scattered bands of Indians along the upper tributaries of the Trinity. The Wacos on Village Creek were one of the most troublesome of the smaller tribes in Texas at the time. In the summer of 1840 Major Jonathan Bird led an unsuccessful attack against the Waco Village, but a year later General Edward Tarrant, with a large force of rangers and militia, broke up the village and destroyed the Indians' crops. A combination military and civil settlement was then attempted near the site of the Indian village, and Jonathan Bird organized a company of men, accompanied by their families, for the purpose of constructing a fort there. Because of Indian depredations and a shortage of supplies, and because it was an encroachment on the Peters colony contract, the settlement was abandoned in the spring of 1842.

Some of the "Bird's Fort" settlers located to the east, but still within the colony, and later claimed land as Peters colonists. Whether or not they had come to Texas under Peters' auspices is not known, though it seems possible that they had. The first contract had been signed on August 30, 1841, and

Peters and his Louisville associates had not been totally inactive. The following item, originating in the *Caddo Gazette*, but taken from the *Louisville Journal,* January 20, 1842, is the earliest evidence of actual colonization:

EMMIGRATION EXTRA—A few days since the steamer Embassy, from Louisville, arrived at Shreveport, La. with one hundred families on board. A company had been formed at Louisville and had purchased eight hundred sections of land in Eastern Texas, and those families were destined to be the first settlers. The Caddo Gazette says the intention of the emigrants was to ascend by Red River to the Cross Timbers, where they expected to locate as the advance guard of civilization. The raft not being removed has disarranged all their plans. Most of the families were supplied with wagons and horses, and started on their way—the men, with rifles, on foot, the women and children either in the wagons or on horseback; while a number have obtained employment on the raft, and will ascend the river when that raft is removed. One marriage was celebrated on board the boat the evening before the party broke up and one child was born while the boat was at Shreveport.

The country they have selected is beautiful, healthy, and fertile. A few years of struggling, and they will find themselves surrounded with all the comforts of competency, and all the refinements of society.[1]

How much editorial fantasy exaggerated the size of the group or marred the accuracy of the report is not known. That there was such a group and that some of them eventually reached the colony is clear from later accounts. The *New Orleans Crescent City* of April 15 carried the following item which seems to refer to the portion of the emigrants who made their way overland:

The colony from Kentucky, under the control of Mr. Peters, has located in the upper end of Robertson County, and in the garden spot of Texas, being in the vicinity of that Eldorado, the Three Forks of the Trinity.[2]

A final report on this group completes the skeletal outlines of their story. On September 27, 1842, the *Louisville Journal* copied the following from the *Caddo Gazette:*

We learn from a gentleman who has been making a tour through the eastern portion of Texas, that the settlement known as the 'Cross Timbers Settlement' in Fannin County, has been broken up by the Indians. This settlement was composed of some twelve families of emigrants who came up to this place last winter in the steamer *Embassy,* from Louisville, Kentucky. They had opened up some five hundred acres of land, which they planted in corn, and which was reported to be in a fine state of cultivation, when a large party of Indians made their appearance and compelled the whites to abandon their agricultural pursuits, and betake themselves to the fort. In those quarters they remained two or three weeks (during which time their cattle and the buffalo destroyed the corn) when their supply of provisions being exhausted, they were compelled to evacuate the post and seek protection among the settlers of Bowie County.[3]

In the fall of 1842 Phineas J. Johnson and Henry J. Peters visited the colony bringing with them twenty-two emigrants from Kentucky in a small wagon train. According to the newspaper report these emigants were of "the better order," and were going to settle in the colony "at the Cross Timbers." They had made better time from Louisville than a similar sized group which had left before them. Peters told the newspaper editor at Clarksville, Charles De Morse, that "two hundred families will leave Kentucky this fall for the colony."[4]

On September 10, De Morse noted that the group of twenty emigrants "passed through this place on Tuesday last, on their way to the colony at the Cross Timbers."[5] This brought the total number of emigrants to the colony by September 1842 to fifty-four families. Of these, twelve families had abandoned a settlement made in the spring and it is not known how many of them remained in the colony. During the winter of 1842-43 migration into the colony continued at an increasing pace. In December De Morse reported that forty families were moving into the colony, and that "they are persons desirable on account of their personal characteristics and their property."[6] Begun with this influx of settlers of the "better order," the colony promised to be an immediate success. On December 10 the following item was carried in the *Standard:*

> FROM THE COLONY:—A gentleman direct from the colony of Msrs. Peters and Browning, called on us in the first part of the week, and informed us that the colonists were quietly progressing with their improvements, entirely unmolested by Indians of any sort. They are gradually getting along with the labor incident to their position, and as directly as could be expected. The Delawares are hunting around them, but disturb nothing, the horses of the Colonists feeding undisturbed.[7]

Migration into the colony continued during the spring and summer of 1843. In April it was reported that "forty or fifty families from Missouri and Illinois lately removed to the settlement in the Cross Timbers,"[8] bringing the total estimated to have arrived in groups to about one hundred and thirty families. It is more than likely that numbers of others moved into the colony singly or in small groups that were not noted in the papers.

In July the first notes of impending trouble were struck: apparently many families began moving away from the colony. The *Northern Standard* stated on July 6, 1843, that there seemed to be only thirty-five families left. Throughout the remainder of its existence the colony was to be plagued with a continual exodus that sometimes exceeded in number the movemnt of settlers into the colony. The situation became acute by the spring of 1844 when the empresarios were trying to fulfill the fourth contract which required that two hundred and fifty colonists be settled by July 1, 1844. Major E. B. Ely, who had come to Texas as mentioned earlier on a special mission for the company, noted in a letter to Charles De Morse:

> I was perfectly aware that I had sent into the Republic a much greater number of families than was required to comply with the requirement of the President for the

first year, but I was also appraised of the fact that a large portion of those families, though they had many of them visited the Colony, had not actually taken up their residence there, but were temporarily sojourning in the region of the Red River.[10]

The confused status of the contract and the company had generated distrust among the settlers which was increased when the law authorizing the president to make empresario contracts was repealed. Adding to their discouragement was the fact that many of them had been told, in accordance with the first three contracts, that their land had to be selected and their improvements started by the end of June. News of the extension of the contract secured by Converse on January 20, 1843, had not reached them or had reached them in a garbled form. Hence, many settlers, in doubt as to whether the contractors would be able to make good on their offer of free land, decided to locate in Fannin County. The settlers reasoned that since they were going to buy land anyway, they might as well buy it where they could get a clear title.

Rumors of forfeiture had a detrimental effect, and Ely blamed the "numerous misrepresentations and false statements" on the locators who wanted to defeat the colony and open the restricted area for the free laying of land certificates. Ely was indignant at what he believed to be the calculated inventions of the land speculators. "Do the citizens of Texas understand that if we lose the contract, the land will pass into the hands of speculators?" he asked.[11] As agent for the colonizing company, he tried to spike the rumors by advertising as follows:

TO EMIGRANTS: NOW within the Republic of Texas, who have left the United States with the intention of settling in the Trinity and Red River Colony, the undersigned, agent of the colony, takes this method to say, that to all families who proceed to the colony, make their selections, build their cabins, and occupy same, on or before the 1st day of June next, 640 acres or one section of land will be given—and young men over 17 years a half section, or 320 acres—Mere visit and selection without improvement will secure no rights—actual settlement and improvement is indespensible.

Persons holding certificates in which they are required to settle at a period earlier than above named, are informed that the time specified is extended to the 1st June—The company *have not* and *will not* incur a forfeiture—all statements of that character are erroneous—the surveyors are now at work laying off the Colony into sections, and Emigrants, on their arrival, will hereafter experience no difficulty in making their locations with certainty in regard to the precise boundary of their lands.

Temporary absence after settlement, does not forfeit rights.[12]

Ely was apparently on his way to Louisville when he inserted the advertisement; on his return to Texas he was optimistic. The *Northern Standard* reported:

TRINITY COLONY.—Since our last we have seen Major Ely, the agent, who has just returned from Louisville. He assures us that there will be more than enough families within the bounds of the colony, by July 1st, when the limitation allowed, expires, to comply with the stipulation of the contract. He also informs us that the company intend forwarding the emigration as much as possible, and expect, next year, to have two thousand families within the grant. These families will be taken up the Trinity by steamboats, several of which will run regularly upon that stream whenever the water will permit.[13]

That the company's efforts to stimulate migration and to meet the terms of the contract were successful is indicated by the following item in the *Standard* of June 26.

> IMMIGRATION—We have received information, several times, within the last few weeks, that great numbers of immigrants, are coming into the District; crossing above here, and making their way to the South Sulphur, and the Trinity. The stream is continual, and they come, not singly, but in bodies.[14]

It is improbable that all of this migration had been stimulated by the Louisville empresarios, or that all of the emigrants were headed for the Peters colony. Some of them, doubtless, were going into the Mercer colony. Charles Fenton Mercer had begun his colonization activities, and in the spring of 1844 he printed and distributed six hundred handbills offering 160 acres to families and 80 acres to single men; in the fall of that year he boosted his offer to 320 acres per family, and the following spring extended it to the full 640 acres in order to meet the terms of his competitors, the Texas Emigration and Land Company.[15] Sincer Mercer in the spring of 1844 was offering only 160 acres to emigrants, it is most likely that most of the newcomers went into the Peters colony.

As a result the company more than fulfilled its contract. The official report to the secretary of state contains a list of the emigrants that arrived prior to July 1, 1844, totaling 381 colonists: 197 heads of families and 184 single men. Over three years had elapsed since the passage of the original empresario law; the results were not impressive. By way of summary, it may be said that prior to July 1844 the empresarios made moderate efforts to stimulate migration to the colony, but that they did little toward constructive administration of the internal affairs of the colony. The fact that emigrants to the colony in general came from the area around Louisville and the Ohio River valley is substantial evidence that the Louisville contractors were in some degree responsible for generating interest in Texas through that area. During the first three years the empresarios had established the colony and secured the contract, but the settlements had not flourished, and the settlers had begun to distrust the company.[15a]

The fiscal year, 1844-1845, was the period in which the company was reorganized and the controversy between the English and American interests was settled. The reorganization brought new leadership into the affairs of the colony, and the change was sharpened by the deaths of two of the colony's most active founders: Samuel Browning and E. B. Ely. Charles De Morse recorded their passing as follows:

DIED

In Trinity Colony, on Thursday, the 21st of June, Mr. Samuel Browning, formerly of Louisville, Ky. and since of the City of Austin, in the 43rd year of his life. Mr. Browning was one of the original contractors for the first Trinity Colony, under the grant of 1841. He settled on it when it was a wilderness; had remained in it, and administered to its interests under all its vicisitudes; and at last after having endured much privation; and seen hundreds come and go; and the Colony at one time, with only sixteen families left in it out of the large number who had ventured, but shrunk away again, from the hardship and hazard of a wild country; he lived long enough to see the success of the enterprise. When he died there were sixteen families more within its limits than were required to comply with the terms of the contract. Mr. Browning was an amiable worthy man, and has left a family to mourn his loss.[16]

DIED

Major Edward B. Ely, agent for the contractors of Trinity Colony, died of bilious fever, at the residence of Mr. Keenan, in the Colony, on Sunday, 7th of July, after an illness of 11 days. He had the medical aid of Dr. Conover; and the day before his dissolution, Dr. McBride was called in consultation.

Major Ely was possessed of mind, enlarged views, and great energy. His death will prejudice the interest of the contractors, if not the interest of the colonists.

He leaves a wife and numerous friends to weep for his premature dissolution. They should know, that in his last illness he reposed in the bosom of an intelligent and sympathising family—that at his bedside night and day, Major Barksdale; and as often as need be, other friends—and was attended by physicians of learning and experience.

Major Ely had been in the colony but a few days. His sickness may be attributed to unaccustomed and fatiguing rides over treeless prairies.

He preserved his consciousness throughout his illness—made preparations for his final exit—confided his business and papers to the care of Major Barksdale, and died in prospect of a richer reward than Trinity Colony could promise.[17]

Despite the loss of these two leading spirits, the colony's prospects seemed bright. The *Northern Standard* continued to carry reports of sizeable migrations to the colony. A report on August 7 stated that twenty-five families had just arrived and fifteen more were expected.[18] An item of October 30 reported that an observer had counted over two hundred wagons en route for the colony.[19] A week later thirteen wagons passed through Clarksville from Illinois bearing the motto "Polk and Dallas, Oregon and Texas."[20] In subsequent issues De Morse reported the wagon trains of emigrants passing through Clarksville bound for the colony, "until the repetition is tiresome, yet the tide swells and breaks upon us . . ."[21]

The period of hardship, however, was not passed. False reports about the company continued to circulate, and most of the colony was still unsurveyed. In the spring of 1845 Indian depredations increased. During the last of January a party of about twenty-five Indians, believed by the settlers to be Creeks or Cherokees from across Red River, approached the settlement near McGarrah's under the pretense of friendship. On nearby Rowlett's Creek they shot and scalped a boy named Rice. The same day Norman Underwood and his young son were killed and scalped on Little Mineral Creek in the western part of present Grayson County. On February 9, on Wilson Creek, north of McGarrah's, one of the Helms family narrowly escaped a band of about six Indians, who took his horse. The settlers organized a posse and caught three of the Indians, who were Caddos and who blamed the trouble on "the damned Wichetaws."[22]

On March 13, 1845, De Morse reported: "Depredations in the way of killing cattle and stealing horses, are taking place daily . . ." He believed that the Indians came from across the Red River and warned settlers to beware of supposedly friendly Indians. "In nine cases out of ten the friendly Indians are the ones who depredate upon us."[23] Charles Hensley, the company agent, ran an advertisement during May in the *Northern Standard* in which he tried to reassure the prospective colonists about the Indian troubles.

> There is now a ranging company on the frontier of the colony, under the command of Col. Smith, and another is now in progress of being raised, so that emigrants need entertain no fear of Indians. All here is perfect peace and quietude.[24]

Hensley may have been guilty of overstatement. Even if the Indian menace had subsided, excitement continued because the company was engaged in its second annual spring drive for colonists. Increasing numbers of colonists had become discouraged and left the colony. The exodus which had begun earlier continued, and at times, apparently, the movement from the colony was almost as great as the movement to it. An account in the *Northern Standard* describes this dual process of settlement:

> IMMIGRATION—Two gentlemen from Missouri, who have just arrived for the purpose of selecting a location to move to, state, that they counted all the emigrant wagons as they passed, between Fayetsville, Arkansas, and Doaksville, some coming and some returning from the Trinity country. There were 225 wagons coming and 75 returning. As they met on the road, the faint-hearted who were going back, would tell their difficulties, which were all embraced in the want of provisions, arising from the want of means to get them, with the addition that those who turn back from a good work always make, namely, that everybody that started with them was doing, or about to do likewise—which was untrue.
>
> But they stopped none—they deterred none. Those whose faces were turned hitherward, kept on; and being warned of the high price of corn on the Trinity, will generally wait until spring before they go there, spending the winter where corn is cheaper and easier obtained.[25]

In an attempt to stop the exodus, Hensley had notified the hesitant and the discouraged that the surveyor was busy working and that emigrants would find no difficulty in making locations. He urged them to give no credence to the "many false reports in circulation by those unfriendly to the interests of the Colonization Company," and announced the company's intention to "defeat the

36

interests and wishes of land speculators, by securing to all who desire a home in the most genial climate and upon the most productive soil in the Republic." Misunderstanding had already begun over the company's land policy, and Hensley tried to correct this by notifying prospective colonists that the company was no longer offering the full 640-acre section to families. Through a judicious choice of words, he tried to make the policy seem generous, which it was except in comparison with the company's previous policy. Hensley stated:

> The contractors having fully complied with all the provisions and conditions of the law, and their contract with the government; they will still continue to allow land until 1st July 1845, to all who comply with the requirements of the law, in the ratio of one half section, or 320 acres of prime tillable land to each head of a family, and to each single man over the age of 17 years, one half that amount.
>
> To secure the benefits of the present year's donation it is absolutely necessary that the settler should have his cabin built and he himself upon the ground by 1st July; but a temporary absence thereafter will not prejudice his claim.[26]

Hensley was able to report for the fiscal year 1844-1845 an addition of 443 new colonists. According to statistics there should have been around 800 colonists in the area, though it may be doubted that there were actually half that number in the colony. On paper it was a successful year, but if all the factors could be considered it would probably be judged the opposite. Dissatisfaction with the company seems to have increased among the colonists, and during the critical period when creative leadership in the administration of the colony's affairs was needed, the company had continued to be backward and negligent.

Left to develop their own leadership, the colonists began to organize local governments, and during the year 1846, the counties of Collin, Dallas, Denton, and Grayson were established.[27] The Peters colony ceased to be the integral unit that the term *colony* implies. The boundaries of the counties were laid out without regard to the colony's boundaries, and the settlers lost any identity they may have had as colonists. They were in fact immigrants who immediately became citizens of Texas, and their only connection with the colony and the Texas Emigration and Land Company was in the acquisition of land. The company's functions became solely that of a land agent's, and in the minds of many of the citizen-colonists, the company's performance in that capacity was unsatisfactory.

Through the channels of government the locators and the colonists united to attack the company. In August 1845 the Constitutional Convention passed an ordinance which stated that "it shall be the duty of the Attorney General. . . to institute legal proceedings against all colony contractors. . . and if upon such investigation it shall be found that any such contract was unconstitutional, illegal, or fraudulent, or that the same has not been complied with according to its terms, such contract shall be adjudged and decreed null and void."[28]

37

A court action against the Texas Emigration and Land Company was instituted in 1846, and the idea that the company's contract was going to be annulled become prevalent. The case was never brought to trial, but the rumors stimulated the land locators who began to trespass on the colony reservation.[29] For several weeks during the late spring of 1846, Charles Hensley ran the following advertisement notifying persons who might be tempted to enter the colony area for the purpose of laying certificates that the colony's boundary was established:

> The boundaries of Peters' Grant are as follows, commencing at a point on Red River 12 miles East of the mouth of Big Mineral Creek, thence due South one hundred miles, thence due west one hundred and sixty four miles, thence due North to Red River, and thence down Red River, with its meanders to the point of beginning.
> The eastern line of this grant was surveyed and partially marked in June last—fifty miles of the Southern boundary line from East to West has been since run, so that all persons interested can readily ascertain the precise and exact boundaries as far as is established by survey.[30]

Despite this notification, a number of surveyors, some of them district surveyors for the state, entered the colony reservation and began locating certificates wherever there was unpatented land. Since neither the colonists' nor the company's patents had yet been issued, it is not difficult to imagine the confusion which must have resulted. Most of the trespassing could be traced to the district surveyor of the Robertson land district, David R. Mitchell. Mitchell contended that the colony's grant was cancelled, and he seemed to believe he had the backing of William Ward, the land commissioner. Ward's animosity to the colony had been earlier demonstrated when his annual report for the year 1843 had helped provoke the nullifying law of January 30, 1844. But Ward's animosity was on principle, and Mitchell was mistaken in believing that Ward supported his erroneous idea. Nevertheless, Mitchell and his deputies entered the reservation during 1846 and 1847 laying certificates and sending the field notes to the land office. In May 1847, Henry O. Hedgcoxe, Hensley's successor as agent, sent the company's attorney a full report on the activities of the trespassing surveyors. According to Hedgcoxe, one of Mitchell's deputies, a man named Walker, stated that Mitchell had threatened him with dismissal if he refused to lay certificates within the reservation.[31]

Later Willis Stewart directed his attorney to begin proceedings to enjoin the trespassers from working in the area. He enclosed a note from Hedgcoxe identifying the chief offenders as follows:

> James E. Patton, a deputy surveyor of Robertson district and Navarro County
> [David R.] Mitchell, the principal surveyor of Robertson district. I think he resides in Franklin.
> A. G. Walker, deputy surveyor of Nacogdoches district and of Dallas County, now residing in Dallas.[32]

38

Two weeks later the trustees of the Texas Emigration and Land Company executed a new power of attorney to Hedgcoxe authorizing him to "institute any suits that may be necessary to protect our interests."[33] A suit was finally initiated against Mitchell and his deputies and the desired enjoinder was obtained in January 1848.[34]

The litigation with the trespassing surveyors indicates that the company had been forced to change its attitude toward the colony. Earlier the company had been primarily concerned with promoting immigration and had made little or no effort in colonial administration. In the closing period of the colony's legal existence, the company, though relegated to the role of land agent, was primarily concerned with administrative matters. Immigration during 1847 and 1848 increased substantially, not as a result of any special activity on the part of the company, but because of the natural westward expansion of the American frontier.[35] The company's chief problem therefore became the administrative one of supplying land for the immigrants.

In 1846 the company unknowingly complicated administrative problems by selecting Henry O. Hedgcoxe to be the colonial agent. Hedgcoxe, who was to become one of the important figures in the colony's history, was an English emigrant who was residing in Indiana when he was employed by the Texas Emigration and Land Company. He came to the colony in the fall of 1845 or the spring of 1846 as an employee of the company and received full power of attorney as chief agent on April 10, 1846.[36] Hedgcoxe's personality was a significant factor in the controversy that followed. His English accent probably grated the ears of frontiersmen in the region, and his desire for preciseness in all matters of business must have been extremely irritating to all but his employers who were well pleased with their new agent.[37] Hedgcoxe was the typically officious but efficient clerk, and he seems to have over-estimated greatly his own importance. From the beginning he adopted an arrogant attitude toward the company's attorney, William G. Hale, who was one of the leading citizens of Texas. A good example of Hedgcoxe's attitude occurs in a letter he wrote Hale in connection with the trouble over the trespassing surveyors:

> Be pleased to stir in this mater as quick as you can—If any of the papers in the surveyors' offices are needed force them into your possession if you can and if my services are needed write me on that subject.[38]

It was not with Hale, however, but with the settlers that Hedgcoxe's personality was to be the most damaging to the company's interests, for Hedgcoxe came to personify the company in many persons' eyes. The company's problems with which Hedgcoxe had to cope were indeed complicated, but more tact and less efficiency would probably have had better results.. The problems derived from the dual difficulty of locating lands in the area where previous titles had already been issued and of completing the necessary surveys of the settlers' tracts so that titles could be applied for. Although some surveying had been done under Barksdale and Hensley, the surveying project does not seem to have become well organized until Hedgcoxe arrived. He claimed to be a civil engineer and had began to direct the work of surveying. On November 14, 1846, the *Northern Standard* noted that a Colonel Ball of Kentucky had gone to the colony along with a "company of surveyors. . . They will commence surveying immediately, so as to give the emigrants an opportunity to select lands."[39]

One of the first things Hedgcoxe did was to issue certificates to colonists stating the amount of land they were entitled to.[40] The issuance of certificates was obviously intended to reassure colonists, but a demand that titles be issued began to grow, and as the titles were not issued until 1854, this demand became a vital force in the colony's history. Hedgcoxe's next move further irritated the colonists. He sent out blank form letters written in a haughty tone and couched in legal language ordering those who had located on an even numbered section (reserved for the government) to move immediately.[41] The certificates and the form letters brought a reaction. On January 24, 1848, a group of colonists memorialized the legislature asking that the state intervene to settle some of the problems in the colony.[42]

The colonists came straight to the point by asking that the county courts be authorized to issue titles since the company had not done so. They requested that new certificates be issued to settlers who discovered, as the surveying progressed, that they had located on old patents or on the state's alternate surveys. The petition closed emphatically: "We believe said contract is forfeited and should be annulled so far as the company is concerned."

There were one hundred and eleven signatures on the memorial, but it was forgotten when the company gave the colonists a more serious grievance to fight. Hedgcoxe began to demand that many of the colonists abandon half of their claim in accordance with the law of February 4, 1841, and the contract of January 20, 1843. Prior to June 30, 1844, the company had not attempted to exercise its vague rights to the half-sections, but thereafter, in all its notices to emigrants, the company had stated that only 320 acres would be given to settlers. It was evident that the company misunderstood its rights in this regard, and that until Hedgcoxe autocratically demanded their relinquishments, the settlers in general misunderstood the company's intentions. The company had no right to these half-sections because it had not performed the required services and the settlers, though they had by the act of entering the colony in a sense accepted the company's illegal terms, were aroused by Hedgcoxe's demands.

Hedgcoxe tried to get written relinquishments to the half-sections because the company's attorney, William G. Hale, informed him that the company's claims would be legal only if backed by written releases from each settler.[43] As far as can be determined none of the settlers signed reliquishments and few apparently acceded to any of Hegcoxe's demands. The most tactful agent could not have secured the company's unreasonable claims; Hedgcoxe, however, injected emotionalism into the controversy which was to disturb North Texas until 1854.

The controversy and its settlement, including the well-known "Hedgcoxe War," are discussed in the next section. The company's grant expired on June 30, 1848. The company, during the last three years, had become merely an ineffective land agent, and within the colony counties and cities had been established without regard to the colony's unity.

FOOTNOTES FOR *PART III*

[1]*Louisville Journal*, January 20, 1842.
[2]*Louisville Journal*, April 22, 1842.
[3]*Louisville Journal*, September 27, 1842.
[4]*Northern Standard*, August 27, 1842.
[5]*Northern Standard*, September 10, 1842.
[6]*Northern Standard*, December 3, 1842.
[7]*Northern Standard*, December 10, 1842.
[8]*Louisville Journal*, April 29, 1843.
[9]*Northern Standard*, July 6, 1843.
[10]*Northern Standard*, March 2, 1844.
[11]*Ibid*. It is interesting to note that Major Ely did not classify himself as a land speculator; he was either very stupid or very clever.
[12]*Northern Standard*, March 2, 1844 and following issues. The advertisement is dated Bonham, February 25; apparently it was run in the Bonham paper and picked up by the *Northern Standard* after the custom of the times—"Such and such a paper or papers will please copy in the amount of three dollars (or some other figure) and bill the subscriber."
[13]*Northern Standard*, June 15, 1844. From the very earliest days of settlement residents of the upper Trinity region seem to have dreamed hopefully of navigating the Trinity.
[14]*Northern Standard*, June 25, 1844.
[15] Charles Fenton Mercer to Ashbel Smith, March 31, 1845, Third Semi-Annual Report of the Texas Association, in "Minutes of the Texas Association," 33-35, microfilm copy in the University of Texas Library.
[15a]Barksdale's report, previously cited.
[16]*Northern Standard*, July 3, 1844.
[17]*Northern Standard*, July 24, 1844.
[18]*Northern Standard*, August 7, 1844.
[19]*Northern Standard*, October 30, 1844.
[20]*Northern Standard*, November 6, 1844.
[21]*Northern Standard*, January 16, 1845.
[22]*Northern Standard*, February 9, February 13, 1845.
[23]*Northern Standard*, March 13, 1845.
[24]*Northern Standard*, May 13, May 20, 1845.
[25]*Northern Standard*, October 30, 1844.
[26]*Northern Standard*, May 13, 1845.

[27]No further attempt is made to trace the minutiae of settlement in these counties, a task left to the writers of county histories.

[28]An ordinance, Consitutional Convention of 1845, in Gammel, *Laws of Texas*, II, 1304.

[29]The state completed a suit against Mercer's Texas Association based on the ordinance (see Peel and Maxey, *Mercer Colony Case*), but the suit against the Texas Emigration and Land Company was withdrawn in 1852. The details of this controversy are discussed in a later section.

[30]*Northern Standard*, May 6, 1846.

[31]Henry O. Hedgcoxe to William G. Hale, May 5, 1847, Hale Papers.

[32]Willis Stewart to Hale, August 6, 1847, Hale Papers, I, 125; Hedgcoxe to Hale, August 6, 1847, Hale Papers, I, 138.

[33]File 12, Colony Contracts File, G. L. O.; Power of attorney to H. O. Hedgcoxe, August 17, 1847.

[34]Stewart, *et al., vs* David R. Mitchell, *et al.*, District Court of the United States in Equity, December term, 1847, filed January 10, 1848.

[35]Statistical details of this immigration are presented in an article by the writer in the *Southwestern Historical Quarterly*, July, 1953.

[36]Power of attorney, H. O. Hedgcoxe, April 10, 1846 and Power of attorney, September 21, 1846, Colony Contracts File, G. L. O. The second document was recorded in Collin County on November 20, 1846.

[37]These matters are difficult to document; the writer's impression results from the reading of scores of letters from or about Hedgcoxe.

[38]Hedgcoxe to Hale, August 6, 1847, Hale Papers, I, 138.

[39]*Northern Standard*, November 14, 1846.

[40]File 12, Colony Contracts File, G. L. O.

[41]Henry O. Hedgcoxe to ————— (form letter), Hale Papers.

[42]Memorial 162, January 24, 1848, archives, T. S. L.

[43]Hedgcoxe to Hale, February 26, 1848, Hale Papers.

(To Be Continued)

KENTUCKY COLONIZATION IN TEXAS

A HISTORY OF THE PETERS COLONY
SEYMOUR V. CONNOR

Part IV

The Peters Colony Controversy

The expiration of the contract solved none of the controversial issues, and the three-way conflict between the company, the land locators, and the colonists was continued in the courts, in the legislature, and at a local level. When the fourth contract of January 20, 1843, expired there were over seventeen hundred settlers and their families within the colony, and immigration into the area was increasing. Local governments had been established and organized, and the political consciousness of the region was maturing. The colonists' opposition to the company soon expressed itself through the channels of government. In the words of one critic:

> The settlers rebelled, threw off the yoke which was too heavy to bear, refused to have anything to do with the contractors or their agents; and boldly appealed to the citizens, and Government for relief.[1]

The earliest manifestation of a direct clash was the ineffective memorial to the legislature discussed earlier. The next attack on the company was at a local level. Dallas County levied taxes against the company's land claims in the county and threatened a forced sale if the taxes were not paid. Actually the company owned no land in the county, nor did any of the persons who had settled as colonists, since titles had not been issued by the general land office, but each colonist claimed the land he had settled on, and the company claimed certain sections as premium land. To maintain itself, the county government was forced to assess these claims for taxes. About the first of September Ben Merrill, the Dallas County Tax Assessor and Collector, sold 320 acres out of a section claimed as premium land by the Texas Emigration and Land Company. A rather fine legal point was involved: could the county tax, and sell for unpaid taxes, land for which no patent had been issued? Stewart wrote to his attorney telling him to act immediately to put a stop to such forced sales since it would be disastrous to the company if the practice was continued and spread to other counties.[2]

Hale advised the company not to fight the county government, but to pay the taxes under protest. Later a suit for recovery might be initiated.[3] Hale's advise came a little late, for during the fall all of the land in Dallas County on which taxes had not been paid was put up for sale, and most of it was sold. "This sweeping sale included all the land which belonged to the State [the alternate sections], as well as that which belonged and should belong to the Company," Stewart complained.[4] The State of Texas purchased about 15,000 acres, and over 30,000 acres were sold to individuals. On January 18, 1849, Hedgcoxe, acting under Hale's instructions, wrote to Merrill demanding detailed information on the land that he had sold for taxes, and offering to redeem it by paying the back taxes.[5] The arrogant tone of Hedgcoxe's demand seems to have offended Merrill. He replied: "Sir, Yours of the 18th instant demanding of me certain information in regard to the sale of certain lands, etc., I comply with not as a demand but as a request." He stated that the taxes due for 1846 amounted to $442.75 as assessed against 354, 262 acres, and that the rest of the land was to be placed on sale on June 22, 1849.[6]

Hedgcoxe, with sarcastic courtesy, pointed out that Merrill had made a minor error in arithmetic and stated: "I wish you would have the kindness to so complete your list that it will show precisely and identify every piece which was bid off or sold to the state."[7] Hedgcoxe hoped to be able to redeem the land which the state had purchased. For some time it had been the practice of the government of Texas to bid on land that was sold in the various counties for unpaid taxes. From time to time congress and later the legislature had passed acts enabling former owners to redeem their property by paying the back taxes plus interest. Such redeeming laws had been passed in 1845 and 1846,[8] and Hedgcoxe, probably with Hale's advice, anticipated that another redeeming law would be passed and that the company would be enabled to reclaim its forfeited land. On January 16, 1850, the legislature did pass a law "to restore Lands sold for Taxes, and purchased by the State, to the former owners"[9] A supplement to this act, passed on February 11, authorized the restoration of the land that had been purchased by individuals.[10] Apparently the company paid the back taxes due and redeemed the fifty thousand acres that had been sold.[11]

No further attempt was made in Dallas or in the other counties to sell the company's premium claims at a delinquent tax sale, but the question of the title to that land, which was basic to the tax issue, was yet unsolved. The general land office had issued no patents to any land claimed by or through the Texas Emigration and Land Company, and the whole status of land ownership in the colony area constantly became more confused. The trustees of the company were keenly aware that their own claims to premium lands, as well as to the half-grants, were contingent upon the completion of the surveying as required by the law and the contracts. The surveying had progressed slowly until the arrival of Hedgcoxe, who seems to have given some organization to the whole project. How much had been completed by the expiration of the contract cannot be determined, but the task was apparently far from finished. On September 7, 1848, Stewart estimated that the work of copying the field notes of the surveyors and making the plats and the general map of the area would be over a year's work unless it were handled by a well-trained and well-organized staff.[12] By January, 1849, however, Hedgcoxe had prepared a general map which the company had lithographed and submitted to the land office.[13] By this time a majority of the surveys had been completed, and the company planned to submit the field notes as part of the evidence necessary to support its claims for premium land.[14]

The stockholders were anxious to settle the controversies, complete their duties, collect their premium, and close the Texas venture. They were pessimistic about the possible final profit, and many were disgusted with the entire affair. Stewart wrote:

> The whole enterprise is likely to be like the Indian gift. Cost twice as much as its worth. There's not one member of the company who, if he had known at the beginning, the amount of money which it would require to complete it that would have touched it with a forty-foot pole.[15]

Stewart claimed that the company's advertising expense in newspapers and circulars "desseminated all over the U. States and in Germany and Great Britain" was over two thousand dollars. He added that it had been a continual surprise to the trustees that the stockholders had borne the various calls upon them as well as they had. "Why for the amount of money expended," Stewart wrote, "land could have been bought in Texas equally as much, if not more, and of better title, than we may eventually acquire."[16]

The Louisville company further was haunted by the possibilities of judicial proceedings. The first rumors of the suit projected by the ordinance of the Constitutional Convention of 1845 reached Louisville in the winter of 1848, although it had actually been instituted in 1846.[17] In January, 1849, Stewart wrote Hale to inform him that no process had been served on Hedgcoxe and no notification had been given the company in the papers. He asked Hale to reassure him that the state would not proceed with the suit without giving the company notice.[18] Stewart believed that the company's defense should be based on the contention that the government had placed obstacles in the path of the company's progress. He hoped to avoid the suit altogether, and wrote: "If the suit could be suspended until the Legislature meets, we could probably effect a compromise and save having to go to the Supreme Court of the United States."[19]

On January 24, 1849, the stockholders of the company held a meeting in Louisville and resolved to send an agent to Austin to settle the company's accounts in Texas, present the evidence that the company had completed its obligations, and "demand title to all the lands which may have been acquired under contracts with the Republic." It was hoped that the business might be ended before the suit was brought to court.[20]

Stewart came to Texas in the fall of 1849 as the company's agent[21] and seems to have worked diligently on the tangled affairs.[22] At the suggestion of Ebenezeer Allen, an associate of Hale's, Stewart employed a man named Brewster[23] to advise him. Allen thought Brewster would be useful because he was Governor Wood's secretary and as such helped shape the executive documents if not the decisions. At any rate his services were thought to be worth $100.[24]

There were three main items on Stewart's agenda: (1) to complete the colony business with the land office, (2) to attempt a settlement of the issue by legislative action, and (3) to investigate the projected court action by the government. While Stewart was in Austin, the state served notice to the company on December 28, 1849, of the suit to be brought against it. In the main the published notice stated that on October 11, 1846, Albert C. Horton, acting governor, had filed a petition with the Navarro District Court charging that the Texas Emigration and Land Company had failed to comply with the terms of the fourth contract of January 20, 1843; that the case was to be heard at the March 1850 term of court; and that the defendants were to be notified by publication in the *Northern Standard*.[25] Fearing that Hale would not return from Mexico in time, Stewart cast about for another lawyer. His distrust of Brewster he expressed as follows: "From my own observations at Austin I had discovered that he was very indolent, and I was apprehensive that he would not prepare our defense properly."[26] George and I. A. Paschal, attorneys from San Antonio, were retained to prepare the defense which Brewster was then entrusted to deliver to Navarro County. G. W. Paschal went to Galveston to work up the defense and discovered that Hale had returned from Mexico. Apparently Hale became angry that additional attorneys had been employed, though Stewart did not learn of this until after his return to Louisville.

In the meantime, Stewart was confronted by a problem of more serious proportions. The colonists had begun agitating for legislation on the controversy, and early in January 1850 had sent an imposing series of petitions to Austin requesting Governor Peter Hansborough Bell to appoint a traveling land commissioner to examine the proof of each colonist to the land he claimed and to issue some form of official certificate from the land office.[27] A joint committee of both houses was appointed in the legislature to study the problem, and on January 21, 1850, a law was enacted, detrimental to the company's interests, entitled: "An act to secure to all actual settlers within the limits of the colony granted to Peters and others, commonly known as Peters' Colony, the land to which they are entitled as colonists."[28] The first section of the act provided that each head of family was entitled to 640 acres and each single man, 320 acres, regardless of contracts to the contrary which the colonists might have signed or assented to. This seems to have been intended not only to secure the colonists' claims to a full grant, but to destroy the company's claim to the half-grants. Several sections of the act provided a legislative answer to problems that had arisen concerning the claims of the colonists. For example the heirs of a dead colonist were entitled to his land, settlers who had located on old surveys had to move, and where two or more settlers had located on one section the first arrival had preference.

The company's position as empresario was completely ignored by the act. Settlers whose land had not been surveyed could demand that service from county surveyors, rather than the company surveyor. The governor was authorized to appoint a commissioner to travel through the colony to issue certificates to the colonists describing the amount of land each was entitled to. To establish his claim a colonist had to produce two witnesses who would take oath before the commissioner that the colonist had settled prior to July 1, 1848. During the summer of 1850 this commissioner, Thomas William Ward, traveled through the colony making temporary headquarters at Dallas, Mc-Kinney, Sherman, Alton and Waxahachie.

By opening a procedure through which the colonists could deal directly with the state, this law mitigated against the interests of the Texas Emigration and Land Company, despite a final clause which stated: "That nothing herein contained shall be construed so as to place the contractors of said colony in a better or worse condition in regard to the State of Texas, than they would be if this act had not been passed." Furthermore the act had canceled the company's claim to the half-grants of the settlers.

Stewart had to take immediate action, and he decided to institute on his own initiative the counter suit against the state that the company had been tentatively planning. He employed I. A. Paschal to draw up a petition to introduce in the Travis District Court. At this time the Travis District Court was in vacation, and Judge William Jones was in Seguin. Paschal presented the petition to Judge Jones in Seguin, and Jones issued a temporary injunction against the Commissioner of the General Land Office restraining him from issuing patents as contemplated by the act. In the petition, Stewart also prayed that the court issue a writ of mandamus to compel the Commissioner to issue patents to the company and to receive the evidence of the fulfillment of the contract. After Jones had seen the petition and issued the temporary injunction, the petition was sent back to Brewster in Austin to be filed in the March term of the Travis District Court. Before he left Austin, Stewart made all the arrangements for security on the necessary bond.[29]

Stewart soon learned that Brewster failed to file the petition in the Travis District Court and that he did not attend the Navarro Court hearing in March, which was postponed until October because the defendant was absent from the hearing. Realizing that he had been duped by Brewster, Stewart then wrote Hale, explaining why he had employed another attorney and requesting Hale to resume the defense of the company:

> In my great anxiety to do all that should have been done to protect the interest of those I represent, I may have consulted too many lawyers and thereby given offense to all. If so I regret it exceedingly. It was an error of the head and not of the heart. *And whether you have anything further to do with the case or not I would be obliged if you would write me what proof we ought to make in the Navarro case, and what course we ought to pursue.* And whether you assisted George W. Paschal, Esq. in preparing the Navarro defense or whether it was prepared at all as he has never written me a word on the subject.[30]

Stewart asked Hale to let the company send him some money in advance on his fee or as a retainer. There is a slightly frantic note in the last paragraph of this letter:

> I am at a loss to know what we should prove or to do in this trial. Ought we to prove fulfillment of the contract? If so, all of our proofs are filed or will be in the Travis Suit and that Court is held about the same time as the Navarro Court and they can not be taken then and if they could I should be very unwilling that they should go there as I would not consider them safe . . . I am totally unadvised as to what we ought to do.[31]

In desparation, the company turned to Hedgcoxe, on July 31, 1850, authorizing him "to employ lawyers and to institute, prosecute, or defend all suits that are now pending in Texas."[32] Soon after these instructions to Hedgcoxe, Hale consented to return to the company's defense for a bonus of four shares of stock in the Texas Emigration and Land Company. For appearances' sake this stock seems to have been set aside to be issued to Hale after the controversy was settled.[33] Together Hale and Hedgcoxe secured the postponement of the suit in the Navarro District Court in October, probably on the grounds that none of the defendants were residents of the state.[34]

The postponement of the Navarro suit gave the company some relief, since the suit in which the company was plaintiff and the general land office defendant was still pending in the Travis District Court. Though Brewster had failed to introduce the petition in the March term of that court, Paschal had written a new petition, sent it to Louisville for signatures, and entered it in the fall term of the court on August 18, 1850. In this petition the company recited the history of the colony, giving in detail the laws and contracts involved, and claimed that 1520 families and 1350 single men had been introduced as colonists. The company alleged that the land commissioner had refused to receive evidence of the company's fulfillment of the contracts and had refused to issue patents to the company.[35] Paschal posted the five thousand dollar bond that Stewart had arranged for before he left Austin, and Judge Jones issued another temporary injunction to restrain the land commissioner.[36]

The suit came to a hearing on October 16, but by agreement of both parties it was continued to the next term of the court.[37] The injunction preventing the land commissioner from issuing titles excited the colonists. On December 2, 1850, they secured from the legislature an act "to authorize the Settlers in Peters' colony to intervene in Suit or suits, in reference to any Matters connected with said Colony contracts, where they have an interest."[38] John Neely Bryan, one of the leading colonists, and M. T. Johnson,[39] filed petitions of intervenor in the suit in the Travis Court on October 12. 1851.[40] Bryan claimed that he had come to the colony under the auspices of the empresarios prior to March 1, 1843, and presented as evidence a certificate given him by Samuel Browning dated Feb. 27, 1843, entitling him to 640 acres. Bryan had had his section surveyed privately and submitted to the court a copy of his field notes. He prayed that the court would order his patent issued. Johnson's case was not so strong,[41] and the court, on October 25, dismissed Johnson's intervenor, but continued Bryan's until the next term.[42]

The company became alarmed at the prospects of endless litigation, and in 1849 a stockholder named Guthrie first suggested that the company memorialize the legislature, setting forth all the facts, in order to secure a compromise act settling the controversy.[43] Later Willis Stewart had written that it might be wise for the company to send an agent to the next meeting of the legislature,[44] and at a stockholders' meeting in August, 1851, the company resolved to send Stewart back to Texas to represent the cause to the legislature.[45]

In Austin, Stewart met with Hedgcoxe and I. A. Paschal and drew up a memorial to the legislature stating the company's grievances and desire for settlement.[46] The problem was brought to the attention of the legislature by Governor Bell in his annual message on November 10, 1851:

> Under the authority of the Ordinance adopted by the Convention which framed the Constitution of the State, one of my predecessors directed a suit to be commenced against the contractors of what is known as "Peters' Colony", to ascertain whether or not they had forfeited their right under the contract. That suit I am informed is still pending, and that no progress has been made in it. No report has yet been received from the Commissioner appointed under the law passed at the last regular session of the Legislature, to secure to the settlers in that Colony, the lands to which they are entitled. That officer is at this time performing the duties required of him under the law, and as soon as his report is received at this Department, it will be submitted to the Honorable Legislature. I am informed that the law, in its practical operation, has been found defective, and has failed in some particulars in effecting the objects for which it was intended. Shortly after it was passed, an injunction was granted by one of the Judges, at the instance of one of the contractors, which has greatly restrained its operation, and that suit, I am advised, is still pending, and may not be brought to a final decision for years.

As the act in its terms declares that nothing therein contained, shall be so construed as to prejudice the rights of the contractors, it would seem proper that some method should be adopted to ascertain their rights, at an early day, and if possible, to obtain an amicable and satisfactory arrangement of the whole matter. The immense litigation which will be involved in this controversy, if permitted to continue, will greatly retard the growth of one of the finest districts in the State, as nothing is more detrimental to the permanent improvement and advancement of a country, than uncertainty of tenure in its lands. I would therefore recommend that this subject receive the early attention of the Legislature.[47]

A joint committee of both houses, headed by R. P. Crumb for the House and G. W. Hill for the Senate, was appointed to study the question. To this committee went Stewart's memorial, the message from the governor, and a special report of the attorney general, together with various documents relating to the difficulties to the Peters colony.[48] The committee reported to both houses on January 6, 1852.[49] The report, though cloaked in terms of judicious impartiality, was highly favorable to the company. The contractors had submitted various records to the committee which seem to have been arranged to present the company in the best light. In order to show the bias of the committee in favor the company, several sections of the report are quoted below in which the committee described the company's activities and its proofs that the contract had been fulfilled:

Multifarious and extensive as these proofs are, and embracing in their details, repetition and affidavits of many persons, frequently relating to but one colonist, it might be supposed that they were entangled together, and little better than a confused mass of facts and testimony, but this is not the case. By the arrangement which is introduced throughout this business, we are enabled to trace each and every colonist through the various kinds of proof which has been collected concerning him. In their book the names of the colonists are alphabetically arranged; the land claimed or settled upon by the colonist is shown opposite his name, also the cabins he has built, the number of his children, male and female, his slaves, guns and ammunition, the time he settled in the colony and upon his section, the State he emigrated from, and the names of persons, who in various certificates have testified to his introduction and settlement. To these are added references to the various papers, etc., containing more particularly the proofs relating to the immigrants and their colonization. Indeed so perfect is the disposition of every thing connected with this colonial evidence, that it seems that the contractors have nothing to hide, but trust entirely and alone to a full and perfect expose of their affairs.[50]

The committee's report was exaggerated in other ways. According to the committee the company had settled nearly 4000 colonists (1590 families and 1230 single men) in full compliance with the law. The committee also reported more colonists settled by 1848 than there were persons in the area enumerated on the census in 1850,[51] and over twice as many colonists as Thomas William Ward issued land certificates to in 1850.[52] Furthermore, the report was not correct in stating that the company had made sufficient surveys to settle the colonists as they were introduced or in stating that the company had completed the surveying by 1848.

Nevertheless on the basis of its findings the committee offered a bill to the senate designed to satisfy both the company and the colonists, and made the following plea for the bill's favorable consideration by the legislature:

> The fulfillment of the contracts is a question which might certainly be left to the tribunals of the country, but the expense and delay consequent upon such a course would be to these persons disastrous and ruinous in the extreme; the subject therefore urges itself upon us as a measure of wise State policy, and one in which the principles of conciliation and compromise should freely enter. The colonists are miserably situated; they cannot improve their lands, nor sell them to advantage; they are confined to a country they love, but dare not improve.
>
> The taxes are unpaid; their county treasuries are impoverished, and the State herself is in this respect no small sufferer. In short, an extensive and important district of rich and beautiful country, settled upon by a hardy, industrious and virtuous population, must inevitably languish for many years under the baneful and withering influences of delayed litigation, unless relieved by some measure of adjustment and compromise.[58]

The plea urged expediency not equity; the exigency of the situation demanded a settlement for the good of the state. The bill was therefore designed to satisfy all parties at the expense of the state and was based on the compromise suggested by Stewart.[54] Since the state had the right to donate land to settlers, the company did not object to that part of the law of January 21, 1850, which guaranteed every family 640 acres and every single man 320. But the company did object to having the guarantee made good out of the half-grants that the company claimed under its contracts. In order to reach a compromise, however, the company was willing to relinquish its claims to the half-grants if the state would provide an equal amount of land for the company. The committee suggested that this amount be 2000 sections. The company agreed to withdraw its suit against the commissioner of the general land office if the compromise arrangements were adopted by the legislature.[55]

Such a bill was passed and approved on February 10, 1852, the only change being that the 2000 sections were reduced to 1700. The bill as passed provided that if the company relinquished all its rights in the colony within twenty days and withdrew the suit in the Travis District Court, the state would dismiss the suit in the Navarro Court and issue to the company certificates for 1700 sections of land. These certificates were transferable and could be located on any land within the colony not claimed by a colonist prior to August 4, 1852. The colony area was to be reserved to the company for two and a half years in order to permit the location of the certificates, but the company was required to alienate at least one-half of the land within ten years. The company had to furnish a map to each district surveyor who was supposed to locate on it all old surveys he had knowledge of and return it to the company agent, who was in turn to add the information about colonists' claims and send the maps to the land commissioner. Every six months thereafter the agent was to send a detailed report to the land commissioner of the new surveys by the company. The numerical discrepancy between Ward's list of colonists and the company's claims was noticed by a clause permitting all colonists who had not signed a Ward-certificate to receive a certificate from any county or district court within the colony.[56]

Though they sought to hide the fact, the company was tremendously enriched by the law. It had exchanged unwarranted and illegal claims to about 600,000 acres for an outright grant of 1,088,000 acres, worth then between $250,-000 and $300,000. In urging the compromise, the joint committee had overlooked the basic question of the legality of the company's claims to the half-grants, and this question was never tested by either court or legislature. As pointed out earlier in this work, the company had no valid claim to these half-grants, since such a claim rested on the promise that the company had performed certain services for the colonists and that the colonists had elected to pay for these services with land instead of money. Few if any of these services had been performed and the money option had not been tendered to nor accepted by any colonist.

In their anxiety to comply with the law's provisions, Stewart and Hedgcoxe signed the relinquishments on February 7, three days before Governor Bell signed the bill.[57] Stewart returned to Kentucky, Hedgcoxe went to the colony to set up his land office as required by the law, and the legislature adjourned on February 16. None seemed to realize the violent reaction the "compromise" was to produce.

FOOTNOTES FOR PART IV

Northern Standard, July 3, 1852.

[2]Stewart to Hale, September 7, 1848, Hale Papers, I, 192.

[3]Stewart to Hale, November 13, 1848, Hale Papers, I, 202.

[4]Stewart to Hale, January 3, 1849, Hale Papers, I, 210; Hedgcoxe to Merrill, January 23, 1849, Hale Papers, Env. I.

[5]Hedgcoxe to Merrill, January 18, 1849, Hale Papers, I, 220.

[6]Merrill to Hedgcoxe, January 19, 1849, Hale Papers, I, 222. (The 354, 262 acres seems to have been land that Hedgcoxe was claiming for the company as premium land.)

[7]Hedgcoxe to Merrill, January 23, 1849, Hale Papers, Env. I.

[8]Gammel, *Laws of Texas*, II, 1066, 1444.

[9]*Ibid.*, III, 475.

[10]*Ibid.*, 607.

[11]Since there is no documentary evidence of the redemption, it must be inferred from the fact that there was no further controversy on this point.

[12]Stewart to Hale, September 7, 1848, Hale Papers, I, 192.

[13]Stewart to Hale, January 3, 1849, Hale Papers, I, 212. A fragmentary copy of this map was located in the general land office.

¹⁴Extract from "Report of the Texas Emigration and Land Company, January 24, 1849." Colony Contracts file, General Land Office.

¹⁵Stewart to Hale, January 3, 1849.

¹⁶Stewart to Hale, January 3, 1849.

¹⁷*Northern Standard*, December 28, 1849.

¹⁸Stewart to Hale, January 3, 1849.

¹⁹*Ibid.*

²⁰Extract from the "Report of the Texas Emigration and Land Company," Colony Contracts file, G. L. O.

²¹Power of attorney from John J. Smith and William C. Peters to Willis Stewart, February 2, 1849, Colony Contracts file, G. L. O.

²²Stewart to Hale, July 19, 1850, Hale Papers, II, 295. Stewart was accompanied from Galveston to Austin by Ebenezer Allen, Hale's law partner, because Hale was in Mexico.

²³This may have been Henry Percy Brewster (1816-1887), who had been Attorney General under Governor G. T. Wood from 1847 to 1849.

²⁴Stewart to Hale, July 12, 1850. Brewster later received $400 more for his services, which in the end seemed to be worthless. (Stewart to Hale, July 12, 1850.)

²⁵*Northern Standard*, December 28, 1849, and February 16 through April 13, 1850.

²⁶Stewart to Hale, August 26, 1850.

²⁷There are nine such documents containing perhaps 500 names, State Department Colonization Papers, 1846-1873, Archives, Texas State Library.

²⁸Gammel, *Laws of Texas*, III, 489.

²⁹Stewart to Hale, July 19, 1850.

³⁰Stewart to Hale, July 12, 1850.

³¹*Ibid.*

³²Power of attorney by Willis Stewart and John J. Smith to Henry O. Hedgcoxe, July 31, 1850, Colony Contracts file, G. L. O.

³³Stewart to Hale, July 30, 1852, Hale Papers, Env. 1851-52. "I have not forgotten the Four shares of stock, altho they have never been transferred to you on the books of the company, they shall be held for your use until wanted."

³⁴Hedgcoxe to Hale, September 4, 1850, Hale Papers, II, 305; Stewart to Hale, October 7, 1850. The postponement of the suit has been inferred from collateral evidence since no direct document has been found, and the records of the Navarro County Court are not available. The inference is also drawn from correspondence indicating the company's intentions. The company was later condemned for seeming to be anxious to have the suit reinstituted in a federal court, since a nefarious connection was made between the federal judge for the district of Texas, John C. Watrous, and the company's attorney, William G. Hale. As the controversy was settled before reaching the federal court, it does not seem necessary to discuss here the allegations made by Sam Houston when demanding the impeachment of Watrous. A discussion of the Watrous affair, tending to the defense of Watrous, can be found in Wallace Hawkins, *The Case of John C. Watrous, United States Judge for Texas: A Political Story of High Crimes and Misdemeanors.*

³⁵Petition, with indorsements, Travis District Court, Archives, File No. 54.

³⁶Injunction Bond, August 18, 1850, Travis District Court, Archives, File No. 54, and Injunction served on George W. Smythe, General Land Commissioner, same file.

³⁷Travis District Court, Civil Minutes, Vol. C., p. 10.

³⁸Gammel, *Laws of Texas*, II, 844.

³⁹This was probably the M. T. Johnson who ran for governor a few years later. The name does not appear on the list of colonists submitted by land commissioner Ward.

⁴⁰Travis District Court, Civil Minutes, C, 137.

⁴¹Copy of decree for intervenors and petitions of Bryan and Johnson, Travis District Court, File 54.

⁴²Travis District Court, Civil Minutes, C, 171.

⁴³Stewart to Hale, January 3, 1849.

⁴⁴Stewart to Hale, July 14, 1850, and August 26, 1850, Hale Papers.

⁴⁵Appointment of Willis Stewart, August 11, 1851, Colony Contracts file, G. L. O.

⁴⁶The memorial itself was not located in the memorial file in the archives of the Texas State Library, but reference is made to it in the report of the joint committee of the Fourth Legislature, discussed below. See Senate Journal, Fourth Legislature, Regular Session, 267, and House Journal, Fourth Leg., Reg. Sess., 477.

⁴⁷Senate Journal, 4 Leg., Reg. Ses., 41. Actually the legislature's attention had already been directed to the question. On November 7, Senator Samuel Bogart introduced a bill to amend the law of February 21, 1850. This bill was read a second time and passed on November 10 before the Governor's message was read. Later the bill was read a third time and tabled. Senate Journal, 4 Leg., Reg. Ses., 19, 23, 277, 299.

⁴⁸Senate Journal, 4 Leg., Reg. Ses., 267. The investigator has not been able to find these documents. Probably many of them were the same that had been submitted to the Travis District Court as evidence, but withdrawn by Paschal. File 54, Archives, Travis District Court.

⁴⁹House Journal, Fourth Legislature, Reg. Ses., 477-486; Senate Journals, Fourth Leg., Reg. Ses., 267-276.

⁵⁰Senate Journal, 4 Leg., Reg. Ses., 272. Unfortunately the evidence with which the Committee worked cannot be located. This evidence probably included large portions of the company's files, for which the investigator has been vainly searching.

⁵¹Based on a rough estimate by the investigator.

⁵²Furthermore, the committee figures do not correspond with the claims of the company in their petition to the Travis District Court.

⁵³Senate Journal, 4 Leg., Reg. Sess., 725 (so numbered in the Journal; should be 275).

⁵⁴Stewart's memorial has not been located, but its context can be inferred from the tenor of the bill.

⁵⁵It is to be noted that the committee did not mention the Navarro suit, which suggests that it had been dismissed or indefinitely postponed.

⁵⁶Gammel, Laws of Texas, II, 950-957. It is noteworthy that only a few persons took advantage of this procedure, and many of these were later proved to have made fradulent claims.

⁵⁷Dismissal of suit, File 54, Archives, Travis District Court; Relinquishment, File 18, Colony Contracts file, G. L. O., February 7, 1852.

(To Be Continued)

KENTUCKY COLONIZATION IN TEXAS

A HISTORY OF THE PETERS COLONY

SEYMOUR V. CONNOR

Part V

THE HEDGCOXE WAR

The essence of the conflict in the colony may be described in a paragraph. Land speculators holding unlocated land certificates were violently opposed to the compromise law which not only closed to them the 16,400 square mile colony reservation but permitted the company to patent one million, eighty-eight thousand acres in the choice locations or to sell unlocated certificates in that amount which would flood the market and depress prices. Since there was possibly 800,000 to one million acres in outstanding paper, the addition of the Texas Emigration and Land Company paper could inflate the market by over one hundred per cent.

Among land locators outside the colony organized opposition to the company had started developing before the compromise law of February 10, 1852 was passed. In the spring of 1849 a public meeting was held in Henderson County, about one hundred miles from the colony, from which a committee of thirty, none of whom were colonists, was selected to defend the colonists from the "villanious tyranny" of the company. This committee passed resolutions requesting the citizens of each county in the colony to hold mass meetings and elect delegates to a general colony convention to be held in Dallas on May 21, 1849.

In the ensuing controversy it is impossible accurately to determine the roles of legitimate colonists, speculators, and politicians. John H. Reagan, one of Texas' most eminent statesmen, was to rise to prominence by making a political issue of the controversy, and others, among them J. W. Throckmorton,[1] were to gain or lose popularity over the colony question. Reagan, at that time a relatively unknown lawyer,[2] was a leader in the Henderson County meeting. He was selected with several others to attend the proposed Dallas convention, and it was announced that the Henderson meeting would support John H. Reagan for state senator in the fall election.[3]

The Dallas convention, held on May 21, elected Peter Dakan president, J. W. Throckmorton secretary, and sent a memorial to the legislature praying for relief for both the Peters and the Mercer colonists. In the senatorial elections that fall the chief issue was the colonists' demand for titles to their land, and

Reagan was defeated by Samuel Bogart. Reagan apparently had not been willing to make promises so extensive as Bogart's. Of this campaign Reagan made the following statement:

> It was the only time I was ever defeated in a popular election, and in this case I deliberately accepted defeat rather than promise the people to do what I felt sure would operate to their injury.[4]

Although defeated in the campaign of 1849, Reagan saw the political opportunities offered by the controversy. He announced himself as opposed to the compromise law of 1852 before it was passed, deprecated the company's claims, and warned that the citizens' rights were in danger.[5] Also, as a former locator of certificates and as a man who profited from land paper speculation,[6] Reagan may have had some personal interest in thwarting the law.

Therefore his actions during 1852 were linked closely to the organized opposition against Hedgcoxe, the company, and the compromise law. Whatever Reagan's motives for entering the 1852 controversy, his contentions were basically correct. As has been pointed out, the company's claim to the 1,088,000 acres was neither legally nor morally valid, but rested instead on a highly favorable committee report which ignored the basic issue in the case. Reagan said of this: "If the Committee and the Legislature had known as well as every colonist knew, how false the statements contained in the Report were, their actions would have been different."[7]

It was the locators, however, not the colonists, who began the attack on the compromise law, and as before the opposition was initially organized outside the colony. A "mass meeting" was held in the town of Springfield in Limestone County under the leadership of John Boyd, J. P. Philpott, John Caruthers, William Croft, Benjamin F. Lynn, A. G. Gholston, and J. P. Lynch, none of whom were colonists. The meeting adopted resolutions framed in emotional language and calculated to arouse the people against the company and the law. According to the resolutions, the company had maintained "a piratical system of extortion upon the settlers, and harassed them with arbitrary requirements." The Convention of 1845 had "heard the cry of the oppressed," but the Legislature "disregarding the provisions of said ordinance," had "actually *compromised* with the company, granting them the enormous amount of seventeen hundred sections of land—an amount sufficient to have built a railroad from the center to the circumference of the state." The law was therefore "unconstitutional—a fraud—speculative—an attempted robbery—partial in its bearing—unjust—impolitic—calculated to engender litigation, and carrying upon its face unmistakeable evidence of imbecility or corruption." The governor was requested to call a special session of the legislature,[8] "that our Statute Book may be purged of this foul blotch," and colonists were urged to hold mass meetings to protest the law. Concern over the possible coming sale of unlocated certificates was expressed as follows:

> Resolved. That as we believe said company will never attempt to locate said land but will attempt to sell certificates to innocent persons, and that as we believe said certificates are absolutely worthless—*an unconstitutional law can vest no right*, we most solemnly warn all citizens of this State and of the United States, and of the whole world, not to purchase them.[9]

The resolutions were ordered published in all the papers of the state as an indication that the Limestone people intended to make an organized fight.[10] Their opposition was unintentionally abetted by Hedgcoxe's actions at this time. To fulfill the requirements of the compromise law, Hedgcoxe established his headquarters about four miles from McKinney, and published (broadside) a proclamation "explaining" the compromise law to the colonists. The proclamation simply stated that colonists would be allowed until August 4, 1852, to establish their claims with Hedgcoxe. This was no more than the law had already established, but the tone was autocratic and arrogant.[11] It undoubtedly aroused considerable feeling throughout the colony and contributed to the misinterpretation of the compromise law. In issuing the proclamation, Hedgcoxe acted as a bonded officer of the state government,[12] but he continued to be the agent of the company, and his dual role made his actions difficult for the settlers to interpret. His "bombastic circular,"[13] was immediately attacked by the speculators who gained much popularity for their cause by calling Hedgcoxe such names as "Lord Hedgcoxe Duke Grand Mogul, etc., of the Three Forks of the Trinity,"[14] and the "most obnoxious man to the colonists."[15]

The compromise law was identified with Hedgcoxe. The speculators argued that the law virtually abrogated the claim "of the widows and orphans of the Fathers whose blood waters the plains of the Alamo, Goliad, and San Jacinto, so that none can receive a patent to their lands, . . . unless they prostrate themselves before Lord Hedgcoxe, Lord Stewart, or whosoever else may be the company's *anointed* and *He* shall say, 'I allow it.' "[16]

The Limestone meeting had been held on April 28, 1852; a meeting was planned for Dallas on May 15,[17] and Reagan accepted a request[18] to make an address by a number of colonists who professed themselves to be dissatisfied with the opinions expressed in the Hedgcoxe proclamation.[19] His speech, published in the Dallas *Herald*, was pacifist on the surface but used language designed to further agitation. While urging moderation against the "bold and unauthorized assumptions of power" by Hedgcoxe and his "singular construction" of the law, he advised the citizens to avoid violence, and "to trust to the moral force of justice to vindicate them from the agent's abuses." In a later address he urged the people not to attack Hedgcoxe and drive him from the colony. "I deprecate mobs, but I think that there is a difference between a lawless mob, and the united resistance, by an injured, wronged, and insulted people, of the lawless conduct of the petty tyrant of foreign nabobs who happened by accident or ignorance, to be clothed with a little brief authority."[20] (Cry Havoc and let slip the dogs of war.)

The Dallas meeting adopted resolutions to the effect that Hedgcoxe did not have the power to adjudicate any colonist's claim and that the alternate section reservation in the contract of July 20, 1843, had ceased to exist when that contract expired. It also took the occasion "to express our regret that the last Legislature should have gone so far beyond the demands of right, reason, and equity, as to give the Peters' Company *one million and eighty-eight thousand* acres of land for what they did towards the settlement of this colony, and that we regard the appointment of H. O. Hedgcoxe with the power given him under the act of February 10, as having been both unfortunate and unwise."[21]

To the resolutions the meeting appended a note of thanks to John H. Reagan for "his frank, able, and eloquent address," and requested him to publish it in the Dallas *Herald*. Furthermore, the meeting resolved that "we will aid and assist" any colonist oppressed by the company "by all the means in our power to obtain his rights as a colonist—peaceably if we can—forcibly if we must."[22]

Excitement was increased among company opponents when Ebenezer Allen, Attorney General and erstwhile partner of William G. Hale, delivered on June 3 an opinion upholding the law.[23] Willis Stewart said that his opinion fell "amongst the colonists like a Congreve Rocket, and is bitterly denounced by some of the rebellious spirits there."[24]

B. Warren Stone, a leader of the rebellious spirits, proclaimed Allen's opinion as "very strange—unprofessional—canting."[25] Reagan returned to the colony on July 1, and formally addressed meetings on July 10 and on July 13. At the second "large and highly Respectable meeting of the citizens of Dallas County," a resolution was adopted calling for the resignation of Samuel Bogart, Reagan's old opponent, from the senate.[26]

On July 12 and 13, a committee, claiming to represent the citizens of Dallas County and consisting of A. Bledsoe, Samuel B. Pryor, Alexander Harwood, James H. Smith, J. W. Crockett, and B. Warren Stone, forced their way into Hedgcoxe's office in Collin County and proceeded to make an "investigation" of his records.[27] On July 15 this committee apparently reported to a mass meeting in Dallas that fraud and corruption were undermining the claims of the colonists who had filed with Hedgcoxe, and that he was planning to do the colonists every sort of evil. Reagan made another "conciliatory" speech lasting several hours urging the people "to abstain from a resort to violence." This was followed by an episode known in Texas history as the "Hedgcoxe War."[28]

During the night of July 15, John J. Good, a militia commander, led a contingent of armed men from the Dallas meeting to Hedgcoxe's office, which was apparently located in or adjacent to his home. Hedgcoxe was ordered to leave the colony, and his files of the colonists' claims, together with the books, maps, and papers of the company, were seized. Hedgcoxe fled the next day to Austin.[29] Good and his men returned to Dallas, deposited Hedgcoxe's papers in the courthouse, and joined the general celebration of what was imagined was a brilliant coup. Good wrote:

> We reached this place [Dallas] early this morning, and met a brilliant reception from the citizens of Dallas County, at whose expense we have been feasting and revelling until this time (3 o'clock) and still the excitement is up. Sam Bogart was promenaded around the square, in effigy, on a rail, then [they] swung him to a black jack and burned him. William Myres a spy of the company's here, was seized, rode around for some time, on the sharp edge of a rail, and the other spies of the company are notified that one month is given them in which to arrange their business and to leave this country.[30]

The attack on Hedgcoxe and the confiscation of his files threw the colony into an uproar. Many feared that the action jeopardized their claims under the compromise law; some who had filed with Hedgcoxe feared their claims would be lost; but others sanctioned the actions wholeheartedly. On July 20 a citizens' meeting in McKinney resolved that the attack on Hedgcoxe was unwarranted, that the stolen records should be returned, that Bogart and Throckmorton were not to be condemned, and that the convention of the colonists suggested by the Dallas meeting be held July 29 in McKinney.[31] On July 24, a Denton County meeting resolved that "we heartily concur in the action of our fellow-citizens of our Colony, in ordering Hedgcoxe to leave the colony, with all those associated with him," that Bogart and Throckmorton resign their seats in the legislature, and "that as we are unwilling to enter into a long and expensive law suit with a lordly company of European Aristocrats, which would cost more to support than our lands are worth and the crisis having arrived at which forbearance ceases to be a virtue, we will defend our homes to the last extremity, *peacably if we can—forcibly if we must.*"[32]

Meetings were probably held in the other counties though no record of them has been found. Delegates from each county were in attendance at the McKinney Convention. Below is a list of delegates with the names of bona fide colonists italicized.

COLLIN COUNTY—*Pleasant Wilson*, J. H. Wilcox, George H. Pigues, Samuel Bogart, *Jacob Baccus*, and J. W. Throckmorton.

COOKE COUNTY—*Aaron Hill*, Daniel Montague, *Robert F. Shannon, William Middleton, R. D. Turner*, and William C. Twitty.

DALLAS COUNTY—*J. M. Crockett, J. W. Smith, T. C. Hawpe, William H. Hord*, B. Warren Stone, and J. W. Latimer.

DENTON COUNTY—*James W. Chowning, A. P. Lloyd, John W. King, Daniel Strickland, Jesse Gibson*, and *Samuel A. Pritchen* (Pritchitt).

ELLIS COUNTY—John H. Reagan, Edward H. Tarrant, E. W. Rogers, *E. C. Newton*, J. E. Patten, and W. Whatler.

GRAYSON COUNTY—*William S. Reeves*, Rev. A. Bone, *William Southwood, J. B. Earhart, T. H. Wilson*, Burrell P. Smith.

TARRANT COUNTY—*John W. Elliston*, S. *Gilmore*, M. T. Johnson, Francis Jordan, *Micajah Goodwin*, and Alexander Young.[33]

A substantial part of the opposition to the company came from persons who were not colonists and whose attack on the company and the law was a result of interest in unlocated land paper. This fact is further emphasized by an examination of the leaders of the convention. John H. Reagan, J. H. Wilcox, *Aaron Hill*, J. W. Latimer, *John W. King*, John H. Wilson, and M. T. Johnson were on the committee which drafted the resolutions adopted by the convention. Of these, only *Hill, King*, and *Wilson* were colonists. Because the minutes of the convention were recorded and published in the *Northern Standard*,[34] it is possible to analyze further the leadership; again the names of colonists have been italicized. M. T. Johnson and J. W. Latimer were president and secretary *pro tem*. The permanent officers were Azariah Bone, president; Burrell P. Smith, vice-president; J. W. Latimer and J. H. Swindells, secretaries; and Daniel Howell, sergeant at arms. The following men served on three of the five committees appointed by the convention: B. Warren Stone, John H. Reagan, and M. T. Johnson. The following men served on two committees: *J. W. Crockett*, Burrell P. Smith, *John Wilson*, Daniel Montague, *A. P. Lloyd*, E. W. Rogers and *Aaron Hill*. During the three sessions of the convention B. Warren Stone was reported as speaking fifteen times; M. T. Johnson, fourteen times; John H. Reagan, eleven times; *J. W. Crockett*, seven times; J. W. Throckmorton, four times; *J. B. Earhart*, three times; and all others, five times.

An examination of the italicized names in the above lists illustrates the origin of the leadership. This was not a spontaneous movement of colonists. The motives of the leaders can be discovered in the resolutions adopted. The first, which was unanimously accepted, set the tone for the rest. It is quoted below:

> Resolved: That the outrages and insults inflicted upon the rights and feelings of the people of the Peters Colony by Henry O. Hedgcoxe, the agent of the company, and the preconcerted schemes of villainy and fraud which he was daily carrying out, and by which he was greatly endangering the colonists in the secure enjoyment of their rights to land in the colony made it necessary for the people of the colony, for the security of these rights, to take the books, maps, and papers of said agent, into their own hands, and to drive him out of the colony.[35]

The second resolution placed B. Warren Stone in charge of the stolen papers and left their disposal largely to his discretion. A memorial was prepared asking the Governor to call a [special] session of the legislature and demanding the repeal of the compromise law, especially the provisions reserving the colony area to the company for two and a half years and granting them certificates for 1700 sections of land. A permanent committee was appointed to collect evidence of the company's villainy; John H. Reagan was retained as counsel at a fee of ten thousand dollars; another meeting of the convention was planned; and finally a committee headed by Reagan drafted an "Address to the People of the State" which was adopted and ordered published broadside and in all the papers of the state.

The main contention of Reagan's statement in this "Address" is unquestionably valid. He held that the company did not completely fulfill the requirements of the contracts within either the letter or the spirit of the law. The various minor contentions are not altogether true, and were obviously based on hearsay rather than on actual evidence. Furthermore, the hearsay evidence came from a group in which a large number were not colonists and whose leadership was almost completely non-colonist.

As the excitement aroused by the McKinney Convention faded, there was a realignment of political forces in the area. In response to the demands of the Stone faction in Dallas, Throckmorton and Crockett resigned their seats in the legislature and campaigned for re-election on the basis of a modification of their earlier stand on the compromise law. Samuel Bogart refused to resign to stand in a special election against John H. Reagan who had emerged a politically powerful figure.[36]

For more than a year after the convention both Bogart and Reagan resorted to the vituperative language of the time accusing one another of falsehood, treachery, and general dishonesty. The fight between them was over the issue of the Peters colony compromise law that Bogart had supported in the legislature. More newspaper space was devoted to the name calling than had been given to the news itself, and the true history of the controversy has ever after been clouded by the various exaggerations presented by both men as "facts." Bogart accused Reagan of having been imported into the colony by land speculators to denounce the legislature and the compromise law and added that he was the prime mover in raising the people to excitement. According to Bogart, Reagan's efforts to allay the excitement were actually designed to create disturbance. Bogart said:

> His course in the colony . . . reminds me much of Anthony's harangue of the body of Caesar. He holds enchained a gaping crowd of listeners, while he portrays the sufferings of the colonists—while he caluminates the Legislature as liars or fools, or both, for passing this 'telegraphic law'—while he advises them 'no longer to submit to the trickery, falsehoods, stratagem and corruption,' which he asserts have been practiced upon them. Then blowing hot and cold at the same breath, tells the citizens 'not to get excited—do no harm to any one—do not *rise and mutiny*. Forgive me that I am *mild* with these thy butchers.' From such persuasive powers in allaying excitement Heaven deliver us![37]

Bogart also stated that Reagan had been one of the self-appointed committee who had examined Hedgcoxe's books on July 13 and misrepresented them to the meeting on July 15.

Reagan's answers were long and detailed, and documented by sworn statements from persons living in the area. He refused to take up the veiled challenge to a duel for typically Reaganesque reasons: as a government official he had sworn to take part in no duels. He villified Bogart with a scurrility as low as the senator's, calling him "an apostate from the Christian Ministry, a murderer and a refugee from justice, a known hypocrite in both religion and politics, and now a convicted liar and slanderer of the basest character."[38]

Fortunately for the state, Reagan survived Bogart's slander, and though Bogart refused to resign and campaign against him for the senate, Reagan was able to capitalize on his popularity by seeking the office of district judge of the Ninth Judicial District, made vacant by the death of the incumbent in September. As this district included most of the colony area, Reagan won easily over his opponent, R. A. Reeves.[39]

Except for the political mudslinging, affairs in the colony seemed to quiet down after the convention. An article in the *Northern Standard*, dated October 10, 1852, stated:

> The colony excitement has so far subsided that little is said about the difficulties creating it. An adjourned meeting of the Convention held here some weeks since was held on Monday; no quorum present, the only delegation present from other counties being from Dallas and Tarrant. Among these were Col. M. T. Johnson, Messrs. Latimer, Crockett, Hawpe, and Stone. On Tuesday they adjourned sine die; having had no quorum nor attempting to effect anything. There is a circular distributed here signed "A lawful colonist of Peters Colony," believed to be written by the agent, Hedgcoxe, which is intended to counteract the feeling against him, and differs in its tone most remarkably from the previous circular issued by him, and from his conduct in pursuance of its declarations. It can produce no effect here in his favor, for there is a thorough conviction here of his unworthiness as a man and a public officer. Dr. Throckmorton the representative of Collin and Denton has resigned, to give his constituency an opportunity to pass upon his course. Mr. Crockett has taken the same course in Dallas.[40]

The company took advantage of what reaction there was to the convention to institute a policy of conciliation. In a published letter, dated September 18, 1852,[41] Stewart said the company deeply deplored the circumstances which gave rise to the difficulties in the colony. Hedgcoxe, he said, was acting not as company agent but as a government official, and the company had had no knowledge of the obnoxious circular until a printed copy was sent to Louisville. The company immediately wrote to Hedgcoxe, asking him to withdraw it. "We desire peace and harmony above all things." Stewart offered to be of what aid he could in straightening out the tangle the confiscation of the files had caused. "Now if they [the colonists] will unite with us, if we do not in a very short time satisfy them, that we are their true and best friends, we will give them leave to curse us for all time to come.[42]

De Morse added an optimistic note:

> On our first page, will be found a letter from the Trustees of the Company . . . setting forth their desire that the colonists shall obtain Patents for their lands, and for just such tracts as they desire; and the willingness of the company to cooperate in the procurement of the Patents. This we presume will settle all the difficulties in the Colony, being all that the settlers would wish. The commissioner of the Land Office, we presume, will under this state of affairs, not hesitate to issue Patents to the colonists.[43]

On January 1, 1853, the company published a letter addressed "To the Colonists of Peters Colony."[44] It began humbly in an attempt to undo the mischief of Hedgcoxe's arrogance: "The undersigned Trustees of the Texas Emigration and Land Company, beg leave most respectfully to address you." It was a well-written letter, laying the blame for the confiscation of the files on a "few misguided colonists who were by the misrepresentations of interested persons, induced to participate in that outrage." If the files had not been taken, Stewart argued, every colonist would "by this time have had a patent for his land." The company announced that it would resign all its rights in favor of the colonists and would dispute with no colonist the title to his land. Therefore, even though the compromise law permitted the company to make its locations after September 4, 1852, the company was magnanimously waiting for the colonists to recover the confiscated files and receive titles from the general land office before filing its own claims. Said Stewart: "Had the Company been the bad men they have been represented, they would at once have taken these means of harrassing and ruining you, but such was never their intention; on the contrary, they desire at once to waive all such rights in your favor; to forego all the advantage which accident or imprudence have given them, and effectually to put an end" to the controversy over the titles. Stewart announced that he would be in Austin from January 1 to April 1, 1853, and would act as adviser and intermediary with the land office for any colonist who so desired. This was followed in February by a published apology to Stephen Crosby, the general land commissioner, by Stewart, who had earlier accused Crosby of refusing to cooperate since the robbery of Hedgcoxe's office in July.[45]

Obviously, the confiscation of Hedgcoxe's files had created a problem. The claim evidence of most of the colonists was among the papers taken into custody by John Good. Presumably this evidence was deposited in the Dallas County Courthouse, but it seems never to have been made available in a body to the general land office, though occasionally individual files were sent to Austin.[46] There are various traditions concerning the fate of the Hedgcoxe files. The most creditable seems to be that Good deposited the records at the Dallas County Courthouse, and that they were later burned.[47] This is substantiated by a statement made in 1913 by 83-year old M. L. Gracey, one of the party who took the books and records from Hedgcoxe's office:

As to the books and papers I can't tell what became of them. The last I ever saw of them, the hack was there by the court-house. Old man Bledsoe and old man Crum drove the hack—But I understand they were put in a box and left with Alex Harwood and Ed Browder, and I heard, afterwards that they were burned up when the court-house burned.[48]

Whatever their fate, Hedgcoxe's stolen files do not seem to have been used as the basis for patents as the compromise law had contemplated. A further problem was created by the "Hedgcoxe War"; the law had stated that the colonists should make their claims through Hedgcoxe. That became impossible since they had driven him from the colony and taken his papers. As stated above, Stewart offered to serve as intermediary for the colonists in the place of Hedgcoxe, but since the compromise law had been specific in outlining the procedures and naming Hedgcoxe, it became necessary to amend the law.

The legislature was called for a special session and during the latter part of January began to consider the problem of land titles in the colony. On January 21, 1853, one observer commented:

The Senate has been engaged in the discussion of that endless subject—Peter's colony.—I was much amused, (although I to some extent coincided in his views) in the remarks of a Senator, who stated "that for thirteen years, he had been seeking for light by voting for every measure calculated to terminate the difficulties existing in that colony, and give to the colonists the right to their homesteads, but instead of this accomplishing its object, legislation has but involved us in more impenetrable darkness," and he was now disposed to retrograde, and seek in repeal what they had failed to effect by enactments. I find that many agree with that gentleman, as will be seen by reference to the vote on the engrossment of the bill for the repeal of the bill passed at the late session. The colonists, or I should say the demagogues who have been inciting the colonists to pursue a suicidal policy, have induced them to act with great indiscretion and to be lavish in their denunciations, and abundant in the use of Billingsgate abuse of those who acted with an eye solely directed to their benefit and prosperity.[49]

In the legislature an attempt to repeal completely the compromise law failed,[50] and a satisfactory amendment was eventually passed and approved on February 7, 1853.[51] By this act, colonists were permitted to file their claims directly and individually with the land office. The remainder of Hedgcoxe's papers were made a part of the land office archives, and the company was required to file an official map in the land office. All colonists' claims had to be described in relation to the company's surveys so they could be located on this official map. The priority period in which colonists who had not yet located their land might have preference over the company was extended three months. The commissioner of the general land office was required to issue titles to all persons filing in accordance with either the compromise law or the supplement to it. The company, as soon as the three-month waiting period was up, was permitted to begin making its locations. The land office was required to furnish the company a quarterly report on all patents issued by colonists, "as fast as the returns of the Colonists are made," and the company was required to report its locations to the land office every six months.

During the next two years, 1852-1854, the majority of the colonists filed their claims and were issued patents in the colony area. About twelve hundred colonists patented their lands and about five hundred sold their claims unpatented and unlocated. The patents were geographically distributed as follows: Collin County, 302; Cooke, 101; Dallas, 546; Denton, 189; Ellis, 122; Grayson, 192; Johnson, 32; Parker, 5; Tarrant, 239; all others, 68.

Except for relatively minor adjustments that continued for a decade to be made in the legislature and in the courts, this ended the colonists' title difficulties. After May 7, 1853, the company hastened to complete its locations and claim its land. The story of the final surveying and the completion of the company's responsibilities to the state of Texas and to the Kentucky stockholders is presented in the next section.

FOOTNOTES FOR PART V

[1]Throckmorton's activities have been traced in Claude Elliott, *Leathercoat, The Life History of a Texas Patriot*, and will not be repeated here.

[2]Reagan's connection with the Peters colony began shortly after he arrived in Texas. In 1840, as deputy surveyor in Nacogdoches County, he had made a survey excursion to the upper Trinity to locate certificates. In 1841 he participated in the attack on the Indians on Village Creek, and in the summer of 1843 he guided Sam Houston to the area to make a treaty with the Indians. In 1847 Reagan was elected for one term to the Legislature from a district that embraced a portion of the colony. (John H. Reagan, *Memoirs* ed. by Walter F. McCaleb, 43 ff.)

[3]Bonham *Advertiser*, May 17, 1849.

[4]John H. Reagan, *Memoirs*, 58. Reagan's statements about the Peters colony controversy are in many places inaccurate, but this is not surprising since he wrote his *Memoirs* many years after the controversy. In particular, Reagan merges the controversy of 1849-50 with that of 1852-53 and is confused about the final settlement. He mentions a court action in the Federal Court at Galveston which cannot be traced and in general attributes to himself a nobleness of purpose which in view of present information appears as a rationalization of opportunism.

[5]Nat M. Burford to John H. Reagan, January 1, 1852; Reagan to W. G. W. Jowers, January 26, 1852, Reagan Papers, Archives, Texas State Library.

[6]Reagan, *Memoirs*, 61.

[7]*South Western American*, March 9, 1853, from Reagan Papers (Benjamin Good, col.), Archives, University of Texas.

[8]It was already obvious that a special session was to be called over the question of apportionment of senatorial districts.

[9]*Northern Standard*, July 3, 1852.

[10]*Ibid*. The final resolution in the series stated: "Resolved that copies of this preamble and resolution be forwarded to three or more papers of this State for publication, and that all others are requested to publish them."

[11]Unfortunately this proclamation has not been located. Its contents can be inferred from collateral documents.

[12]H. P. N. Gammel (comp.), *The Laws of Texas, 1822-1897*, II, 956. His bond was set at $20,000.

[13]B. Warren Stone to Charles De Morse, July 20, 1852, *Northern Standard*, July 31, 1852.

[14]John J. Good to John H. Reagan, August 17, 1852, Reagan Papers, Archives, University of Texas.

[15]Stone to De Morse, July 20, 1852.

[16]*Northern Standard*, July 3, 1852.

[17]The Dallas meeting was probably a result of the Limestone meeting's agitation, although no documention has been found.

[18]Reagan to Bledsoe, May 11, 1852, Reagan Papers, Archives, Texas State Library.

[19]Samuel T. Bledsoe and others to John H. Reagan, May 11, 1852, in the *Northern Standard*, September 10, 1852.

[20]*State Gazette*, September 7, 1852, publication of a speech of July 10, 1852.

[21]*Northern Standard*, August 7, 1852.

[22]*Ibid.*

[23]*Northern Standard*, July 31, 1852.

[24]Stewart to Hale, July 30, 1852, Hale Papers, Env. 1851-52, Archives, University of Texas.

[25]Stone to De Morse, July 20, 1852, in the *Northern Standard*, July 31, 1852.

[26]J. W. Latimer (Secretary of the meeting) to Samuel Bogart, July 16, 1852, *Northern Standard*, August 7, 1852.

[27]A. Bledsoe and others to Charles De Morse, August 16, 1852, *Northern Standard*, September 11, 1852.

[28]Reagan later claimed that he had continually advocated peaceful measures and that he had tried to prevent the mob action that followed the July 15 meeting. He took a full page advertisement in a number of papers (see *Northern Standard*, September 10, 1853) and published statements sworn to by scores of persons to the effect that he urged temperance and tried to check the impatience of the citizens. One feels that he did protest too much and that the paid advertisements should be accepted with reservations.

[29]Hedgcoxe to Stephen Crosby, September 4, 1852, Colony Contract File, General Land Office.

[30]John J. Good to John C. Easton, July 17, 1852, in *Northern Standard*, August 7, 1852. By a misprint the letter is there dated July 17, 1851.

[31]Mass meeting of the Citizens of Collin County, *Northern Standard*, August 7, 1852.

[32]Mass Meeting in Denton County, *Northern Standard*, August 7, 1852.

[33]*Northern Standard*, October 16, 1852. Italics mine.

[34]*Ibid.*

[35]*Ibid.*

[36]Claude Elliott's *Leathercoat* gives the details of Throckmorton's re-election, pp. 29-31.

[37]*Northern Standard*, October 8, 1853. Bogart closed this attack on Reagan with a remark that seems apropos: "When your name and infamy shall have been consigned to the tomb . . . and the future historian . . . shall search the archives of the Peters Colony he will be astonished to find that in the year 1852 the Reagans, the Stones, the Crocketts, and the Goods were regarded by the people of the Three Forks as either great or wise."

[38]*Northern Standard,* September 10, 1853.

[39]Reagan, *Memoirs,* mentions without detailed information, his election. An item in the *Northern Standard,* September 10, 1853, described the campaign as friendly.

[40]*Northern Standard,* November 13, 1852.

[41]*Northern Standard,* November 20, 1852.

[42]*Ibid.*

[43]*Ibid.*

[44]*Northern Standard,* January 1, 1853.

[45]*Northern Standard,* February 12, 1853.

[46]*Northern Standard,* January 22, 1853.

[47]John M. Cochran to Mrs. Mattie Austin Hatcher, September 16, 1914, Archives, University of Texas.

[48]John M. Cochran to Mrs. Mattie Austin Hatcher, September 2, 1913, private collection, San Antonio, Texas.

[49]*Northern Standard,* February 26, 1853.

[50]*Northern Standard,* February 5, 1853.

(To Be Continued)

KENTUCKY COLONIZATION IN TEXAS

A HISTORY OF THE PETERS COLONY

SEYMOUR V. CONNOR

Part VI

THE FINAL SETTLEMENT

On May 7, 1853, the destinies of the company and of the colonists became completely divorced.[1] The company, having fulfilled its legal responsibilities to the colonists turned all of its energies to the task of realizing a profit from the rewards of its efforts in the venture. This meant surveying, patenting, and distributing the premium land among the stockholders. The difficulties of the colonists were presumed to be solved by the compromise law and its settlement granting them land and extending the location deadline to May 7, 1853.[2] The confusion which had arisen over land titles, however, was not so easily laid; nearly twenty years and ten legislative enactments were required to bring a final settlement.

In the main the United States, after Jefferson's land ordinance of 1785, recognized the problem of inaccurate or incorrect deeds and rarely opened land for sale and settlement until after it had been surveyed. The settlement of Texas had been more haphazard, especially under Mexico; clearly one of the expected benefits of the Republic's empresario laws was that land tracts would be surveyed before settlement. The empresarios in this sense were agents of the land office fulfilling for Texas a responsibility handled by the government in the United States. Had the empresarios done the surveying as required, there would have been fewer land title problems in Texas. Surveying fell behind settlement in the Peters colony, and a number of settlers, when making their claims, described their land erroneously.

The first of a number of acts dealing with land titles was passed on February 1, 1854, permitting "settlers of Peters' Colony who may have filed their claims with the agent of said Colony, in error upon lands other than that claimed by them, or where the same does not correspond with the field notes of their survey" to correct their mistake.[3]

It was soon realized that all of the colonists had not filed their claims by May 7, 1853. On February 8, 1854, the legislature passed a law requiring the land commissioner to issue a title to any colonist who presented a set of field notes accompanied by one of Ward's certificates or a certificate issued by a county court.[4]

A problem was raised by conflicts between colonists' titles and a new class of titles originated by the State in 1852. It is necessary here to pick up the thread of the evolution of the land policy from the first part of this work. Texas had begun the land policy by giving to settlers in the Republic prior to March 2, 1836, a full league and labor of land. These titles became known as First Class Certificates. Second Class Certificates, worth 1280 acres, terminated January 1, 1837. Third class certificates, worth 640 and 320 acres were issued from that date to January 1, 1842. After that date, except within the limits of an established colony, land was not available to individuals until 1853. Within the Peters colony Third Class Certificates were effectively extended until June 30, 1848, and all colony titles issued were Third Class titles. On January 22, 1845, the state passed its first pre-emption law which granted persons who had settled on unappropriated public domain a period of three years to cover their claim by a valid certificate, during which time they had a prior right to their location.[5] This law in no way granted land to settlers; it simply provided pre-emption rights or freedom from molestation by land locators for a restricted period.

The pre-emption law was converted into the western world's first "homestead" law by a Texas statute enacted on February 7, 1853. This law, which emerged naturally from the general trend of Texas land policy, made outright land grants of 320 acres to pre-emptors. By the law's terms, any person who had settled on and improved any portion of the unappropriated public domain under the terms of the previous pre-emption acts could acquire a title by paying the usual surveying costs plus twenty dollars.[6] On February 13, 1854, this act was broadened in scope though the quantity of land was reduced to 160 acres.[7]

During the period following July 1, 1848, a number of settlers who had located in the Peters colony area began claiming land under the homestead act. Land lawyers and the employees of the land office were dubious as to whether these claims were valid, since the colony area was closed to the laying of certificates for the two an half year period given the Texas Emigration and Land Company to locate its lands and since a portion of the area was included in the railroad reserve of December 21, 1853.[8] A group of preemptors therefore petitioned the legislature in November 1855 to define their rights,[9] and on January 21, 1856, a law was passed to confirm the titles of pre-emption settlers within the colony. All pre-emptors who settled prior to December 21, 1853, were given full legal rights under the pre-emption and homestead laws provided their claim did not conflict with the prior claim of a colonist.[10]

The next legislative enactment affecting the colony was of a less general nature. Five land certificates, totaling 2713 acres had been laid during the period between July 1, 1848, and February 10, 1852. The legislature on August 25, 1856, authorized the land commissioner to issue patents on the claims named in the law.[11]

In 1857 it became apparent to the land commissioner that fraudulent use had been made of the county courts' powers to issue Peters colony certificates. This power had been given the county courts to take care of the difference that seemed to exist in 1852 between the number of certificates Ward had issued and the number of colonists the company had claimed. On January 5, 1858, the legislature repealed this power of the courts,[12] and on February 4, 1858, set up machinery to determine which county court certificates had been issued illegally.[13] A travelling board of land commissioners was established to inspect the records of each county court within the colony and to hear testimony concerning the validity of county court certificates issued after February 1, 1855. The travelling board was to notify the public of its route and schedule by publication in the *Dallas Herald*, to keep a complete record of its proceedings, and to finish its business within three months. Until the board completed its investigation the land commissioner was prohibited from issuing patents on certificates of Peters colony claimants issued by county courts. Claimants whose certificates were invalidated by the board could appeal their case to the district court within a limited time, which for the claimant would be a court of last resort. Twelve hundred dollars was appropriated to cover the board's expenses.[14]

A supplement to this law, passed on January 24, 1860, gave holders of county court certifcates who had failed to file with the Board or to appeal to a district court, a period of twelve months from the passage of the law to take action on their claims through the district court.[15]

The confusion caused by the investigation of the fraudulent certificates necessitated a law to protect what was known as augmentation certificates. Colonists who had come to the colony as single men but who had married prior to July 1, 1848, were entitled to 640 acres, but most of these persons had received certificates from Ward for only 320 acres. This oversight had been corrected by augmentation certificates issued by the county courts, and on February 11, 1860, the legislature enacted a statute exempting these augmentation certificates from investigation and requiring the land commissioner to issue titles.[16]

Though the Peters colony had seemed to become a perennial subject of legislation, as well as a campaign issue for politicians, the Civil War and reconstruction problems crowded colony affairs from the legislative docket. Finally on October 24, 1871, the last statute concerned directly with the Peters colony lands was passed. It settled all questions arising over the county court certificates by declaring them valid and affirming patents issued on them.[17]

Thirty years had passed since the colony had been originated; the empresario device had been proven a failure by the litigation and the long series of statutes required to "quiet" the land titles in the disturbed area; and the state had given away nearly three million acres of land to acquire less than eighteen hundred settlers who quite probably would have immigrated for a much smaller inducement. A factor of no small consequence to later Texas history was the 1,088,000 acres which was placed in the hands of Kentucky owners through the Texas Emigration and Land Company.

To acquire title to the 1700 sections of land offered by the compromise law, the company had to survey each section and submit regularly to the general land office reports and a map of the area. The whole colony area was reserved by law until August 10, 1854, to permit the company to make its locations. Henry O. Hedgcoxe remained in the company's employ to superintend the surveying. A number of crews were necessary to complete the job, and in all, Hedgcoxe seems to have contracted with thirteen surveyors to work in the field. These were David Hearsum of Illinois and S. M. Carter of Kentucky, employed on February 25, 1853; Joseph Bledsoe of Kentucky, and John Granger of Hunt County, Texas, on March 25; William Smyth of Travis County, April 8; D. W. C. Baker of Travis County, John R. Hubbard of Burnet County, and Peter B. Lowe of Travis County, May 4; Wm. M. Ruse of Guadalupe County, May 20; Thomas Leckie, Oliver Hedgcoxe, and James Powell of Travis County, and B. B. Barker of Williamson County, July 15.[18]

Hedgcoxe put these parties in the field with instructions to work as rapidly as possible. He directed them to locate only land of the first quality for the company—"deep, rich dry rolling lands, with good Water & Timber like the lands of Collin County."[19] To avoid the plague of conflicting claims, he sent them into the western portion of the grant to make their locations.[20]

During the summer and fall of 1853 Hedgcoxe kept six surveying camps in operation. His superintendent in the field was George Hearndon whose responsibility it was to see that the surveyors selected only choice land. As this was Indian country, Hearndon depended on Major Robert S. Neighbors, the Indian agent, to supply him and his crews with protection. Indians, however, did not threaten the success of the surveying operation as much as did the land locators. Apparently the legal reservation of the colony area was ineffective in stopping the activities of persons holding unlocated land paper.

On February 15, 1853, the company filed a petition with the clerk of the Travis District Court praying that the land commissioner be prohibited from issuing patents in the area until the reservation period expired. Because the "locators and their confederates, agents, and attorneys are already so numerous as to render it impossible to make all defendants" the company named George Hancock, Stephen Crosby, et al., of the general land office as defendants in the suit. The company complained that the locators pretended they did not know where the colony's boundaries were, or that their locations were made prior to February 4, 1841, or that they were made in the period between July 1, 1848, and February 10, 1852.[21]

The company obtained a temporary injunction against the land office on February 19, by posting a $15,000 bond.[22] The injunction was served on Stephen Crosby on February 28, and Crosby averred that the suit ought not be directed at him. He retaliated by refusing to accept the field notes that Hedgcoxe began to accumulate from the field parties. The company filed an amended petition on September 7 protesting this action, and on September 19 Crosby answered by claiming the company had no rights at all in the colony, basing his argument on the old claims that the company had not fulfilled its contracts. The suit continued in the courts until the Supreme Court handed down a decision on January 5, 1856, upholding most of the inferior court's rulings, and in the main declaring that the land office had the right to issue patents within the colony to the land locators.[23] Of course by this time the company's surveys had been completed and the temporary injunction had served its purpose.

By these measures the company succeeded in avoiding a great deal of title litigation over conflicting claims with individual land locators, but despite its precautions the company got involved in a controversy with one of the state's most active land locators, Jacob De Cordova. On December 29, 1854, this conflict was resolved by mutual agreement, De Cordova withdrawing his claims to land located after February 10, 1852, and the company withdrawing its claims to land surveyed for De Cordova prior to that date.[23]

While the court action and the negotiation with De Cordova was taking place in Austin, the surveying was being completed in haste. A section of a letter of instruction from Hedgcoxe to Hearndon is quoted below in which the tone of urgency and the busy-body nature of Hedgcoxe's character are apparent:

> You can have no doubt of the very high Opinion which I entertain of your abilities & perserverance, as well as of the unbounded confidence I have in you, and constant disposition to serve you, but you must recollect, that in carrying out things there I have a great complexity of interests to study, and not only incurring a great expense but that I am liable to the Company for the success of the whole enterprize. I am responsible for you all, not one out there but are my choice for the work I have assigned them, and must answer to the Co. for their actions—Now if I cannot keep your interests separate, the whole affair must blow up, and to keep peace and quietness in everything I rely in a great measure upon you—You must keep cool. Let others do as they please, you do your duties, and if you need anything get it, if Others go astray or fail, talk mildly to them

about it, and if not rectified and likely to injure the Company inform me. I conceive it to be your express duty to keep everything to right, to the utmost of your ability, not to kill your self or suffer, and to keep me advised plainly and fearlessly of everything done out there by everyone. Let nothing be hid from me, speak out plainly, so that I may at once apply the remedy. At the same time try to keep all in Harmony and at work, and rather bear many evils *if the surveying goes on fast & correct,* than create the least difficulty. Recollect the Object of the Company is *to get their lands surveyed.* Let all your efforts be applied to this[25]

By the fall of 1853 many of the field notes had been sent to Hedgcoxe in Austin and by December most of the surveying was finished. A correspondent at Fort Belknap noted on December 12, 1853, that the company suveyors had finished and gone to Austin with their notes.[26]

Hedgcoxe compiled the notes into an excellent map.[27] Since Hedgcoxe had required his surveyors to run connecting lines through their surveys, the sprawling and scattered locations could be considered as one survey, rather than as 3,400 separate surveys.[28] A map, Figure 1, shows the approximate location of the company's land, which the·company chose to select in 3400 square sections of 320 acres each rather than 1700 full sections of 640 acres each.

The progress of the surveying can not be detailed accurately. During the winter of 1853-54 Hedgcoxe submitted notes to the land office on at least 2276 half-section tracts,[29] and by August 10, 1854, notes on the rest of the 3400 tracks were submitted, though some of the work later had to be corrected.[30] In his report of February 10, 1854, Hedgcoxe suggested that in so large an undertaking there was a possibility of error; on November 28, 1854, he applied to have such an error corrected. He withdrew from the land office notes on survey numbers 1401 and 3400 and commenced a resurvey of these sections.[31] Running throughout the work of Thomas Leckie he found an error of 100 varas in each thousand; in other words Leckie's chainman had "reported nine pins for out instead of ten." In the tracts affected this reduced the area from 320 acres as reported to 265 acres.[32] Leckie was sent out to correct his work, and in 1858 returned corrected field notes to 346 surveys.[33] This entitled the company to locate land equivalent to the total error, which was 19,030 acres, or fifty-nine and one-half 320 acre tracts. Actually only forty-five additional tracts were patented, some of them being out-sized. The 3445 tracts were located as follows:[34]

Archer County	270 tracts
Baylor County	96 tracts
Callahan County	133 tracts
Clay County	93 tracts
Cooke County	1 tract
Eastland County	22 tracts
Jack County	194 tracts
Montague County	67 tracts
Palo Pinto County	245 tracts

Parker County	22 tracts
Shackleford County	225 tracts
Stephens County	564 tracts
Throckmorton County	553 tracts
Wichita County	6 tracts
Young County	954 tracts
	3445 tracts

Hedgcoxe continued to correspond with the general land office over minor points connected with the surveying until 1859,[35] but the great majority of the patents were issued to the company in 1854 and 1855.[36] As the land was in an unsettled part of the country and as the company was forced by law to alienate at least half of its holdings within ten years, no attempt seems to have been made to continue the existence of the Texas Emigration and Land Company. In 1858, after the termination of the suit discussed earlier, the company distributed its land among the stockholders.[37]

Unfortunately no company records have been found to indicate the basis of the division. The latest document available listing the names of the stockholders was dated November 3, 1853.[38] Stockholders at that time were:

NAME	NUMBER OF SHARES	NAME	NUMBER OF SHARES
Armstrong & Allen	20	W. C. Hite	15
Wm. W. Bacon & Cobb	20	H. H. Honore	6
A. P. Barker	20	H. S. Julien	15
W. Bishop	10	M. Kean	8
John S. Brannin	6	George Killick	5
S. S. Bucklin	10	John Kitts	30
John S. Carpenter	3	David Land	2
James P. Chambers		E. H. Lewis	20
John O. Cochran	5	James Lusse	10
Thomas Coleman	60	James W. McGill	5
Isaac Cromie	30	A. Martin	5
R. H. Crump	5	Martin-Owen Co.	20
D. M. Dowell	10	John M. Monahan	20
D. P. Faulds	13	J. Monks	43
E. A. Gardner	3	D. P. Monsarrat	9
James Garvin	25	C. H. Monsarrat & Co.	10
Wm. Garvin	30	W. J. Murphy	5
G. Gates	26	H. J. Peters	15
James Guthrie	20	Wm. C. Peters	
Guthrie & Tyler	20	Wm. S. Peters	18
Henry A. Hambright	5	Wm. F. Pettit	20
J. B. Harper	5	Daniel J. Pratt	10
R. C. Hewitt	5	S. A. Pratt	8

NAME	NUMBER OF SHARES	NAME	NUMBER OF SHARES
William Pratt	10	Willis Stewart	137
M. W. Redd	8	John M. Stokes	10
Abner Reeves	24	William Terry	17
Samuel Richardson	20	Levi Tyler	20
O. W. Root heirs	18	Thomas Vail	10
George M. Sealy	5	J. W. Van Osten	1
W. W. Sherrill	2	A. B. Van Winkle	20
Felix Simon	2	J. B. Walker	5
James B. Slaughter	13	B. U. Webb	5
T. & E. Slevin	15	John White	5
John J. Smith	82	A. Zanova	10

The above list included 68 names and 1079 shares of stock. The numbers of shares owned by William C. Peters and James Chambers were not listed, but since Peters was a trustee and Chambers was secretary, it is probable that they had at least fifty shares each. The total number of shares out in 1853 therefore was probably about 1200. If this figure was the same at the time of the dissolution of the company, and it seems reasonable to believe it was, then the land was prorated at about 900 acres per share of stock.

No attempt has been made to trace individual transactions after the dissolution of the company. In the main the stockholders were forced to hold on to their land in Texas for a number of years because of Indian depredations and the Civil War. A resident of Louisville, Charles J. Meng, undertook to act as agent for the Kentucky owners. His first visit to Texas was probably made in 1859, when he rendered the land for taxes; he came again in 1861 to pay the taxes for 1860.[39] On April 24, 1866, Meng sent a form letter to all the owners of the "Peters colony land" informing them that he had paid their taxes for 1861 and 1865, that the taxes for 1862, 1863, and 1864 would be remitted, and that he had visited their lands in the fall of 1865 and was endeavoring to get troops placed near them for the protection of prospective settlers. He also stated that he had sold some of the land.[40] Meng paid the taxes in 1866, 1867, and 1868, and continued to act as agent until some time in 1868.[41]

In 1869 an enterprising speculator from Kentucky, Edwin S. Graham, began to take an active interest in the Texas lands though he seems to have first become an owner as early as 1860.[42] Graham came to Texas in the fall of 1869 to examine the Kentucky land holdings, and during the next year and a half he bought a large amount of the T. E. & L. land[43] at an average price of fifty cents an acre.[44]

How extensive Graham's holdings became is not known; by the end of 1870 an inconclusive estimate of about 17,000 acres was made.[45] His wife later wrote:

When he bought these lands he borrowed a large sum of money, feeling sure he was getting great bargains and could sell again at a good profit at any time: but we find that we can never see far ahead, for in the early 70's a severe panic struck us, which so greatly paralyzed all branches of business that there was no demand at all for Peters colony lands, and it was just as much as he could do for a long time to pay taxes and keep alive.[46]

Graham advertised the T. E. & L. lands widely, acting as agent for his own as well as other persons' holdings. One of his earliest pamphlets stated in part:

We call special attention to the lands known as the Peter's Colony Texan Emigration and Land Company's lands which after being patented to the Company, the trustees dissolved it by a division of all the lands as to interest among those composing the company, and now not owned by the Company, as many suppose, but by individuals, and most of them non-residents of Texas.[47]

Graham supplanted Meng as agent for the Kentucky owners and for the next two decades was active in promoting the sale of the lands.[48] A meeting of the owners seems to have been held in Louisville in 1875 giving Graham exclusive agent's rights. He charged a fee of six per cent commission plus costs of resurveying where necessary.[49] It was chiefly by this process that the lands of the Texas Emigration and Land Company were put into the hands of settlers and ranchers, though a few of the stockholders eventually settled on their holdings in Texas. There seems to have been little profit in the venture for any connected with it. The Peters colony cost the state heavily in land; the original Peters group could not have profited; and the gain of the later stockholders of the company was small.

Although the venture in the main, was a failure, a number of persons moved to Texas because of the colony who might otherwise not have come. A trend of migration to North Texas from the Ohio River valley was established in the years 1841 to 1848 that continued for several decades. These people were farmers, small land owners, merchants and artisans, and in small ways were different in character from earlier migrants to other parts of Texas. Commercially the Peters colony region developed more rapidly than the rest of the state, despite being in a less advantageous geographic position. Union sentiment was quite strong in the area and was reflected in the political temperance found in such important Texas politicians as J. W. Throckmorton, a notable middle-of-the-roader, and John H. Reagan. The significance of the colony thus lies in the nature of the people who migrated to it. These persons and the available social data connected with them are listed in an appendix to this work.

In size, in the number of persons involved, in the length of time it played an active role on the Texas scene, the Peters colony was the largest impresario colony in Texas under either the Republic or Mexico. Nevertheless it has been relegated to a minor position, and, barely mentioned or often forgotten in textbooks and general narratives of Texas history, the story of the Peters colony has almost sunk into oblivion. A small stone marker, erected in 1936 in Dallas County, tells this perverted story to posterity:

SITE OF THE FIRST AGENCY
JANUARY, 1845, OF THE
TEXIAN LAND AND
EMIGRATION COMPANY
GENERALLY KNOWN AS "PETERS' COLONY"
IN HONOR OF WILLIAM S. PETERS, WHO,
UNDER A COLONIZATION CONTRACT
SECURED IN 1841 FROM THE REPUBLIC
OF TEXAS, INTRODUCED MORE THAN TEN
THOUSAND SETTLERS TO 17 COUNTIES
OF NORTH TEXAS

FOOTNOTES FOR PART VI

[1]One exception might be noted. On February 10, 1854, Stewart and Hedgcoxe, acting for the company, signed a final relinquishment of the company's claims to any and all land claimed by colonists. File 20, Colony Contracts file, General Land Office.

[2]This date was fixed by Land Commissioner Crosby's interpretation of the law rather than by the law itself which only stated that the time limit was extended three months.

[3]Gammel, *Laws of Texas*, II, 1472.

[4]*Ibid.*, III, 57-58.

[5]*Ibid.*, II, 1073-1075. The period was extended from 1848 to 1854 by a supplemental act dated February 10, 1852. *Ibid.*, IV, 960.

[6]*Ibid.*, III, 1317.

[7]*Ibid.*, III, 1550-1552.

[8]*Ibid.*, IV, 7-13.

[9]Memorial No. 168, Archives, Texas State Library.

[10]Cammell, *Laws of Texas*, IV, 209.

[11]*Ibid.*, IV, 468.

[12]*Ibid.*, IV, 908.

[13]*Ibid.*, IV, 978-982.

[14]*Ibid.*

[15]*Ibid.*, IV, 1388. On February 14, 1860, James S. Robinson, District Attorney of the 16th Judicial District, was awarded $250 for defending the interest of the state in cases concerning the doubtful Peters colony certificates. (*Ibid.*, IV,1475.)

[16]*Ibid.*, IV, 1442.

[17]*Ibid.*, VII, 14.

[18]Report of appointment of surveyors, February 10, 1854, Colony Contracts file, General Land Office.

[19]Henry O. Hedgcoxe to George Hearndon, May 14, 1853, Peters Colony file, Archives, the University of Texas.

[20]See map in Part I.

[21]Petition in the case of Willis Stewart, *et al. v.* Geo. Hancock, *et al.*, Travis District Court, Archives, file 252.

[22]*Ibid.* As the District Judge of the Travis Court, John Hancock, was a brother of George Hancock, a defendant in the suit, Stewart sought and obtained the injunction from Thomas Devine of the Bexar District Court. The bond was actually not posted until February 28, nor was the petition officially filed until that date.

[23]Various documents in the archives of the Travis District Court, File 252. An editorial in the *Texas State Gazette*, April 14, 1855, rejoices in the ruling of the district court against the company, though the ruling was immediately appealed.

[24]Agreement, file 419, Colony Contracts file, G.L.O.

[25]Hedgcoxe to Hearndon, May 14, 1853.

[26]*Northern Standard*, December 31, 1853.

[27]The Hedgcoxe map was lithographed, but only a few copies have been found, all in fragmentary condition. The best copy is preserved in the general land office.

[28]Hedgcoxe to the commissioner of the general land office, March 14, 1854, Colony Contracts file, G.L.O.

[29]Connecting Lines file, G.L.O., documents date October 28, October 29, November 19, 1853, January, and March 7, 1854.

[30]Henry O. Hedgcoxe to Stephen Crosby, December 5, 1854, Connecting Lines file, G.L.O.; Hedgcoxe to Crosby August 10, 1854, Colony Contracts file, G.L.O.

[31]H. O. Hedgcoxe to Stephen Crosby, November 28, 1854, Colony Contracts file, G.L.O.

[32]Hedgcoxe to Crosby, December 3, 1857, Connecting Lines file, G.L.O.

[33]Certificate by Thos. Leckie and letter from Henry O. Hedgcoxe to Francis White, Land Commissioner, Connecting Lines file, G.L.O. Neither document bears date other than the year, 1858.

[34]County patentee maps on file in the G.L.O.

[35]Connecting Lines file, G.L.O., various documents dated January 31, February 11, March 8, and June 28, 1859.

[36]*Abstracts of Texas Land Titles*, G.L.O.

[37]Broadside Advertisement, December 1877, Graham Papers, Envelope XI, U. T. Archives.

[38]No. 25, Colony Contracts file, G.L.O.

[39]Charles J. Meng to E. S. Graham, Ft. Belknap, Texas, February 27, 1861, Graham Papers, Env. I, Archives, U. T.

[40]Broadside: "To Owners of Peters Colony Lands," June 25, 1886, Graham Papers, Env. XII, Archives, U. T.; C. J. Meng to E. S. Graham, printed form letter, April 24, 1866, Graham Papers, Env. XII.

[41]Printed form letters dated August 20, 1866, and January 14, 1869, Graham Papers, Env. XII.

[42]Meng to Graham, February 27, 1861, Graham Papers, Env. XII.

[43]Reminiscences of E. S. Graham, Graham Papers.

[44]G. E. Lewis to E. S. Graham, May 14, 1870; R. W. Gates to E. S. Graham, May 29, 1870; G. E. Lewis to E. S. Graham, June 1, 1870; Lewis to Graham, June 15, 1875; J. Monk to E. S. Graham, March 15, 1871, Graham Papers, Env. II.

[45]Diary, E. S. Graham, 1870. Graham Papers, Env. XI. In a broadside dated 1887 Graham advertised about 50,000 acres for sale which he owned personally.

[46]"The Autobiography of Mrs. Addie M. Graham," Graham Papers, Env. X.

[47][E. S. Graham] *Rambles in Texas* (pamphlet), n.d., Graham Papers, Env. XII.

[48]Among other things he founded and laid out the town of Graham in Young County.

[49]"To the Owners of Peters' Colony lands," June 25, 1886; *Galveston Daily News*, September 9, 1876.

(To be continued)

KENTUCKY COLONIZATION IN TEXAS
A HISTORY OF THE PETERS COLONY
SEYMOUR V. CONNOR

APPENDIX
LISTS OF COLONISTS

Listed in this appendix are the names of all settlers in the Peters colony region who were or may have been colonists. The appendix is divided into the following sections:

    I. *Bonafide colonists who received land*

    II. *Colonists who moved away before receiving land*

    III. *Persons issued county court certificates as colonists who received land: Probable colonists*

    IV. *Persons issued county court certificates as colonists who received land: Doubtful colonists*

    V. *Persons issued county court certificates as colonists who did not receive land.*

Information taken from records in the general land office, including Ward's certificates, is listed on the line with the name of the colonist; information taken from the census is listed on the line immediately below if available.

Names in italics are of persons who died before 1850.

The date of migration (Yr/Mig) is based on the company's reports and is divided, except in a few cases where special information was available, into three periods; (1) 1844 indicates migration any time prior to July 1, 1844; (2) 1845 indicates migration between July 1, 1844 to July 1, 1845; (3) 1848 indicates migration between July 1, 1845 to July 1, 1848, though in most cases it probably indicates migration in the later part of this period.

The county given on the line with the land office information indicates the county in which the colonists land was located. The word *Sold* following the county name means that the colonist sold his certificate and that the land was patented in another person's name. The county given on the line with the census information indicates county of residence at the time of enumeration.

Where census information was available the state of birth (*Birth*) and the state from which the colonist migrated (*Removal*) is given on the line beneath the name in the appropriate column.

In the last two columns illiterates are marked with an X and the number of children are given if the colonist was found on the census. An asterisk (*) before the name of a colonist indicates that that name was listed as having illegally received a land certificate from one of the county courts in the *Report of the Commissioners to Investigate the Land Boards within Peter's Colony* in 1857.

1. Bonafide colonists who received land

Name (Marital Status) Occupation; Age	Yr/Mig	County County	Birth	Removal	Illit.	Chld.
Abbott, Benjamin (S)	1848	Dallas				
Abbott, William O. (S)	1843	Dallas				
Adams, Rolston W. (M)	1848	Grayson				
Farmer; 22		Grayson	Ohio	Ohio		1
Akers, George (M)	1848	Tarrant				
Farmer; 59		Tarrant	Ky.	Ind.		4
Akers, John (S)	1848	Tarrant				
Farmer; 22		Tarrant	Ind.	Ind.		
Akers, Simon (S)	1848	Tarrant				
Farmer; 29		Tarrant	Ind.	Ind.		
Akers, Thomas	1848	Tarrant				
Farmer; 24		Tarrant	Ind.	Ind.		
Alexander, Elias (S-M)	1848	Collin—sold				
Farmer; 28		Collin	Ill	Ill.		1
Alexander, Reuben (M)	1848	Cooke—sold				
Laborer; 37		Grayson	N.C.	Mo.		4
Allen, Jesse G. (M)	1848	Tarrant				
Farmer; 52		Tarrant	N.C.	Tenn. to Mo.		2
Allen, Malachi W. (S)	1848	Dallas—sold				
Surveyor; 25		Collin	Ark.	Ark.		
Allen, Margaret E. (W)	1848	Ellis				2
Allen, Pamelia (W)	1848	Tarrant				
73		Tarrant	N.C.	N.C.		
Allen, Richard W. (S)	1848	Denton				
Farmer; 21		Denton	Tenn.	Mo.		
Allen, Richard F. (M)	1848	Tarrant				
Blacksmith; 35		Tarrant	Tenn.	Tenn.		
Allen, Reuben (M)	1845	Grayson			X	
Farmer; 48		Grayson	Va.	Tenn.		9
Allen, Simon B. (S)	1848	Grayson				
Clerk; 24		Dallas	Ky.	Ky.		
Allen, Thomas J. (M)	1848	Denton			X	
Farmer; 48		Denton	N. C.	Tenn. to Mo.		8
Allen, Thomas (M)	1848	Grayson—sold				
Farmer; 33		Grayson	Ohio	Ind.		4
Allen, Thomas (S)	1848	Collin—sold				
Laborer; 20		Grayson	Tenn.	Tenn		
Allen, Wm. H. (S)	1845	Montague—sold				
Farmer; 21		Grayson	Tenn.	Tenn		
Alvey, George (M)	1848	Dallas				
Farmer; 24		Dallas	Ind.	Ill.		2
Anderson, Andrew W. (M)	1848	Tarrant—sold				
Farmer; 50		Tarrant	Tenn.	Mo.		6
Anderson, James (M)	1848	Dallas			X	
Farmer; 55		Dallas	Va.	Tenn. to Ark.		4

Name (Marital Status) Occupation; Age	Yr/Mig	County County	Birth	Removal	Illit.	Chld.
Anderson, James (M)	1848	Collin				
Farmer; 42		Collin	Ky.	Ky.		1
Anderson, James W. (S)	1848	Dallas—sold				
Anderson, John S. (M)	1848	Dallas				
Farmer; 28		Dallas	Ky.	Ky.		2
Anderson, Philip (S)	1848	Collin—sold				
Anderson, Thomas K. (S)	1848	Dallas				
Farmer; 34		Dallas	Tenn.	Ark.		
Andrews, Benjamin F. (M)	1848	Dallas & Knox				
Plasterer; 23		Dallas	Eng.	Ill.		3
Archer, Thomas M. (M)	1848	Collin&Dallas—sold				
Armstrong, James (M)	1845	Dallas				
Farmer; 29		Dallas	N.C.	Tenn. to Ark.		3
Armstrong, Joseph A. (S)	1848	Dallas				
Arnspiger, David (M)	1848	Collin				
Farmer; 39		Grayson	Ky.	Ill.		3
Ashlock, Josiah (M)	1848	Dallas				
Farmer; 43		Denton	Tenn.	Ill.		6
Ashlock, Meriday (M)	1848	Collin				
Farmer; 48		Collin	Tenn.	Ill. to Mo.		6
Atkinson, Henry (S)	1844	Grayson				
Laborer; 19		Grayson	Tenn.	Miss. to Ark.		
Atchison, James L. (M)	1848	Grayson				
Farmer; 48		Grayson	Ky.	Tenn. to Mo. to Ark.		7
Atcheson, Robert (M)	1844	Grayson				
Clerk; 45		Grayson	Ky.	Ky.		1
Atchison, Wm. C. (S)	1848	Grayson				
Laborer; 21		Grayson	Tenn.	Miss. to Ark.		
Attebury, Churchwill (S)	1848	Dallas			X	
Atterbury, Jesse (M)	1848	Dallas			X	
Farmer; 59		Dallas	S.C.	Ky.		3
Atterbury, Nathan (S)	1848	Tarrant—sold			X	
Farmer; 28		Dallas	Ky.	Ky.		2
Atterbury, Stephen C. (S-M)	1848	Dallas				
Farmer; 30		Dallas	Ky.	Ky.		
Ayres, Vel H. (M)	1848	Dallas				
Blacksmith; 35		Dallas	N.J.	N.J.		1
Babbit, William (M)	1848	Dallas—sold				
Plasterer; 32		Dallas	Ill.	Mo.		2
Bachus, Benjamin (S)	1845	Denton—sold				
Bacus, Godfrey S. (M)	1848	Collin—sold pt.				
Farmer; 36		Collin	Ill.	Ill.		
Bacus, Jacob (S)	1845	Collin				
Farmer; 54		Collin	Penn.	Ill.		3
Bachus, Peter (M)	1845	Collin				
Farmer; 32		Collin	Ohio	Ohio		2

Name (Marital Status) Occupation; Age	Yr/Mig	County County	Birth	Removal	Illit.	Chld.
Bacon, Fielding (M) Farmer; 38	1848	Grayson—sold pt. Grayson	Mo.	Mo.		7
Badgley, David A. (M) Farmer; 30	1848	Dallas Dallas	Ill.	Ill.		3
Badgley, Daniel (S) Farmer; 25	1848	Collin Dallas	Ill.	Ill.		
Badgley, Job (S-M) Farmer; 61	1848	Dallas Dallas	Va.	Ill.		
Baggett, Sebourn (S-M) Farmer; 23	1845	Dallas Dallas	Ga.	Ga.	X	1
Baggett, Uzzel (W) Farmer; 53	1845	Dallas Dallas	N.C.	Ga. to Ala.		4
Bailey, DeWitt C. (S) Laborer; 21	1848	Grayson Grayson	Va.	Va.		
Bailey, Hiram W. (S) Blacksmith; 26	1848	Grayson—sold Grayson	Va.	Va.		
Bailey, John P. (M) Blacksmith; 45	1848	Grayson Grayson	Va.	Va.		7
Baker, Artemas Jr. (S) Shoemaker; 29	1848	Dallas Dallas	Ohio	Ohio		
Baker, Charles (M) Farmer; 23	1845	Dallas Dallas	Va.	Va.		2
Baker, Henry (M) Farmer; 38	1848	Cooke Cooke	Germ.	Germany		4
Baker, James M. (S-M) Farmer; 30	1844	Tarrant—sold Tarrant	Tenn.	Tenn.		2
Baker, Joseph C. (S)	1844	Denton—sold				
Baker, John W. (S)	1844	Denton				
Baker, Rosannah (W)	1848	(?) Denton		Denton		4
Baker, Rutha (W)	1848	Tarrant—sold				1
Balch, Evan R. (S) Farmer; 26	1848	Ellis Ellis	Tenn.	Tenn.		
Balch, John B. (S) Farmer; 26	1848	Denton—sold Ellis	Tenn.	Tenn.	X	
Balch, Wm. M. (S) Farmer; 19	1848	Johnson Ellis	Ill.	Ill.		
Balch, William (M) Farmer; 47	1848	Ellis Ellis	N.C.	Ill.		6
Ballard, Frederick (S)	1844	Ellis—sold				
Balsmier, Henry (S-M) Farmer; 34	1845	Dallas Dallas	Ger.	Germany		1
Bandy, Richard T. (S)	1848	Dallas				
Bancroft, Daniel (M) Farmer; 37	1848	Tarrant Tarrant	Va.	Mo.		6
Barefoot, Jonathan (M) Farmer; 35	1848	Grayson Grayson	Tenn.	Tenn.	X	

Name (Marital Status) Occupation; Age	Yr/Mig	County County	Birth	Removal	Illit.	Chld.
Barker, Joshua (M)	1844	Dallas			X	
Farmer; 21		Dallas	Ky.	Ky.		1
Barksdale, Ralph H. (S)	1842	Denton				
Barlough, John H. (M)	1848	Tarrant—sld				
Farmer; 38		Dallas	S.C.	Ark.		3
Barnard, Abraham (M)	1848	Tarrant			X	
Farmer; 53		Tarrant	Ky.	Ark.		3
Barnes, Larkin (W)	1848	Tarrant				
Farmer; 40		Ellis	Mo.	Mo.		1
Barnes, Wm. D. (S)	1845	Dallas—sld				
Barnes, William H. (S)	1843	Dallas				
Barrow, James C. (S)	1848	Collin				
Bartram, John (S)	1845	Denton				
Bast, Abraham (M)	1848	Dallas				
Farmer; 50		Dallas	Ky.	Ind.		7
Batterton, John (M)	1848	Collin				
Baugh, John (M)	1848	Dallas				
Farmer?; 44		Tarrant	Ga.	Ga.		
Baugh, John R. (M)	1848	Tarrant—sld			X	
Baugh, Mitchell (S)	1848	Tarrant—sld			X	
Bean, Wm. (M)	1845	Grayson				
Merchant; 44		Grayson	Tenn.	Ark.		6
Beard, Allen (M)	1848	Tarrant				
Beasely, Felix G. (M)	1848	Tarrant—sld				
Farmer; 34		Grayson	Tenn.	Mo.		4
Beck, Manly (S)	1848	Collin			X	
Farmer; 21		Collin	Ill.	Ill.		
Beck, Sanford (M)	1848	Collin—sld			X	
Farmer; 48		Collin	Tenn.	Ill.		6
Beeman, Isaac (S)	1848	Dallas				
Farmer; 25		Dallas	Ill.	Ill.		
Beeman, James (M)	1844	Dallas				
Beeman, John (M)	1844	Dallas				
Farmer; 32		Dallas	Ill.	Ill.		5
Beeman, John S. (M)	1844	Dallas				
Farmer; 50		Dallas	N.C.	Ill.		10
Beeman, Samuel (M)	1846	Dallas				
Farmer; 55		Dallas	N.C.	Ill.		8
Beeman, Samuel H (S)	1848	Dallas—sld				
Farmer; 21		Dallas	Ill.	Ill.		
Beeman, Wm. H. (S)	1848	Dallas—sld				
Farmer; 23		Dallas	Ill.	Ill.		
Bell, John (M)	1848	Ellis				
Farmer; 38		Ellis	Va.	Mo.		6
Bell, John R. (W)	1846	Dallas—sld			X	
Farmer; 35		Dallas	Ky.	Ill.		3

Name (Marital Status) Occupation; Age	Yr/Mig	County County	Birth	Removal	Illit.	Chld.
Bell, Joseph (M)	1848	Ellis				
Farmer; 31		Ellis	Va.	Mo.		5
Bell, Robert (S-M)	1848	Ellis				
Farmer; 31		Ellis	Va.	Va.		1
Bellow, Wm. (W)	1848	Parker				
Bennett, Elisha (S)	1848	Dallas				
Ranger; 17		Dallas	Ga.	Ga.		
Bennett, Hamilton (M)	1848	Tarrant			X	
Farmer; 40		Tarrant	Va.	Ky. to Mo.		8
Bennett, Hiram (M)	1845	Dallas				
Farmer; 55		Dallas	Ga.	Ala. to Ark.		7
Bennett, James (M)	1845	Dallas				
Farmer; 27		Dallas	S.C.	Ark.		4
Bennett, Wm. H. (M)	1845	Dallas				
Farmer; 24		Dallas	Ga.	Ark.		2
Bernard, Charles H. (M)	1848	Dallas				
Farmer; 31		Tarrant	Ky.	Ill.		4
Bernard, Thomas (S)	1848	Dallas				
Farmer; 24		Tarrant	Tenn.	Tenn.		
Berry, Alexander (S)	1848	Collin—sold				
Lawyer; 36		Collin	Va.	Va.		
Berry, James S. (M)	1848	Ellis				
Farmer; 53		Ellis	Ky.	Mo.		1
Berry, William C. (S)	1844	Ellis				
Farmer; 21		Ellis	Mo.	Mo.		
Bethuven, Benjamin F. (S)	1845	Dallas				
Farmer; 25		Dallas	Ohio	Ohio		
Bethuven, Robert (M)	1845	Dallas				
Beverly, James (S)	1848	Collin				
Farmer; 19		Collin	Mo.	Mo.		
Beverly, John (S)	1848	Collin				
Farmer; 21		Collin	Tenn.	Tenn.		
Beverly, William (M)	1848	Collin				
Farmer; 45		Collin	Tenn.	Tenn.		5
Biggs, Jacob H. (S)	1848	Collin				
Meth. Preacher; 37		Collin	N.C.	N.C.		
Biggs, Rebecca (D)	1848	Dallas			X	
Biles, James H. (S)	1848	Tarrant				
Farmer; 62		Grayson	N.C.	N.C.		
Billingsley, James (M)	1844	Ellis				
Farmer; 52		Ellis	Ky.	Ga.		6
Billingsley, John R. (M)	1845	Ellis				
Farmer; 42		Ellis	Ky.	Ark.		9
Billingsley, Jonathan (M)	1848	Ellis				
Farmer; 34		Ellis	Mo.	Mo.		7

Name (Marital Status) Occupation; Age	Yr/Mig	County County	Birth	Removal	Illit.	Chld.
Billingsley, Nathan S. (M) Farmer; 32	1848	Ellis Ellis	Tenn.	Tenn.		
Billingsley, Robert M. (M) Farmer; 32	1848	Dallas Ellis	Ark.	Mo.	X	4
Billingsley, Samuel (M) Farmer; 57	1844	Ellis—sld Ellis	Ky.	Ark. to Mo.		6
Billingsley, Susan (W)	1848	Dallas				2
Billingsley, William (S) Farmer; 25	1844	Ellis Ellis	Ark.	Ark.		
Billingsley, Wm. C. (M) Farmer; 38	1845	Dallas Ellis	Ky.	Ark. to Mo.		4
Bishop, James (M) Farmer; 32	1848	Grayson Grayson	Tenn.	Ill. to Ark.		7
Bishop, Richard (S) Laborer; 20	1848	Grayson—sld Grayson	Ill.	Ark.	X	
Blackwell, Benjamin E. (M) Schoolteacher; 51	1848	Collin Collin	Va.	Tenn.		6
Blackwell, Hiram (M) Farmer; 28	1848	Tarrant—sld Tarrant	Tenn.	Ark.		2
Blackwell, James (S)	1848	Tarrant				
Blackwell, Joel (M)	1848	Tarrant				
Bledsoe, Anthony (S) Farmer; 28	1845	Dallas—sld Dallas	Mo.	Mo.		
Bledsoe, Allen (S) Farmer; 49	1845	Dallas—sld Dallas	Ky.	Mo.	X	
Bledsoe, Samuel T. (M) Physician; 36	1848	Dallas Dallas	Ky.	Ill.		2
Bledsoe, Willis (W)	1844	Dallas				
Blundell, John (S) Farmer; 22	1848	Grayson—sld Grayson	Ky.	Ky.	X	
Blundell, William B. (M) Farmer; 55	1848	Grayson-sld Grayson	Va.	Ky.		1
Boggs, Harvey (M) Farmer; 48	1848	Cooke Cooke	Ky.	Mo.		7
Boggs, John (M) Farmer; 24	1848	Cooke Cooke	Ky.	Mo.	X	3
Boggs, Margaret E. (W)	1848	Cooke				
Bontewell, Alexander (M) Farmer; 25	1848	Cooke-sld Cooke	Ark.	Ark.		2
Bostick, Soloman (M) Shoemaker; 36	1848	Wise—sld Grayson	Tenn.	Tenn.		6
Bounds, Joseph M. (S) Floating trader; 28	1845	Collin—sld Collin	Mo.	Mo.		
Bourgeirs, Luc (S)	1848	Denton—sld				
Bowen, William (S)	1848	Collin ?				
Bowles, Franklin (M)	1848	Dallas				

85

Name (Marital Status) Occupation; Age	Yr/Mig	County County	Birth	Removal	Illit.	Chld.
Boyd, Larkin M. (S)	1848	Collin—sld			X	
Farmer; 27		Grayson	Mo.	Mo.		
Boyd, William J. (S)	1848	Ellis—sld				
Farmer; 23		Ellis	Tenn.	Tenn.		
Boydstun, Jacob G. (M)	1848	Dallas				
Farmer; 38		Tarrant	Ky.	Ill.		7
Boyle, Joseph (W)	1848	Cooke				
Boyles, William (S)	1848	Grayson—sld				
Farmer; 24		Grayson	Ky.	Ky.		
Bradford, Edward C. (S)	1848	Ellis				
Farmer; 21		Ellis	Mo.	Mo.		
Bradford, Henry H. (M)	1848	Ellis				
Bradford, William H. H. (M)	1848	Tarrant—sld				
Farmer; 25		Ellis	Va.	Va.		2
Bradley, Edward (M)	1848	Collin				
Farmer; 65		Collin	N.C.	N.C.		8
Bradley, James S. (S)	1848	Collin				
Farmer; 21		Collin	Mo.	Mo.		
Bradley, Thomas T. (S)	1845	Collin—sld				
Constable; 26		Collin	Mo.	Mo.		
Bradshaw, David (M)	1847	Dallas				
Farmer; 57		Dallas	Ky.	Mo. to Ark.		3
Bradshaw, Washington (S)	1848	Tarrant			X	
Farmer; 21		Dallas	Mo.	Ark.		
Brandenburg, Absolem (M)	1848	Dallas—sld				
Farmer; 51		Dallas	Ohio	Mo.		10
Brandenburg, Henry (M)	1848	Collin				
Brandenburg, John (S)	1848	Dallas			X	
Farmer; 18		Dallas	Mo.	Mo.		
Brandenburg, Samuel (S)	1848	Dallas			X	
Farmer; 20		Dallas	Mo.	Mo.		
Bray, Henry (M)	1848	Cooke				
Farmer; 31		Cooke	Ind.	Mo.		4
Brewster, Benjamin (S)	1848	Collin—sld				
Bridges, John (M)	1848	Grayson				
Bridges, William A. (S)	1848	Denton				
Farmer; 23		Denton	Tenn.	Ill.		
Brien, Catherine (W)	1845	Collin				2
Britten, Joseph (S)	1848	Collin				
Farmer; 35		Collin	Tenn.	Tenn.		
Brooke, John (S)	1848	Grayson				
Browder, Edward C. (S)	1848	Ellis				
Farmer; 25		Dallas	Mo.	Mo.		
Browder, Isham B. (M)	1848	Dallas			X	
Farmer; 23		Dallas	Mo.	Mo.		2
Brown, Archibald D. (S)	1848	Dallas			X	

Name (Marital Status) Occupation; Age	Yr/Mig	County County	Birth	Removal	Illit.	Chld.
Brown, Henry (S)	1848	Grayson				
Brown, James M. (M)	1845	Grayson				
Farmer; 48		Grayson	Va.	Ky.		2
Brown, John D. (M)	1848	Collin				
Farmer; 64		Collin	Va.	Va.		4
Brown, Jotham (M)	1844	Tarrant				
Brown, Mary (W)	1848	Dallas				1
Brown, Robert H. (S)	1848	Collin				
Farmer; 25		Collin	Va.	Va.		
Brown, Rutha (W)	1848	Tarrant			X	
59		Denton	S.C.	Mo.		4
Brown, Samuel H. (M)	1848	Collin				
Carpenter; 43		Collin	Va.	Ky. to Tenn.		8
Brown, Samuel P. (M)	1848	Dallas—sld				
Farmer; 30		Dallas	Va.	Va.		3
Brown, Stephen D. (S)	1845	Cooke				
Farmer; 25		Cooke	Tenn.	Tenn.		
Brown, William C. (M)	1845	Cooke				
Farmer; 55		Cooke	Tenn.	Tenn.		5
Brown, Young E. (M)	1845	Dallas				
Farmer; 37		Dallas	Ill.	Ill.		4
Browning, Samuel (M)	1842	Denton				
Bruce, Peter M. (M)	1848	Grayson				
Farmer; 33		Grayson	Tenn.	Ill.		3
Bruce, Thomas (M)	1848	Collin				
Farmer; 39		Collin	Tenn.	Ark.		3
Bruten, Richard (S)	1845	Dallas				
Farmer; 38		Dallas	Ky.	Ky.		1
Bruten, William (M)	1845	Dallas			X	
Trader; 65		Dallas	S.C.	S.C.		
Bryan, John Neely (M)	1843	Dallas				
Lawyer; 39		Dallas	Tenn.	Ky.		3
Burnham, Horace (S)	1844	Dallas—sld				
Burnley, Stephen (M)	1848	Denton—sld				
Farmer; 36		Denton	Mo.	Mo.		5
Burns, Charles A. (S)	1848	Collin				
Grocer; 20		Grayson	Unk.	Unk.		
Burns, Jephtha S. (S)	1848	Grayson—sld				
Farmer; 21		Grayson	Mo.	Mo.		
Burns, Lionel G. (S)	1848	Grayson—sld				
Laborer; 25		Grayson	Unk.	Unk.		
Burns, Simon (S)	1848	Collin—sld			X	
Farmer; 20		Collin	Mo.	Mo.		
Burns, Uriah (M)	1848	Grayson—sld				
Farmer; 55		Grayson	N.C.	Mo.		5

Name (Marital Status) Occupation; Age	Yr/Mig	County County	Birth	Removal	Illit.	Chld.
Burns, Wm. P. (S-M)	1848	Collin—sld				
Farmer; 35		Grayson	N.C.	N.C.		2
Burris, Thomas (M)	1848	Dallas—sld pt.			X	
Farmer; 34		Dallas	Miss.	Mo.		4
Burris, Zachariah (M)	1848	Collin—sld			X	
Farmer; 30		Dallas	Mo.	Mo.		
Burrows, John R. (M)	1845	Collin—sld			X	
Bush, Joseph (M)	1848	Cooke				
Buskirk, Jonas (M)	1848	Dallas			X	
Farmer; 42		Dallas	Ky.	Ill.		5
Bussell, William (M)	1848	Tarrant				
Shoemaker; 37		Dallas	Eng.	Eng.		1
Butt, George N. (S)	1848	Grayson				
Farmer; 36		Grayson	Va.	Va.		1
Butler, Wm. (S-M)	1845	Collin				
Buttler, Wm. W. (M)	1844	Collin—sld				
Byrd, James (M)	1844	Dallas				
Farmer; 37		Dallas	Tenn.	Mo.		7
Calder, Wm. (M)	1842	Ellis				
Caldwell, James M. (S)	1844	Grayson				
Cameron, David R. (M)	1845	Dallas				
Farmer; 44		Dallas	Tenn.	Mo.		8
Campbell, Harry (M)	1848	Grayson				
Farmer; 46		Grayson	Mass.	N.Y. to Ind.		5
Campbell, Samuel R. (M)	1848	Grayson—sld				
Lawyer; 38		Collin	Tenn.	Tenn.		4
Campbell, Thomas J. (M)	1848	Dallas				
Farmer; 39		Dallas	N.C.	N.C.		7
Campbell, William H. (S)	1848	Grayson				
Cannon, Alexander E. (M)	1848	Denton—sld				
Cantrell, Baurch (M)	1848	Dallas				
Carder, C. C. (S)	1844	Tarrant				
Carder, Elijah S. (S)	1844	Tarrant				
Carder, William F. (M)	1844	Dallas—sld				
Carpenter; 44		Dallas	Va.	Mo.		7
Carpenter, Benjamin F. (M)	1844	Cooke—sld pt.			X	
Farmer; 35		Cooke	Tenn.	Mo.		5
Caryver, Philip (M)	1848	Cooke				
Carter, Allen (M)	1848	Grayson—sld				
Shoemaker; 35		Grayson	N.C.	Mo.		3
Carter, Charles (M)	1848	Grayson—sld				
Farmer; 33		Grayson	Tenn.	Mo.		4
Carter, John (M)	1848	Denton			X	
Farmer; 40		Denton	Va.	Ark.		7
Carter, William (M)	1848	Denton—sld				
Farmer; 27		Dallas	Va.	Va.		

Name (Marital Status) Occupation; Age	Yr/Mig	County County	Birth	Removal	Illit.	Chld.
Carter, William B. (M) Farmer; 30	1848	Cooke—sld pt. Cooke	Tenn.	Mo.		2
Carter, Wormley (S) Hunter; 33	1848	Dallas—sld pt. Dallas	Va.	Va.		
Cartwright, Asbury (M) Preacher, C. C.; 40	1848	Grayson Grayson	Tenn.	Mo.		7
Carver, Abraham (M) Farmer; 35	1844	Dallas Dallas	Ohio	Ill. to Mo.		4
Carver, Soloman (M) Farmer; 41	1844	Dallas Dallas	Ohio	Ill.		4
Casey, John Jr. (M) Farmer; 37	1844	Dallas Dallas	Tenn.	Ark.		3
Casey, John, Sr. (M)	1844	Dallas				
Cassidy, Thomas (S-M)	1848	Ellis				
Cassidy, Thomas Sr. (M)	1848	Collin & Parker				
Cate, Thomas (M)	1845	Tarrant				
Chadwell, Carpenter (S) Farmer; 25	1848	Cooke Cooke	Tenn.	Tenn.	X	
Chadwell, John (M) Farmer; 26	1848	Cooke Cooke	Tenn.	Tenn.		2
Chaffin, James (M) Farmer; 45	1848	Grayson & Cooke Grayson	Mo.	Tenn.		14
Chambers, Elisha (M) Farmer; 40	1848	Collin & Dallas Collin	N.C.	Ind.		9
Chandler, Albert (S)	1848	Dallas				
Chandler, Alfred (S) Farmer; 27	1848	Collin Collin	La.	La.		
Chapman, James (M) Farmer; 42	1848	Dallas & Ellis Dallas	Tenn.	Ind.		7
Chapman, John (M) Farmer; 31	1848	Ellis Ellis	Ky.	Ind.		2
Chapman, John C. (S) Farmer; 22	1848	Dallas Dallas	Ind.	Ind.		
Chapman, Robert (M)	1848	Dallas & Ellis				
Chenault, Wesley M. (M) Farmer; 32	1848	Dallas Dallas	Va.	Ind.		6
Chenault, William (S) Farmer; 22	1848	Dallas Dallas	Va.	Ind.	X	
Chenoweth, James F. (M) Farmer; 30	1848	Dallas Dallas	Ohio	Ala.		2
Chenoweth, Thomas S. (S-M) Farmer; 28	1848	Dallas Dallas	Ohio	?		1
Chesire, Thomas (M) Farmer; 35	1845	Dallas Dallas	Va.	Ky. to Mo.	X	4
Chisum, Pleasant G. (S)	1848	Dallas				

Name (Marital Status) Occupation; Age	Yr/Mig	County County	Birth	Removal	Illit.	Chld.
Chowning, James W. (M)	1848	Denton				
Farmer; 34		Denton	Tenn.	Ill.		4
Chowning, Richard (W)	1845	?				
Chowning, Robert (M)	1845	Denton			X	
None; 45		Dallas	Tenn.	Ill.		4
Chowning, Samuel (M)	1848	Denton				
Farmer; 35		Denton	Unk.	Ill.		4
Chronister, John (M)	1848	Cooke & Grayson				
Farmer; 39		Grayson	N.C.	Mo.		2
Clark, Andrew I. (S)	1848	Dallas				
Farmer; 33		Dallas	Tenn.	Tenn.		1
Clark, Henry (M)	1848	Dallas				
Clark, James (M)	1848	Cooke—sold			X	
Clark, John B. (S)	1848	Denton				
Farmer; 23		Denton	Ind.	Ind.		
Clark, John R. (M)	1848	Grayson & Cooke				
Clark, Joseph (M)	1848	Grayson & Denton				
Clark, Mary E. (W)	1848	Cooke				2
Clark, Peter (S-M)	1848	Cooke				
Clark, Samuel (M)	1848	Dallas				
Farmer; 34		Dallas	Ohio	Ill.		6
Clark, Sanson (M)	1848	Collin				
Farmer; 38		Collin	Tenn.	Tenn.		6
Clark, Wm. A. (M)	1844	Denton				
Clary, Elisha C. (M)	1844	Tarrant—sold			X	
Farmer; 43		Denton	Tenn.	Ark.		7
Clary, Elisha T. (M)	1848	Denton			X	
Farmer; 41		Denton	Tenn.	Ark.		4
Clayton, James J. (M)	1848	Ellis				
Farmer; 29		Ellis	Ky.	Mo.		2
Clepper, Daniel (S)	1848	Collin			X	
Clepper, Joseph (M)	1848	Collin			X	
Farmer; 45		Collin	Tenn.	Ill.		5
Clepper, Samuel (S)	1848	Collin				
Farmer; 21		Collin	Tenn.	Ill.		
Cochran, William M. (M)	1843	Dallas				
Farmer; 43		Dallas	S.C.	Tenn. to Mo.		5
Cockrell, Alexander (M)	1848	Dallas			X	
Farmer; 33		Dallas	Ky.	Ky.		1
Cockrell, Wesley (M)	1846	Dallas			X	
Farmer; 34		Dallas	Ky.	Mo.		5
Coffee, Eli (S)	1848	Grayson—sld			X	
Coffee, Hiram (M)	1848	Cooke				
Farmer; 50		Grayson	Tenn.	Ind.		4
Coffee, James S. (M)	1848	Grayson—sld		Ind. Mo. to		
Farmer; 27		Grayson	Ind.	Cher. Nat.		3

Name (Marital Status) Occupation; Age	Yr/Mig	County County	Birth	Removal	Illit.	Chld.
Coffee, Washington (S) Laborer; 21	1848	Grayson—sld Grayson	Ind.	?		
Coffman, John (M) Farmer; 46	1845	Collin-sld pt. Collin	Tenn.	Ill.		
Cohen, Louis (S)	1848	Tarrant—sld.				
Coker, Nancy (W) 29	1848	Denton Denton	Mo.	Mo.	X	2
Coldiron, James (M) Farmer; 35	1848	Dallas Ellis	Ky.	Mo.	X	1
Cole, Calvin G. (M) Farmer; 34	1844	Dallas Dallas	Tenn.	Ark.		7
Cole, James M. (S) Farmer; 27	1844	Dallas Dallas	Tenn.	Tenn.		
Cole, John (M)	1844	Dallas				
Cole, John H. (S) Farmer; 23	1844	Dallas Dallas	Tenn.	Tenn.		
Cole, John R. (M) Farmer; 41	1845	Dallas Dallas	Va.	Tenn.		5
Cole, William L. (S) Farmer; 20	1848	Dallas Dallas	Ark.	Ark.		
Collier, Samuel (S)	1848					
Collins, Albert G. (M) Farmer; 46	1848	Dallas Dallas	Ky.	Mo.		7
Collins, John H. (M) Farmer; 43	1848	Collin Collin	Ky.	Mo.		3
Colwell, Timothy (S) Farmer; 21	1848	Dallas—sld Dallas	Ind.	Ill.	X	1
Combs, Joseph (M) Farmer; 25	1848	Tarrant—sld Dallas	Ohio	Ohio		1
Combs, Zur (S) Farmer; 22	1848	Dallas—sld Dallas	Ohio	Ohio		
Condra, John (M) Carpenter; 48	1848	Tarrant—sld Dallas	Tenn.	Ill.	X	5
Condre, John (S)	1848	Tarrant—sld			X	
Connelly, Cornelius (M) Farmer; 44	1844	Tarrant Tarrant	Ky.	Ky.		1
Conner, Joseph W. (M) Farmer; 42	1844	Tarrant Tarrant	Ind.	Mo.	X	5
Conner, William D. (S) Farmer; 22	1844	Tarrant Tarrant	Ind.	Ind.		
Conover, Wm. W. (M)	1844	Dallas				
Conway, John (M) Farmer; 50	1848	Ellis Dallas	Ky.	Ill.	X	6
Cook, Daniel (S)	1848	Denton				
Cook, David (S-M) Farmer; 33	1848	Denton Denton	Ill.	Ill.		
Cook, Edward (M)	1844	Dallas				

Name (Marital Status) Occupation; Age	Yr/Mig	County County	Birth	Removal	Illit.	Chld.
Cook, Henry (M)	1848	Collin			X	
Farmer; 75		Collin	Va.	Ill.		4
Cook, John C. (M)	1844	Dallas				
Cook, Wilford W. (M)	1848	Dallas				
Coombs, Isaac M. (S-M)	1844	Dallas				
Farmer; 24		Dallas	Ky.	Ky.		1
Coombs, Levin Green (M)	1844	Dallas				
Farmer; 26		Dallas	Ky.	Ky.		
Coombs, William (M)	1844	Dallas				
Farmer; 47		Dallas	Ky.	Ky.		3
Coombs, William H. (S)	1844	Dallas				
Coonrad, George W. (M)	1848	Tarrant				
Carpenter; 33		Ellis	Ky.	Ill.		4
Cooper, Alexander (M)	1848	Denton—sld			X	
Farmer; 36		Collin	Tenn.	Tenn.		1
Cornelius, Abner P. (S)	1848	Dallas				
Couch, Henderson (M)	1844	Dallas				
Farmer; 39		Dallas	Tenn.	Tenn.		2
Coween, Hugh (S-M)	1845	Grayson				
Farmer; 30		Grayson	Ireland	Ireland		1
Cox, Cornelius (M)	1848	Dallas				
Farmer; 50		Dallas	Ky.	Ind. to Mo.		5
Cox, Jesse (S)	1844	Dallas—sld				
Farmer; 24		Dallas	Mo.	Mo.		
Cox, John (S-M)	1844	Dallas—sld pt.				
Farmer; 28		Dallas	Ill.	Ill.		1
Cox, Joseph (S)	1848	Dallas				
Farmer; 22		Dallas	Ind.	Ind.		
Cox, William (M)	1844	Denton & Tararnt				
Crawford, Washington (S)	1848	Dallas				
Crawley, Benjamin F. (S)	1848	Dallas				
Farmer; 24		Tarrant	Ala.	Ala.		1
Crawley, Isham (M)	1848	Tarrant			X	
Farmer; 55		Tarrant	Va.	Ala. to Mo.		4,
Crawley, Richard (S)	1848	Tarrant				
Farmer; 25		Tarrant	Ala.	Ala.		
Crockett, John M. (M)	1848	Dallas				
Lawyer; 33		Dallas	S.C.	S.C.		
Crow, William M. (M)	1848	Dallas				
Farmer; 44		Dallas	Ky.	Ky.		7
Crum, Harmon P. (M)	1848	Ellis				
Farmer; 49		Ellis	S.C.	Ala. to Ill.		7
Crumpacker, Daniel (S)	1848	Dallas				
Crumpacker, Joel (S)	1848	Dallas				
Crutchberry, John (M)	1848	Grayson				

Name (Marital Status) Occupation; Age	Yr/Mig	County County	Birth	Removal	Illit.	Chld.
Crutchfield, Dixon M. (S)	1848	Collin			X	
Farmer; 20		Collin	Ga.	Ga.		
Crutchfield, George (S)	1844	Collin				
Crutchfield, James O. (S)	1848	Dallas				
Farmer; 21		Dallas	Ky.	Ky.		
Crutchfield, John (M)	1844	Collin				
Farmer; 27		Collin	Ala.	Ala.		
Crutchfield, Joseph (S)	1848	Collin				
Farmer; 70		Collin	S.C.	S.C.		
Crutchfield, Thomas (M)	1848	Dallas				
Inn Keeper; 47		Dallas	Ky.	Ky.		5
Culwell, Andrew J. (M)	1848	Collin			X	
Farmer; 32		Collin	N.C.	Ark.		4
Culwell, Hezekiah (M)	1848	Collin				
Farmer; 52		Collin	N.C.	Tenn. to Ark.		7
Culwell, John (S)	1848	Parker				
Culwell, John Sr. (M)	1845	Collin—sld				
Meth. Preacher; 36		Collin	N.C.	Ark.		5
Culwell, Thomas (M)	1848	Collin			X	
Farmer; 40		Collin	N.C.	Ark.		7
Culwell, Wm. (M)	1845	Collin			X	
Blacksmith; 39		Collin	N.C.	Ark.		5
Cunius (Cannius), Talton (M)	1844	Collin				
Farmer; 49'		Collin	Ky.	Ala. to Ark.		7
Cunningham, David (S)	1848	?				
Cunningham, John (M)	1848	Collin—sld				
Curtis, John W. (S-M)	1844	Colllin—sld Dallas—sld				
Dailey, Hiram W. (M)	1848	Grayson—sld				
Farmer; 27		Denton—sld				
		Collin	Ala.	Ala.		3
Dakan, Perry (S)	1845	Denton				
Physician; 29		Dallas	Pa.	Pa.		2
Daniel, John F. (S)	1847	Denton				
Farmer; 25		Dallas	Va.	Tenn.		2
Daniel, John H. (S)	1848	Dallas—sld				
Farmer; 24		Dallas	Ky.	Ky.		
Danks, Albert B. (M)	1845	Collin—sld Dallas—sld				
Davidson, Jesse J. (S)	1848	Ellis				
Davidson, Lorenzo D. (M)	1848	Collin				
Farmer; 48		Collin	Va.	Mo. to Ten.		3
Davis, Benjamin T. (S)	1848	Dallas				
Farmer; 21		Dallas	Va.	Va.		
Davis, Henson C. (M)	1848	Dallas				
Farmer; 46		Dallas	Va.	Va.		8
Davis, John W. (S)	1848	Dallas				
Farmer; 23		Dallas	Va.	Va.		

Name (Marital Status) Occupation; Age	Yr/Mig	County County	Birth	Removal	Illit.	Chld.
Davis, Joseph C. (S) Farmer; 22	1848	Tarrant Ellis	Tenn.	Tenn.		
Davis, Solomen (M) Farmer; 36	1848	Tarrant Ellis	Pa.	Pa.	X	1
Dawson, Jonas (M) Farmer; 36	1844	Collin Collin	N.C.	Tenn.		4
Deaver, Elijah N. (S) Laborer; 21	1848	Grayson Grayson	N.C.	N.C.		
Deaver, John (M) Carpenter; 54	1848	Grayson Grayson	N.C.	Mo.		6
Deaver, Joseph (M)	1848	Grayson				
Deaver, William A. (M)	1848	Grayson—sld pt.				
Degman, Jabez (M)	1848	Collin				
Deister, George (S)	1848	Cooke				
Demarcus, John (M) Farmer; 25	1848	Cooke Cooke	Tenn.	Tenn.		1
Demay, Charles (S)	1848	Denton				
Dickson, Christopher C. (S) Farmer; 25	1848	Denton Denton	Ga.	Ga.	X	
Dickson, James C. (M) Farmer; 52	1848	Cooke Cooke	N.C.	N.C.		?
Dickson, James M. (S) Farmer; 25	1848	Cooke Cooke	N.C.	N.C.	X	
Dickson, James O. (S-M) None; 39	1848	Denton Denton	Ga.	Ga.		
Dickson, John S. (S) None; 22	1848	Denton—sld pt. Denton	Ga.	Ga.		
Dickson, William H. (W) Farmer; 65	1848	Denton Denton	S.C.	Ga. to Ark.		
Dillingham, Joshua (S)	1848	Collin				
Dixon, Joseph (M) ? Farmer; 54	1845	Collin—sld pt. Collin	N.C.	N.C.	X	
Dixon, Soloman (M) Farmer; 44	1845	Dallas—sld Dallas	Ohio	Mo.	X	7
Dollins, James (S-M) Farmer; 32	1844	Dallas Dallas	Va.	Va.		3
Donaldson, Surry E. (M) Farmer; 40	1848	Collin Collin	S.C.	Ill.		5
Dooley, George W. (M) Farmer; 37	1844	Dallas Dallas	Va.	Tenn.		5
Dozier, Adam (M) Farmer; 53	1848	Cooke Cooke	Va.	Ill. to Mo.	X	
Dosser, Francis (M) Farmer; 30	1848	Collin Collin	Ind.	Ind.		1
Douglass, Hezekiah (M) Farmer; 22	1848	Collin—sld Dallas	Ill.	Ill.		1

94

Name (Marital Status) Occupation; Age	Yr/Mig	County County	Birth	Removal	Illit.	Chld.
Dowdy, Allanson (S-M) Farmer; 22	1848	Dallas—sld pt. Dallas	Ill.	Ill.		1
Downing, William (M) Farmer; 43	1848	Ellis—sld Ellis	Ky.	Ind.		10
Downing, William D. (S)	1847	Dallas				
Driggers, John J. (S)	1848	Collin—sld			X	
Dronard, E. (S)	1848	Denton				
Dunaway, Foster W. (S)	1848	Dallas				
Dunham, Joseph A. (S)	1848	Tarrant			X	
Dunn, Tola (M) Farmer; 35	1844	Collin—sld pt. Collin	Ky.	Ky.		7
Dunn, William T. (S)	1848	Ellis—sld			X	
Durbin, Everistus (M) Farmer; 40	1848	Dallas Dallas	Ky.	Mo.	X	2
Durgin, Charles H. (S)	1848	Wise				
Durrett, George W. (M)	1848	Dallas				
Dye, Benjamin Jr. (S) Farmer; 21	1848	Dallas—sld Dallas	Ky.	Ky.		
Dye, Benjamin (M) Farmer; 57	1848	Dallas Dallas	Va.	Ky.		9
Dye, Enoch (S) Carpenter; 28	1848	Dallas Dallas	Va.	Ky.		
Dye, Joseph (S) Farmer; 18	1848	Dallas Dallas	Ky.	Ky.		
Dye, Rama (M) Farmer; 29	1848	Cooke Cooke	Mo.	Mo.		3
Dye, William (S) Farmer; 22	1848	Ellis—sld Dallas	Ky.	Ky.	X	
Dye, William H. (S) ? Physician; 21	1848	Dallas Collin	Va.	Va.		
Dyke, Thomas (M)	1848	Dallas				
Eads, Jesse (M) Farmer; 55	1848	Denton Denton	Ky.	Mo.	X	7
Eads, Richard (S) Farmer; 18	1848	Denton Denton	Mo.	Mo.	X	
Eakey, Robert (M)	1844	Cooke				
Easter, Thomas (M) Farmer; 27	1848	Tarrant Tarrant	Va.	Mo.		2
Edwards, Isaac (M) Farmer; 48	1845	Dallas Dallas	S.C.	Ill.		4
Edwards, Lemuel J. (W) Carpenter; 44	1848	Tarrant Tarrant	Ohio	Mo.		5
Elam, Isaac (M) Farmer; 42	1848	Dallas Dallas	Ky.	Ill. to Mo.		8
Elam, Jesse (M) Farmer; 68	1845	Dallas—sld Dallas	Ga.	Ga.		

Name (Marital Status) Occupation; Age	Yr/Mig	County County	Birth	Removal	Illit.	Chld.
Elam, William B. (M)	1845	?				
Farmer; 37		Dallas	Tenn.	Mo.		4
Elkins, Smith (M)	1848	Dallas—sld				
Lawyer; 59		Dallas	N.H.	N.H.		2
Ellet, John (M)	1848	Collin—sld				
Elliot, Saunders (M)	1844	Tarrant				
Farmer; 39		Tarrant	N.Y.	Ill. to Ky.		3
Ellis, Edward S. (S)	1848	Tarrant—sld				
Ellis, Joshua N. (M)	1848	Tarrant				
Ellis, Thomas N. (M)	1848	Dallas				
Farmer; 51		Dallas	Ill.	Ill.		6
Elliston, John W. (M)	1848	Tarrant				
Blacksmith; 41		Ellis	Ky.	Ky.		4
Elliston, Mortimer (S)	1848	Tarrant				
Farmer; 19		Ellis	Ky.	Ky.		
Elston, Allen (M)	1848	Cooke—sld			X	
Carpenter; 34		Grayson	Ala.	Mo.		2
Ely, Edward B. (S)	1844	?				
Estis, Thomas (M)	1848	Collin				
Eubanks, Alfred (M)	1848	Cooke—sld				
Farmer; 30		Cooke	Ala.	Ala.		4
Evans, Abraham (M)	1848	?				
Evans, James (M)	1848	Dallas—sld				
Farmer; 26		Dallas	Va.	Mo.		5
Evans, Wm. T. (S)	1844	Cooke				
Eveens, Davida (W-M)	1848	Johnson—sld			X	
Everard, Patrick (S-M)	1845	Tarrant				
Farmer; 38		Ellis-Tarrant	Ire.	Ireland		
Fain, Mercer (S)	1848	Dallas				
Farmer; 30		Tarrant	Tenn.	Tenn.		
Farrans, John (S)	1848	Dallas			X	
Farmer; 22		Dallas	Mo.	Mo.		
Farrans, Michael (M)	1848	Dallas			X	
Farmer; 54		Dallas	Va.	Mo.		3
Fay, Jonathon B. (M)	1845	Tarrant				
Feland, James M. (S)	1845	Collin				
Ferguson, John P. (M)	1848	Grayson				
Farmer; 29		Grayson	Tenn.	Tenn.		1
Ferris, Lewis (S)	1848	Dallas				
Ferris, Morris (M)	1844	Dallas				
Farmer; 39		Grayson	Ky.	Mo.		8
Finger, Lewis (M)	1848	Tarrant				
Farmer; 33		Tarrant	Ind.	Ind.		5
Fisher, Peter (M)	1845	Collin			X	
Farmer; 69		Collin	Pa.	Pa.		6

Name (Marital Status) Occupation; Age	Yr/Mig	County County	Birth	Removal	Illit.	Chld.
Fisher, Witsaul (M) R.P.B. Preacher; 31	1845	Collin Collin	Mo.	Mo.		5
Fitch, William D. (S) Clerk; 28	1848	? Grayson	?	?		
Fitzhugh, Gabriel (M) Farmer; 48	1845	Collin Collin	Ky.	Ky.		
Fitzhugh, Gabriel H. (S) Farmer; 29	1844	Dallas—sld Collin	Ky.	Ky.		
Fitzhugh, George (M) Farmer; 59	1848	Collin Collin	Va.	Ky.		4
Fitzhugh, John (M) Farmer; 58	1845	Collin & Grayson Collin	Va.	Mo.		4
Fitzhugh, Robert (S-M) Sheriff; 33	1844	Collin Collin	Ky.	Mo.		2
Fitzhugh, Solomon (S)	1844	Collin				
Fitzhugh, William (S-M) Farmer; 31	1848	Collin Collin	Ky.	Ky.		1
Fleming, William (M) Farmer; 29	1848	Dallas Dallas	Pa.	Pa.	X	1
Floyd, George (M) Farmer; 37	1848	Dallas Dallas	?	Ill.		6
Fondren, John R. (M) Farmer; 37	1848	Dallas Dallas	N.C.	Ala. to Miss.		8
Foote, Gerard A. (S-M) Physician; 26	1848	Collin Collin	Va.	Ark.		2
Ford, Geo. W. (S-M) None; 26	1844	Collin—sld pt. Collin	Ark.	Ark.	X	3
Forgy, William A. (S)	1848	Dallas				
Fortner, Melford F. (M) Farmer; 37	1843	Dallas Dallas	Tenn.	Mo. to Ark.		7
Foster, Ambrose (M)	1848	Tarrant				
Foster, Benjamin J. (S) Farmer; 19	1848	Tarrant—sld Tarrant	Mo.	Mo.	X	
Fox, Abner (M)	1844	Grayson & Tarrant				
Fox, Cahill (S) Farmer; 19	1848	Grayson Grayson	Ky.	Ill.		
Fox, Vel D. (M) Farmer; 41	1848	Grayson Grayson	Ky.	Ill.		7
Franklin, Daniel J. (W) Farmer; 28	1845	Collin Collin	Tenn.	Ark.	X	2
Franklin, Jesse W. (S) Farmer; 20	1848	Collin—sld Collin	Tenn.	Tenn.		
Franklin, Levi Farmer; 26	1848	Dallas—sld Tarrant	Ky.	Ky.		
Frans, James M. (M) Farmer; 35	1848	Wise-Montague sold Grayson	Va.	Mo.	X	3

Name (Marital Status) Occupation; Age	Yr/Mig	County County	Birth	Removal	Illit.	Chld.
Freeman, John A. (M)	1848	Tarrant				
Baptist Preacher; 23		Tarrant	S.C.	S.C.		2
Freeman, Samuel (M)	1848	Tarrant—sld				
Farmer; 52		Tarrant	N.C.	N.C.		
French, James P. (S)	1848	Denton			X	
French, Nathaniel (M)	1848	Denton				
French, Oliver M. (S)	1848	Denton			X	
Farmer; 28		Denton	Tenn.	Tenn.		
Frost, Benjamin (M)	1848	Dallas				
Farmer; 49		Dallas	Tenn.	Ala. to Miss.		7
Fyke, Archer (S)	1848	Dallas				
Fyke, Elisha (M)	1848	Dallas				
Fyke, John (S)	1848	Collin				
Gallagher, William (S)	1848	Cooke—sld				
Galloway, David R.S.C. (M)	1848	Dallas				
Garvin, Benjamin G. (M)	1848	Ellis				
Farmer; 50		Ellis	Va.	Ark. to Mo.		7
Garvin, John B. (S)	1848	Ellis				
Garvin, Thomas B. (M)	1847	Dallas—sld Denton—sld				
Farmer; 38		Denton	S.C.	S.C.		
Gibson, James (M)	1848	Dallas				
Gibson, Jesse (W)	1844	Tarrant				
Farmer; 54		Tarrant	S.C.	Tenn.		
Gibson, John A. (S)	1848	Tarrant				
Gibson, John M. (S)	1848	Denton			X	
Gibson, Levander (M)	1848	Grayson			X	
Farmer; 46		Grayson	Mo.	Tenn.		7
Gibson, Robert W. (M)	1848	Denton & Tarrant				
None; 27		Tarrant	Ala.	Mo.		3
Gibson, William (M)	1848	Denton—sld				
Farmer; 48		Denton	Tenn.	Mo.		
Gibson, Wm. H. (M)	1844	Denton—sld				
Farmer; 29		Denton	Tenn.	Mo.		2
Gilman, Charles (S)	1848	Collin			X	
Carpenter; 22		Collin	N.Y.	N.Y.		
Gilman, Harry (S)	1848	Cooke				
Farmer; 28		Grayson	N.Y.	N.Y.		
Gilman, Samuel (M)	1848	Grayson				
Farmer; 63		Grayson	N.H.	N.Y.		2
Gilmore, Seburn (M)	1848	Tarrant				
Farmer; 50		Tarrant	Ga.	Ill.		3
Glover, George W. (S-M)	1844	Dallas—sld Tarrant—sld				
Farmer; 34		Dallas	Ala.	Mo.		3
Goar, Clement (S)	1848	Ellis				
Farmer; 32		Dallas	Ky.	Ill.		
Goar, John (S-M)	1845	Dallas				
Farmer; 45		Dallas	Ky.	Ill.		5

98

Name (Marital Status) Occupation; Age	Yr/Mig	County County	Birth	Removal	Illit.	Chld.
Goddard, Daniel (S)	1844	Denton				
Goodman, James J. (M)	1848	Tarrant—sld				
Farmer; 35		Tarrant	Tenn.	Ark.		3
Good, Noah (M)	1848	Dallas				
Farmer; 35		Dallas	Va.	Tenn.		6
Goodwin, John J. (S)	1848	Tarrant				
Farmer; 25		Ellis	Ga.	Ga.		
Goodwin, Micajah (M)	1846	Dallas				
Farmer; 45		Ellis	Ga.	Ala.		6
Gorbet, John W. (M)	1848	Tarrant—sld				
Farmer; 32		Dallas	Va.	Ill.		3
Gorham, Joshua (S)	1848	Cooke			X	
Farmer; 25		Cooke	Ky.	Ky.		
Gough, Jesse W. (M)	1848	Collin				
Farmer; 42		Collin	Ohio	Ill.		7
Gouhenant, Adolphe (S)	1848	Tarrant				
Graham, Joseph (M)	1843	Dallas				
Farmer; 58		Dallas	Pa.	Ill.		1
Graham, Milton H. (S)	1848	Dallas				
Graham, Spencer (M)	1844	Collin—sld Denton			X	
Farmer; 30		Denton	Tenn.	Ark.		3
Graves, James M. (S)	1848	Dallas—sld				
? Farmer; 31		Collin	Va.	Va.		1
Gray, Andrew K. (M)	1848	Dallas—sld Ellis				
Farmer; 46		Dallas	Va.	Ill.		8
Gray, Elizabeth (W)	1848	Dallas				
Gray, John (S)	1844	Collin				
Grayum, James (W)	1848	Collin				
Green, Jones (S-M)	1845	Dallas			X	
Farmer; 32		Dallas	Ill.	Ill.		2
Green, Martin P. (M)	1848	Dallas				
Griffin, Thackea V. (M)	1846	Dallas				
Farmer; 49		Dallas	Ill.	Tenn.		2
Grimes, John (M)	1848	Grayson			X	
Farmer; 35		Grayson	Ky.	Ind. to Mo.		6
Ground, Robert (M)	1848	Dallas				
Farmer; 31		Tarrant	Ky.	Ill.		5
Guess, John (M)	1843	Denton				
Gunnells, George W. (M)	1848	Collin—sld pt.			X	
Farmer; 24		Collin	Mo.	Mo.		1
Hackney, Francis N. (M)	1848	(? claim not proved)				
Farmer; 28		Grayson	Tenn.	Tenn.		1
Haile, Benjamin (M)	1848	Collin—sld				
Farmer; 57		Collin	N.C.	Ky. to Mo.		4
Hale, Richard F. (S)	1848	Dallas				
Halford, Jacob W. (S)	1844	Dallas				

Name (Marital Status) Occupation; Age	Yr/Mig	County County	Birth	Removal	Illit.	Chld.
Halford, James R. (M) Farmer; 37	1844	Tarrant—sld Tarrant	S.C.	Mo.		7
Halford, John H. (M) Farmer; 35	1844	Denton Denton	Ky.	Mo.		4
Hall, David L. (M) Farmer; 32	1845	Dallas & Tarrant—sld Dallas	Pa.	Ill.		3
Hall, John (M) Blacksmith; 58	1848	Dallas Dallas	Pa.	Ill.		4
Hall, Little Berry G. (S) Blacksmith; 26	1848	Tarrant Tarrant	Mo.	Mo.		
Hall, Peter (M) Farmer; 30	1848	Dallas—sld Dallas	Pa.	Ohio to Ill.		3
Hall, William W. (S-M) Farmer; 24	1848	Tarrant Tarrant	Mo.	Mo.		
Hambright, Benjamin (M) Farmer; 50	1848	Grayson Grayson	S.C.	Ill.	X	3
Hambright, James M. (S) Farmer; 23	1848	Grayson Grayson	Ky.	Ky.		
Hambright, Thomas J. (S)	1848	Grayson				
Hamilton, Frederick (M) Farmer; 35	1848	Grayson Grayson	R.I.	Ark.		4
Hamilton, James (S)	1848	Grayson—sld				
Hammick, Samuel (S)	1848	Throckmorton				
Hammond, Willis (S)	1844	Denton				
Handy, Frederick W. (M)	1845	Dallas & Johnson				
Haning, Aaron (S) Farmer; 20	1848	Grayson Grayson	Ohio	Ohio	X	
Haning, Jabez (S)	1848	Grayson			X	
Haning, John (M) Farmer; 35	1848	Grayson Grayson	Ohio	Ill.	X	4
Haning, Rachael (W) 60	1848	Grayson—sld Grayson	N.J.	Ohio	X	2
Hannah, Amana (M)	1848	Dallas				
Hardaway, James Marcum (S)	1845	Clay				
Hargroeder, Mary (W) 43	1848	Dallas Dallas	La.	La.		2
Harmonson, Peter (M) Farmer; 49 (Sheriff)	1845	Denton—sld Denton	Ky.	Ind. to Mo. to Ark.		3
Harmonson, Zerrell J. (S) Farmer; 26	1845	Denton Denton	Ind.	Mo. to Ark.		
Harper, Hugh (M) Farmer; 39	1848	Denton Denton	Tenn.	Tenn.	X	3
Harrington, Alfred (S)	1848	Collin				
Harrington, Silas (S)	1848	Collin				
Harris, Andrew S. (M) Farmer; 34	1848	Tarrant Denton	N.C.	N.C.		1

Name (Marital Status) Occupation; Age	Yr/Mig	County County	Birth	Removal	Illit. Chld.
Harris, Esom (M)	1848	Collin			
Harris, Ethelbert Sanders (M)	(?1840)	Tarrant—sld			
Farmer; 29	1848	Grayson	Mo.	Mo.	5
Harris, Francis L. (S-M)	1848	Tarrant—sld Denton			
Farmer; 25		Denton	Tenn.	Tenn.	
Harris, Harrison (M)	1848	Grayson			
Carpenter; 23		Grayson	N.Y.	N.Y.	1
Harris, J. M. (M)	1848	Grayson—sld			
Laborer; 28		Grayson	Tenn.	Ill.	
Harris, James S. (S)	1848	Denton			
Harris, Matthew H. (M)	1848	Grayson			
Harris, Oliver W. (M)	1848	Denton			
Farmer; 28		Denton	Tenn.	Tenn.	1
Harris, Robert R. (S)	1848	Collin—sld			
Laborer; 21		Grayson	Tenn.	Ill.	
Hart, Abraham (S-M)	1845	Dallas—sld Parker		X	
Farmer; 28		Dallas	N.C.	N.C.	1
Hart, Caleb (M)	1848	Collin			
Farmer; 45		Collin	Va.	Mo.	9
Hart, Jacob (M)	1844	Dallas			
Hartzog, Elijah (M)	1848	Grayson			
Blacksmith; 38		Grayson	N.C.	Tenn. to Ark.	8
Hartzog, Josiah (M)	1848	Grayson		X	
Farmer;		Grayson	Tenn.	Ark.	
Harvin, Wesley (M)	1846	Dallas—sld pt.			
Harwood, Alexander (S)	1845	Dallas—sld pt.			
Clerk; 28		Dallas	Tenn.	Tenn.	
Harwood, Alexander M. (M)	1845	Dallas			
Harwood, Nathaniel B. (M)	1845	Dallas			
Hatcher, Solomon (M)	1848	Grayson			
Farmer; 29		Grayson	Tenn.	Mo.	2
Haught, Peter (S)	1845	Dallas—sld Tarrant—sld			
Haux, James M. (M)	1847	Dallas			
Havens, John H. (S)	1848	Denton		X	
Hawkins, Benjamin F. (M)	1848	Ellis			
Farmer; 22		Ellis	Ind.	Ind.	1
Hawkins, James Emerson (S)	1848	Ellis—sld pt.			
Farmer; 20		Ellis	Ind.	Ind.	
Hawkins, Marcellus T. (S)	1848	Ellis			
Farmer; 26		Ellis	Ind.	Ind.	
Hawkins, William (M)	1848	Ellis			
Farmer; 50		Ellis	Del.	Ind.	6
Hawse, Trespant C. (M)	1846	Tarrant—sld			
Farmer; 28		Dallas	Ga.	Ga.	2
Hawse, William B. (M)	1848	Denton—sld			
Farmer; 34		Denton	Va.	Ohio to Mo.	6
Haydon, Samuel M. (M)	1845	Denton			

Name (Marital Status) Occupation; Age	Yr/Mig	County County	Birth	Removal	Illit.	Chld.
Hayhurst, Joseph W. (M)	1848	Grayson				
Farmer; 30		Grayson	Va.	Ark.		2
Haworth, Solomon (W)	1848	Tarrant				
Farmer; 30		Dallas	N.C.	Ill.		2
Hazelton, Nathaniel S. (S-M)	1845	Denton			X	
Farmer; 28		Denton	Ind.	Ind.		2
Hearn, Daniel B. (S)	1848	Collin				
Hearn, Martin (M)	1848	Collin			X	
Farmer; 46		Collin	N.C.	Ill.		6
Heath, Zebedee (M)	1848	Dallas				
Farmer; 27		Dallas	N.C.	N.C.		2
Hedgcoxe, Robert A. (S)	1846	Denton				
Farmer; 23		Collin	Ind.	Ind.		
Hedgcoxe, Oliver (M)	1846	Collin				
Farmer; 27		Collin	Ind.	Ind.		
Helms, Jacob (S)	1845	Dallas—sld				
Saddle tree maker; 62		Dallas	Va.	Ky. to Mo.		
Helms, John B. (M)	1848	Dallas				
Saddler; 33		Dallas	Va.	Ky. to Mo.		3
Helms, Thomas H. (S)	1845	Tarrant				
Farmer; 35		Ellis	Ky.	Mo.		
Helms, Thompson (M)	1845	Collin				
?; 29		Collin	Ky.	Mo.		8
Henderson, Noah (M)	1847	Dallas			X	
Farmer; 31		Dallas	Ohio	Mo.		4
Hendrix, John (M)	1848	Grayson				
Farmer; 52		Grayson	N.C.	Mo.		8
Hendrix, Reuben (S)	1848	Grayson				
Laborer; 25		Grayson	Ky.	Ky.		
Herndon, George (M)	1848	Collin				
Farmer; 32		Collin	Ky.	Ark.		4
Herndon, James (M)	1845	Collin				
Farmer; 48		Collin	Va.	Ky. to Ark.		4
Herring, Daniel (M)	1848	Collin				
Farmer; 38		Collin	N.C.	Ill.		6
Herring, Isaac (M)	1848	Collin			X	
Farmer; 39		Collin	N.C.	Ill.		4
Herring, Sherwood (S)	1848	Collin				
Herron, Martha (W)	1848	Collin			X	
45		Collin	Tenn.	Tenn.		3
Herron, Wm. H. (S)	1848	Collin				
Hibbert, John B. (M)	1845	Ellis—sld Parker—sld				
Farmer; 37		Dallas	Ky.	Ark.		4
Hibbert, Wm. P. (M)	1848	Grayson & Montague			X	
Cooper; 30		Grayson	Mo.	Mo.		3
Hickman, Henry H. (S)	1848	Dallas				
Farmer; 25		Dallas	Tenn.	Tenn.		

Name (Marital Status) Occupation; Age	Yr/Mig	County County	Birth	Removal	Illit.	Chld.
Hicky, Granville S. (S) Farmer; 20	1848	Johnson—sld Ellis	Tenn.	Tenn.		
Higgins, Lewis T. (M) Farmer; 27	1848	Denton Denton	Ill.	Ill.		3
Higgins, Phileman R. (M) Farmer; 24	1845	Denton Denton	Ill.	Ill.		
Higgins, Phileman Sr. (M) Farmer; 65	1848	Denton Denton	Va.	Ill.	X	3
Hill, Aaron (M) Farmer; 55	1848	Cooke Grayson	S.C.	Ala. to Miss.		7
Hill, Charles S. (S)	1848	Cooke				
Hill, James O. M. Farmer; 28	1848	Cooke—sld Grayson	S.C.	S.C.		2
Hill, John (M) Farmer; 36	1844	Cooke Dallas	Tenn.	Ind.		3
Hill, John T. (S) Farmer; 23	1848	Cooke Grayson	Ala.	Miss.		
Hill, Thomas J. (M) Farmer; 27	1844	Grayson—sld Grayson	Tenn.	Tenn.	X	1
Hillis, John M. (M) Farmer; 32	1848	Grayson—sld Grayson	Ky.	Ky.		2
Hinkley, Harrison F. (M) Farmer; 32	1848	Ellis Ellis	N.Y.	Ind.		1
Hobaugh, Hiram (M)	1848	Denton			X	
Hodges, Amos (M) Farmer; 30	1848	Dallas—sld Johnson—sld Dallas	Ky.	Ill.	X	3
Holman, George T. (S)	1848	Ellis—sld				
Holman, William P. (M) Farmer; 27	1848	Dallas & Ellis Tarrant	Tenn.	Ill.		2
Hood, Thomas M. (S-M) Farmer; 27	1845	Tarrant Tarrant	S.C.	S.C.	X	
Hord, Wm. H. (M) Farmer; 40	1845	Dallas Dallas	Va.	Tenn.		5
Horn, George (S) Farmer; 20	1848	Collin Collin	Ga.	Ga.		
Horn, James T. (S) Farmer; 19	1848	Collin—sld Collin	Ga.	Ga.	X	
Horn, Jeremiah (M) E.M.S. Preacher; 56	1848	Collin Collin	Tenn.	Tenn.		4
Horn, William T. (S-M) Farmer; 30	1848	Collin Collin	Unk.	Unk.		1
Horton, Enoch (M)	1848	Dallas			X	
Horton, Enoch (M) Farmer; 64	1844	Dallas & Ellis Dallas	Va.	Va.		2
Horton, James (S)	1848	Dallas				
Horton, John (S) Farmer; 35	1848	Dallas Dallas	Va.	Va.		

Name (Marital Status) Occupation; Age	Yr/Mig	County County	Birth	Removal	Illit.	Chld.
House, Joseph (M)	1848	Collin & Grayson				
Howard, David (M)	1845	Collin				
Farmer; 50		Collin	Tenn.	Mo.		4
Howard, Robert (M)	1848	Denton				
Howell, Daniel (M)	1845	Collin				
Farmer; 30		Collin	Ohio	Mo.		3
Howell, John (M)	1847	Dallas				
Farmer; 35		Dallas	Tenn.	Miss.		6
Howell, Mary (W)	1848	Collin—sld			X	
Huffman, John S. (S)	1848	Collin				
Physician; 24		Collin	Ky.	Ky.		
Huffstutter, Aaron (S)	1848	Collin—sld			X	
Laborer; 19		Grayson	Ky.	Ky.		
Huffstutter, Solomon (W)	1848	Grayson—sld				
Farmer; 57		Grayson	Ky.	Mo.		2
Hughs, William (M)	1848	Dallas			X	
Farmer; 43		Dallas	Tenn.	Ill.		5
Huitt, Andrew Jackson (M)	1843	Tarrant				
Farmer; 29		Dallas	Ark.	Ark.		4
Huitt, John (M)	1843	Tarrant				
Huitt, Roland (M)	1846	Dallas				
Huitt, Solomon (M)	1844	Dallas—sld Tarrant				
None; 87		Dallas	N.C.	N.C.	X	
Hull, John (M)	1845	Grayson				
Farmer; 29		Dallas	Va.	Iowa(?)		1
Hume, Alfred (S)	1848	Grayson				
Hunnicutt, William C. (M)	1846	Dallas				
Farmer; 31		Dallas	Ind.	Ind.		3
Hunt, Edward (S-M)	1848	Dallas				
Farmer; 24		Dallas	N.C.	N.C.		1
Hunt, John L. (S)	1847	Dallas				
Farmer; 20		Dallas	N.C.	N.C.		
Hunter, Burwell (M)	1844	Denton			X	
Farmer; 50		Denton	N.C.	Tenn.		4
Hunter, David (M)	1848	Dallas & Johnson			X	
Hunter, Wiley B. (S)	1848	Denton				
Farmer; 20		Denton	Tenn.	Tenn.		
Hurst, Carter H. (S)	1848	Ellis				
Farmer; 20		Ellis	Ind.	Ind.		
Hurst, Henderson G. (S)	1848	Ellis				
Farmer; 24		Ellis	Ind.	Ind.		
Hurst, Isaac (M)	1848	Ellis				
Farmer; 46		Ellis	Va.	Ind.		10
Hurt, Ann S. (W)	1848	Collin				
22		Collin	Va.	Va.		2
Hust, John A. (M)	1848	Tarrant				
Farmer; 34		Ellis	Tenn.	Ind.		7

Name (Marital Status) Occupation; Age	Yr/Mig	County County	Birth	Removal	Illit.	Chld.
Hunstead, Harrison (M) Farmer; 44	1848	Dallas—sld Dallas	Va.	Ill.		8
Hutchinson, Robert (M)	1845	Cooke				
Hutton, Vincent J. Farmer; 38	1844	Tarrant Tarrant	Ind.	Ark.		5
Hyatt, Frederick (M)	1848	Denton				
Hyden, Abner A. (S) Farmer; 27	1848	Dallas Ellis	Va.	Ill.		
Hyden, James (M) Farmer; 68	1848	Tarrant—sld Ellis	Va.	Ill.	X	3

(To be continued)

105

KENTUCKY COLONIZATION IN TEXAS

A HISTORY OF THE PETERS COLONY

SEYMOUR V. CONNOR

LIST OF COLONISTS

Name (Marital Status) Occupation; Age	Yr/Mig	County County	Birth	Removal	Illit.	Chld.
Ingram, James (M)	1848	Grayson			X	
Farmer; 32		Grayson	Ark.	Ark.		2
Inman, Samuel C. (M)	1848	Tarrant-sld				
Carpenter; 23		Grayson	Tenn.	Tenn.		1
Irwin, William (M)	1848	Ellis—sld				
Farmer; 65		Ellis	Tenn.	Tenn.		
Ivy, James (S)	1844	Denton				
Jackson, Ashford (S)	1845	Dallas				
Jackson, James E. (S)	1848	Dallas				
Farmer; 24		Dallas	Tenn.	Tenn.		
Jackson, John (M)	1848	Dallas				
Farmer; 52		Dallas	Tenn.	Mo.		6
Jackson, John (M)	1848	Dallas				
Farmer; 43		Denton	Eng.	Eng.		8
Jackson, Moses Andrew (S)	1848	Collin—sld			X	
Laborer; 21		Dallas	Ill.	Ill.		
Jackson, Shadrick (M)	1848	Collin			X	
Farmer; 57		Collin	N.C.	N.C.		
Jackson, Trial (M)	1844	Ellis—sld				
Jackson, William (S)	1848	Collin—sld				
Farmer; 23		Collin	Ill.	Ill.		1
Jackson, William C. (S)	1848	Dallas				
Jackson, Zachariah (S)	1848	Dallas—sld			X	
? None; 16 ?		Dallas	N.C.	N.C.		
Jacobs, William P. (S)	1845	Ellis—sld				
James, Amos M. (S-M)	1848	Dallas & Johnson				
Farmer; 27		Dallas	Tenn.	Tenn.		1
James, Hogan (M)	1844	Grayson				
James, Michael (M)	1848	Dallas				
Farmer; 36		Dallas	Tenn.	Mo.		3
James, William (M)	1848	Dallas—sld			X	
Farmer; 36		Dallas	Va.	Tenn. to Mo.		5
Jamison, Harrison (M)	1848	Collin				
Farmer; 56		Collin	Ky.	Mo.		10
Jamison, Thomas J. (S)	1848	Collin			X	
Farmer; 18		Collin	Mo.	Mo.		
Jenkins, Alexander S. (M)	1848	Ellis				
Farmer; 20		Ellis	Ind.	Ind.		

Name (Marital Status) Occupation; Age	Yr/Mig	County County	Birth	Removal	Illit.	Chld.
Jenkins, Coleman (S)	1848	Ellis				
Farmer; 27		Ellis	Ind.	Ind.		
Jenkins, William (M)	1848	Tarrant—sld Dallas				
Farmer; 31		Dallas	Tenn.	Ark.		4
Jennings, Fleming (S)	1848	Grayson—sld			X	
Jennings, Hillard (M)	1848	Cooke—sld Grayson			X	
Farmer; 34		Grayson	Tenn.	Mo.		4
Jennings, John (M)	1848	Grayson & Cooke				
Farmer; 36		Grayson	Tenn.	Mo.		10
Jennings, John (M)	1848	Grayson—sld				
Farmer; 47		Grayson	S.C.	Mo.		6
Jennings, John Marshall (S)	1848	Grayson			X	
Laborer; 19		Grayson	Mo.	Mo.		
Jennings, Martin (S)	1848	Grayson			X	
Laborer; 21		Grayson	Mo.	Mo.		
Jewell, Joseph (M)	1848	Grayson				
Farmer; 52		Grayson	N.H.	Ill. to Ind.		8
Johnson, Henry (S)	1848	?Tarrant				
Farmer; 24		Collins	Ga.	Ga.		
Johnson, James (S)	1844	Tarrant—sld				
Johnson, James P. (S)	1844	Collin				
Johnson, John (M)	1848	Dallas				
Johnson, Robert A. (M)	1848	Denton & Collin				
Farmer; 30		Collin	Mo.	Mo.		1
Johnson, Thomas M. (S)	1844	Dallas				
Johnston, Andrew Jackson (W)	1848	Cooke				4
Jones, David (M)	1848	Grayson			X	
Farmer; 38		Grayson	Mo.	Ark.		7
Jones, George W. (S)	1848	Grayson				
Farmer; 29		Grayson	Mo.	Mo.		
Jones, John (M)	1845	Dallas & Denton				
Jones, Hamel C. (S)	1848	Dallas				
Farmer; 27		Dallas	Unk.	Unk.		
Jones, Matthew (M)	1848	Denton				
Farmer; 27		Denton	Tenn.	Ill.		2
Jones, William (M)	1845	Dallas				
Keel, Solomon (S)	1848	Grayson				
Physician; 55		Grayson	Ky.	Ky.		
Keen, Abner (M)	1846	Dallas				
None; 50		Dallas	Va.	Ind.		6
Keen, Abner M. (S)	1846	Ellis—sld				
Surveyor; 21		Dallas	Ind.	Ind.		
Keen, John W. (M)	1848	Dallas				
Farmer; 24		Dallas	Tenn.	Ky.		1
Keen, William H. (M)	1846	Dallas				
Farmer; 30		Dallas	Tenn.	Ind.		4
Keenan, Thomas (M)	1842	Dallas				
Farmer; 42		Dallas	Ohio	Ind.		5

Name (Marital Status) Occupation; Age	Yr/Mig	County ·County	Birth	Removal	Illit.	Chld.
Keller, Samuel (M)	1844	Dallas				
Farmer; 29		Dallas	Ky.	Ill.		3
Kemble, Catherine (W)	1845	Dallas & Ellis—sld			X	2
Kemble, Phillip (M)	1845	Dallas—sld				
Farmer; 24		Dallas	Ill.	Ill.		
Kennady, James M. (S)	1845	Dallas				
Farmer; 21		Dallas	N.C.	N.C.		
Kennady, Mary (W)	1845	Dallas—sld			X	
57		Dallas	S.C.	S.C.		2
Kennedy, John (M)	1848	Denton			X	
Farmer; 20		Tarrant	Ky.	Mo.		3
Kephart, Samuel (S)					X	
Kerby, John W. (M)	1848	Collin			X	
Farmer; 32		Collin	Tenn.	Mo.		3
Key, George T. (M)	1848	Collin & Denton—sld				
Physician; 47		Collin	Va.	Mo.		10
King, Augustus G. (S)	1844	Denton				
Farmer; 22		Denton	Tenn.	Mo.		
King, Christopher C. (S)	1848	Denton—sld pt.			X	
Farmer; 27		Denton	Ind.	Ind.		
King, Finis E. (M)	1848	Ellis				
C.P. Minister; 30		Ellis	Tenn.	Mo.		2
King, John (M)	1844	Denton				
King, John N. (S-M)	1845	Tarrant				
Farmer; 21		Denton	Ind.	Ind.		
King, John W. (M)	1848	Denton—sld pt.				
Farmer; 53		Denton	Tenn.	Mo.		12
King, Joseph (M)	1848	Palo Pinto				
Farmer; 18		Denton	Ind.	Ind.		
King, Rhoda (W)	1845	Denton			X	
60		Denton	Ky.	Tenn.		7
King, William (S)	1844	Denton			X	
Blacksmith; 24		Denton	Tenn.	Mo.		
King, Wm. E. (S)	1845	Parker				
Farmer; 22		Denton	Tenn.	Tenn.		
Kingwell, Wm. (S)	1848	Dallas				
Kinnaman, Wm. A. (M)	1848	Grayson—sld				
Kirkland, Pollard (M)	1844	Dallas				
Kiser, John (M)	1845	Dallas				
Farmer; 29		Dallas	Ohio	Ill. to Tenn.		4
Name (Marital Status) Occupation; Age	Yr/Mig	County ·County	Birth	Removal	Illit.	Chld.
Knight, Gabriel B. (S)	1848	Tarrant				
Knight, Joseph (M)	1848	Denton—sld pt.				
Farmer; 31		Denton	N.Y.	Mo.		3
Knight, Obediah (M)	1846	Tarrant				
Farmer; 44		Dallas	Va.	Tenn.		8
Knight, Richard (S)	1848	Denton				

Name (Marital Status) Occupation; Age	Yr/Mig	County County	Birth	Removal	Illit.	Chld.
Korn, Levi (M) Carpenter; 38	1845	Dallas—sld Grayson	Mo.	Mo.		3
Kuhn, Anton (M) Blacksmith; 30	1847	Dallas Dallas	Baden, Germany			
Lacy, Hilburn (S)	1844	Dallas		Ill.		1
Lambshead, Thomas (M) Farmer; 45	1848	Throckmorton Navarro	Eng.	Eng.		1
Lane, Cannuth T. (S) Farmer; 19	1848	Tarrant—sld Tarrant	Ga.	Ga.		
Lane, James W. (M) Farmer; 41	1848	Tarrant—sld Tarrant	Ga.	Ga.		7
Lane, Stephen W. (S) Farmer; 18	1848	Tarrant—sld Tarrant	Ga.	Ga.		
Langley, John (M) Farmer; 38	1848	Grayson—sld Tarrant—sld Dallas	Tenn.	Mo.		6
Langston, Martha (W) 37	1848	Denton Denton	Va.	Mo.	X	4
Langston, Martin M) Farmer; 40	1848	Denton—sld Denton	Tenn.	Mo.	X	
Larner, Elizabeth (W) 30	1848	? Dallas	Mo.	Mo.		4
Larner, Wm. (M)	1844	?				
Laughlin, James P. (M) Farmer; 30	1848	Ellis Ellis	Tenn.	Mo.		5
Laughlin, Newton C. (M) Farmer; 32	1848	Dallas & Johnson Ellis	Tenn.	Mo.		7
Laughlin, William B. (S) Farmer; 28	1848	Dallas—sld Ellis	Tenn.	Tenn.		
Lavallay, George W. (M) Farmer; 52	1848	Grayson—sld Grayson	Ohio	Ohio		1
Lavender, William (M)	1848	?				
Lawson, Berry (S) Farmer; 22	1848	Wise (Abandoned) Cooke	Tenn.	Tenn.	X	
Lawson, Jacob (M) Farmer; 69	1848	Cooke Cooke	Va.	Tenn.	X	5
Lawson, Miller (S)	1848	Cooke—sld			X	
Leake, Anthony M. (M) Farmer; 58	1848	Dallas Dallas	Mo.	Mo.		3
Learned, Daniel A. (S)	1848	Dallas				
Lee, Joshua B. (M) Farmer; 35	1848	Dallas Dallas	Ky.	Ill.		3
Lee, Michael (M) Farmer; 44	1848	Collin Collin	Va.	Mo.		9
Leeper, John (M) Farmer; 54	1848	Dallas Collin	N.C.	Mo.	X	8
Leeper, Isaac J. (S) Farmer; 22	1848	Collin—sld Collin	Mo.	Mo.		

Name (Marital Status) Occupation; Age	Yr/Mig	County County	Birth	Removal	Illit. Chld.
Linard (Lennard) Wm. M. (M)	1846	Dallas			
Farmer; 37		Dallas	S.C.	Tenn.	7
Lemmon, Robert A. (S-M)	1845	Ellis			
Farmer; 26		Ellis	Ind.	Ind.	
Leonard, Archibald F. (M)	1848	Tarrant			
Farmer; 34		Tarrant	Pa.	Mo.	5
Leonard, George L. (M)	1844	Dallas			
Farmer; 61		Dallas	S.C.	Tenn.	5
Leonard, George S. C. (S)	1844	Dallas—sld			
Farmer; 25		Dallas	Tenn.	Tenn.	
Leonard, John R. (S)	1848	Johnson—sld			
Farmer; 18		Dallas	Tenn.	Tenn.	
Leonard, John A. (M•	1843	Dallas—sld			
Farmer; 51		Dallas	Conn.	Conn.	4
Leonard, Joshua (S)	1843	Dallas			
Lewis, James S. (M)	1848	Dallas			
Lewis, John (M)	1848	Dallas			
Farmer; 26		Dallas	N.C.	Ind.	1
Lewis, Squire T. (S)	1845	Collin—sld			
Lewis, Wm. C. (M)	1845	Collin—sld			
Farmer; 39		Collin	Mo.	Mo.	6
Ligon, Thomas D. (M)	1848	Denton			
Farmer; 39		Denton	Tenn.	Ala. to Miss.	7
Linney, George (S)	1848	Tarrant—sld			
Stonemason; 33		Dallas	Ohio	Mo.	3
Linney, Perry (M)	1848	Dallas			
Farmer; 29		Dallas	Ky.	Mo.	2
Little, Edmund (M)	1848	Tarrant—sld			
Farmer; 45		Tarrant	Va.	Mo.	9
Little, John (W)	1848	Dallas			
None; 75		Dallas	N.C.	N.C.	
Little, John (S)	1848	Tarrant			X
Farmer; 22		Tarrant	Mo.	Mo.	
Little, Wm. H. (S)	1848	Tarrant—sld			
Farmer; 24		Tarrant	Va.	Mo.	
Lloyd, Alexander P. (M)	1848	Denton—sld pt.			
Clerk; 40		Denton	Ire.	Mo.	
Loftin, William (M)	1845	Denton			
Loller, Elcana (S)	1845	Cooke—sld			
Farmer; 32		Collin	Ky.	Ky.	
Long, Henry (S)	1844	Dallas			
Love, Reuben B. (S)	1848	Dallas			
Lovelady, James (M)	1848	Collin			
Farmer; 34		Collin	Tenn.	Mo.	
Loving, Abraham (M)	1848	Denton			
Farmer; 44		Denton	Ky.	Mo.	3
Loving, Oliver (M)	1845	Collin			
Farmer; 38		Collin	Ky.	Ky.	7

Name (Marital Status) Occupation; Age	Yr/Mig	County County	Birth	Removal	Illit.	Chld.
Loving, Samuel P. (M) Farmer; 36	1848	Dallas—sld Tarrant Denton	Ky.	Mo.		4
Loving, William (S) Farmer; 21	1848	Denton—sld Denton	Ark.	Ark.	X	
Loving, William R. Farmer; 36	1848	Tarrant—sld Denton	Ky.	Mo.		4
Lucas, George F. (M) Coronor; 31	1845	Collin—sld Collin	Ky.	Ky.		2
Lucas, Peter F. (S-M) Farmer; 36	1844	Collin Collin	Ky.	Ky.		2
Lundy, Wm. (M)	1844	Dallas—sld				
Lusk, John Preston (S)	1844	Tarrant				
Luttrel, Shelton (S-M) Farmer; 27	1848	Denton Denton	Ill.	Ill.		2
Luttrel, William (M)	1844	Denton				
Luttrel, William (S-M) Farmer; 23	1848	Denton Denton	Ill.	Ark.	X	6 ?
Lynch, Horatio G. (S)	1848	Tarrant				
Lynch, John (W) Farmer; 46	1848	Tarrant—sld Tarrant	Tenn.	Ill. to Mo.		1
Lynch, Josiah M. (S)	1848	Tarrant			X	
Lynch, Mahaly (W)	1848	Tarrant				
McBride, James (M) Farmer; 37	1844	Collin—sld. pt. Collin	Tenn.	Tenn.		
McCants, Joshua (M) Farmer; 28	1848	Dallas & Denton Denton	Ill.	Ill.		1
McCarty, Gerard (M) Farmer; 55	1844	Grayson Grayson	Va.	Ark.		2
McCarty, Larkin (M) Farmer; 46	1845	Collin—sld Collin	Ky.	Mo.		5
McCarty, Larkin Sr. (M)	1845	Collin				
McClure, Hugh R. (M)	1848	Johnson				
McCollough, Francis (S)	1848	Collin			X	
McCollough, Henry (M)	1845	Collin				
McCollough, James T. (M)	1848	Collin			X	
McCollough, John (S)	1848	Collin			X	
McCollough, Robert (M) Farmer; 33	1848	Dallas Dallas	Tenn.	Mo.	X	4
McCombs, Joshua (S) Farmer; 26	1848	Dallas Tarrant	Ark.	Ark.		
McCommas, Amon (M) Farmer; 48	1844	Dallas Dallas	Tenn.	Ohio to Ill. to Mo.		7
McCommas, Elisha (S) Farmer; 20	1848	Dallas—sld Dallas	Ohio	Ill. to Mo.		
McCommas, James B. (M) Farmer; 26	1844	Dallas—sld Dallas	Ohio	Mo. to Tenn.		3
McCommas, John (S)	1845	Dallas & Tarrant				

Name (Marital Status) Occupation; Age	Yr/Mig	County County	Birth	Removal	Illit.	Chld.
McCommas, John (M) Farmer; 22	1844	Tarrant—sld Dallas	Mo.	Mo.	X	
McCommas, Lavina (W)	1848	Dallas			X	5
McCommas, Stephen B. (S)	1845	Dallas				
McCommas, Stephen B. (M) Grocer; 43	1844	Dallas—sld Dallas	Tenn.	Ill.		3
McCommas, Stephen M. (M)	1843	Ellis & Hood				
McCoy, Ephraim D. (S-M) Farmer; 30	1848	Collin & Young—sld Collin	Tenn.	Tenn.	X	1
McCoy, John C. (S)	1845	Dallas				
McCracken, Anson (M) Farmer; 44	1845	Dallas Dallas	Tenn.	Mo.		4
McCreary, William (M) Farmer; 37	1848	Collin—sld. pt. Collin	N.C.	Mo.	X	3
McDaniel, Aaron (M) Gunsmith; 34	1848	Dallas—sld Tarrant—sld Dallas	N.C.	Va. to Ind.		5
McDermott, Joseph B. (W) None; 56	1848	Tarrant Dallas	Pa.	Tenn.		7
McDonald, Thomas (M) Farmer; 35	1844	Collin Collin	Mo.	Mo.		
McDowell, Hamilton (M) Farmer; 25	1848	Dallas Dallas	Ky.	Mo.		3
McDowell, John (M) Millwright; 70	1845	Dallas Dallas	Tenn.	Tenn.		
McDowell, Thomas (S) Farmer; 25	1848	Dallas Dallas	Ky.	Ky.		
McElroy, John C. (M) Farmer; 28	1848	Cooke—sld Cooke	Tenn.	Mo.		3
McFall, Robert (S)	1848	Cooke—sld			X	
McFearson, George (S)	1844	Collin				
McGarrah, George (M) Farmer; 42	1844	Collin Collin	Ky.	Ark.	X	3
McGarrah, John (M) Farmer; 45	(1842-1844)	Collin Collin	Unk.	Ark.	X	4
McGlothlin, George W. (M)	1848	Grayson—sld				
McGlothlin, Samuel M. (M) Blacksmith; 28	1848	Grayson Grayson	Mo.	Mo.		2
McGlothlin, Smith (S)	1848	Cooke—sld Grayson				
McKay, Samuel (M)	1848	Grayson				
McKinney, John (W)	1848	Collin				2
McKinney, William G. (S) ? Farmer; 46	1848	Collin—sld Collin	Ky.	Ark.		6?
McKinzey, Kenneth (M) Farmer; 56	1848	Grayson Grayson	Ky.	Mo.		3
McKinzey, Wm. (S) Laborer; 21	1848	Grayson—sld Grayson	Mo.	Mo.	X	

Name (Marital Status) Occupation; Age	Yr/Mig	County County	Birth	Removal	Illit.	Chld.
McMillen, Comfort A. (M)	1848	Collin			X	
Farmer; 39		Collin	Ill.	Ark.		2
McNeely, Friar (M)	1848	Grayson				
McNeil, George (S)	1848	Collin				
Farmer; 31		Collin	Ga.	Ga.		
McNeil, John M. (S)	1848	Denton—sld				
Farmer; 20		Collin	Ga.	Ga.		
McNiel, Benjamin F. (S)	1848	Collin—sld				
Farmer; 28		Collin	Ga.	Ga.		
McNiel, Lewis H. (S)	1848	Collin				
Farmer; 25		Collin	Ga.	Ga.		
McNiel, William (M)	1848	Collin-sld Denton—sld				
Farmer; 56		Collin	Ga.	N.C.		3
McReynolds, James M. (M)	1844	Collin				
Farmer; 30		Collin	Tenn.	Tenn.		2
Madden, Absolem C. (S)	1848	Denton			X	
Mahan, Thomas (M)	1848	Tarrant			X	
Farmer; 35		Tarrant	Ky.	Mo.		3
Malone, Perry (M)	1848	Denton—sld				
Farmer; 36		Denton	Ky.	Mo.		8
Malony, John (M)	1848	Denton—sld				
Farmer; 36		Denton	Ky.	Mo.		3
Manley, Joseph (S)	1848	Dallas—sld			X	
Manning, Andrew J. (M)	1844	Dallas				
Blacksmith; 36		Dallas	Ky.	Mo.		7
Mannin, Thomas (S)	1844	Dallas				
Manning, Delilah C. (W)	1845	Dallas — Tarrant—sld				3
Manning, John (S)	1848	Collin				
Farmer; 26		Collin	Tenn.	Tenn.		
Markham, George (S)	1848	Dallas				
Farmer; 29		Dallas	Eng.	Eng.		1
Marks, Watts (M)	1848	Dallas				
Marsh, Edwin(M)	1845	Denton				
Marsh, Harrison C. (M)	1845	Dallas				
Farmer; 45		Dallas	Miss.	Miss.		6
Marsh, Minor (M)	1848	Denton—sld				
Farmer; 54		Denton	Ga.	Ga.		
Marsh, Thomas C. (S)	1848	Dallas				
Farmer; 19		Dallas	Miss.	Miss.		
Marshall, Henry (S)	1848	Grayson				
Farmer; 28		Grayson	Va.	Va.		
Martin, Alexander H. (M)	1848	Grayson—sld			X	
Farmer; 41		Grayson	Tenn.	Ill.		6
Martin, Garland A. (S)	1848	Collin				
Farmer; 21		Collin	Ky.	Ky.		
Martin, Garland R. (M)	1848	Collin & Denton			X	
Farmer; 64		Collin	Va.	Va.		1

Name (Marital Status) Occupation; Age	Yr/Mig	County County	Birth	Removal	Illit.	Chld.
Martin, Hardy (S)	1844	Grayson—sld				
Farmer; 28		Grayson	Tenn.	Tenn.		
Martin, John (M)	1848	Cooke—sld				
Farmer; 32		Grayson	Tenn.	Iowa		2
Martin, John B. (M)	1848	Collin				
Farmer; 26		Denton	Ky.	Ky.		1
Martin, Lent (S)	1848	Dallas			X	
None; 78		Dallas	Unk.	Unk.		
Martin, Thomas (M)	1844	Tarrant				
Mask, William (M)	1848	Tarrant				
Massie, George W. (M)	1848	Collin			X	
Farmer; 36		Dallas	Mo.	Mo.		5
Masters, James B. (M)	1848	Dallas—sld. pt.				
Masters, James (S)	1848	Denton				
Masters, William (S)	1848	Dallas—sld				
Farmer; 24		Denton—sld				
		Dallas	Mo.	Mo.		
Mathews, Andrew (S)	1848	Cooke—sld				
Farmer; 59		Cooke	S.C.	Mo.		4 ?
Mathews, Benjamin (M)	1848	Collin				
Farmer; 24		Collin	Ky.	Ky.		
Matthews, Benjamin (S-M)	1848	Dallas—sld				
Farmer; 24		Denton—sld			X	
		Dallas	Mo.	Mo.		1
Matthews, James (S-M)	1844	Dallas—sld Tarrant			X	
Matthews, John (S-M)	1844	Grayson & Montague				
Matthews, Thomas (M)	1848	Cooke			X	
Matthews, William G. (S)	1848	Tarrant				
Maxwell, Henry (M)	1848	Collin				
Farmer; 39		Collin	Ark.	Ark.		10
Maxwell, James (M)	1848	Collin				
Maxwell, James W. (M)	1848	Collin			X	
Farmer; 33		Collin	Ala.	Ark.		2
May, Jephtha (M)	1846	Dallas—sld				
Farmer; 27		Dallas	Ky.	Ky.		2
Medlin, Charles (M)	1848	Denton				
Farmer; 43		Denton	N.C.	Mo.		7
Medlin, Lewis (M)	1848	Denton				
Farmer; 40		Denton	Unk.	Mo.		7
Medlin, Mary (W)	1848	Denton			X	
64		Denton	S.C.	Tenn.		2
Medlin, Wilson (S)	1848	Denton				
Melvin, Levi (S-M)	1848	Collin				
Meridith, Elijah (S)	1848	Tarrant				
Meredith, Wm. (M)	1848	Grayson				
Blacksmith; 55		Grayson	S.C.	S.C.		3
Merrell, Adolphus M. G. (S)	1845	Dallas				

Name (Marital Status) Occupation; Age	Yr/Mig	County County	Birth	Removal	Illit.	Chld.
Merrell, Benjamin (M) Farmer; 30						
(Clerk, enumerator for Dallas County)	1844	Dallas Dallas	N.C.	Ill. ?		3
Merrell, David (M) Farmer; 49	1845	Dallas Dallas	N.C.	N.C.		8
Merrell, Eli (S) Farmer; 25	1845	Dallas Dallas	Mo.	Mo.		
Merrell, Eli (M)	1844	Dallas				
Merrell, Robert F. (S) Farmer; 31	1848	Dallas Dallas	N.C.	N.C.	X	
Merrell, Wm. W. (S) Farmer; 24	1845	Dallas Dallas	N.C.	N.C.		
Metcalf, John J. (M) Farmer; 35	1848	Dallas Dallas	Ky.	Ky.		2
Meyerheim, Clemens (S)	1848	Grayson				
Middleton, William R. (S)	1844	Cooke			X	
Miller, Charilions (S) Farmer; 20	1848	Dallas Dallas	N.C.	N.C.		
Miller, Etheal S. (M) Farmer; 25	1848	Ellis—sld Dallas Dallas	Ind.	Ind.		1
Miller, Francis (M) Farmer; 56	1845	Dallas—sld. Dallas	N.C.	Ill.	X	3
Miller, Henry B. (M) Farmer; 33	1848	Collin Collin	Ky.	Ill.		3
Miller, James (S) Schoolteacher; 53	1848	Dallas—sld Grayson	Ky.	Ky.		
Miller, James L. (S)	1844	Dallas—sld				
Miller, John (S-M)	1844	Montague				
Miller, John H. (M) Farmer; 39	1848	Grayson Grayson	Tenn.	Tenn.		9
Miller, John J. (S)	1845	Collin			X	
Miller, John K. (S)	1845	Cooke—sld			X	
Miller, Madison M. (W) Merchant; 34	1848	Dallas Dallas	Ga.	Ala.		3
Miller, William (M) Farmer; 35	1848	Collin—sld Denton Denton	Ky.	Ill.		2
Miller, William B. (M) Farmer; 43	1848	Ellis—sld Dallas	Ky.	Tenn.		8
Mills, Edward (M) Wagon maker; 45	1848	Dallas Dallas	Ohio	Ky.		8
Mills, Hope (S) Farmer; 21	1848	Dallas Dallas	Ohio	Ohio		
Mills, James (S) Farmer; 18	1848	Dallas Dallas	Ohio	Ohio		
Mills, John (S) Farmer; 20	1848	Dallas Dallas	Ohio	Ohio		

Name (Marital Status) Occupation; Age	Yr/Mig	County County	Birth	Removal	Illit.	Chld.
Ming, William F. (S)	1848	Johnson				
Farmer; 24		Dallas	Ala.	Ala.		
Minter, Green W. (M)	1845	Tarrant				
Farmer; 48		Dallas	Va.	Va.		1
Mitchell, David (M)	1848	Johnson				
Farmer; 46		Tarrant	Ind.	Ark.		5
Mitchell, John W. (M)	1848	Collin				
Farmer; 32		Collin	Va.	Va.		4
Monroe, Benjamin (M)	1848	Ellis				
Farmer; 40		Ellis	Va.	Mo.		
Moon, Jesse (M)	1845	Dallas				
Moon, William M. (S)	1848	Dallas				
Mooneyham, James T. (T)	1845	Dallas—sld				
Farmer; 30		Ellis	Tenn.	Mo.		3
Mooneyham, Wm. (M)	1845	Dallas				
Farmer; 40		Dallas	Tenn.	Mo.		7
Moore, Albert (M)	1845	Dallas				
Farmer; 33		Dallas	Ky.	Iowa		5
Moore, Lorenzo (M)	1848	Denton—sld				
Morgan, Rial (M)	1848	Dallas				
Morgan, William (S)	1848	Ellis—sld				
Farmer; 20		Ellis	Ky.	Ind.		
Morris, Richard (S)	1848	Tarrant				
Clerk; 22		Dallas	Eng.	Eng.		
Morris, Sarah (W)	1848	Cooke				2
Morris, Wm. H. (M)	1844	Tarrant—sld	Ellis—sld		X	
Farmer; 32		Dallas	Tenn.	Ill.		5
Morrison, Alexander (M)	1848	Grayson				
Physician; 34		Grayson	Scot.	N.Y. to Canada		2
Morrison, James P. (M)	1845	Grayson—sld			X	
Carpenter; 41		Grayson	Ohio	Ind. to Ark.		5
Moss, Frederick (M)	1848	Dallas				
Farmer; 54		Dallas	Ky.	Iowa to Mo.		9
Moss, Hewlett P. (S)	1848	Tarrant—sld				
Laborer; 19		Dallas	Ky.	Ky.		
Mounts, Jackson H. (S)	1844	Dallas—sld				
Farmer; 27		Collin	Ill.	Ill.		2
Mounts, Jesse V. (M)	1844	Collin				
Farmer; 47	1848	Collin—sld		Ill.		2
Mounts, John H. (S)		Dallas	Miss.			
Mounts, Thomas A. (S-M)	1844	?				
Farmer; 23		Collin	Ill.	Ill.		1
Mullican, Felix G. (M)	1848	Tarrant				
Mullican, John (M)	1845	Johnson—sld				
Farmer; 44		Ellis	S.C.	Ky. to Ill.		5
Munden, Joseph (S-M)	1848	Dallas—sld				
Farmer; 27		Ellis	Ind.	Ind.		2
Murphy, Thomas G. (S)	1848	Cooke				

116

Name (Marital Status) Occupation; Age	Yr/Mig	County County	Birth	Removal	Illit.	Chld.
Murphy, Henderson (M)	1845	Denton			X	
Farmer; 39		Denton	Ky.	Ky.		2
Murray, Ambrose R. (S)	1848	Dallas				
Farmer; 23		Dallas	Ohio	Ohio		
Murray, Daniel (M)	1848	Dallas				
Farmer; 64		Dallas	Vt.	Ohio to Mich.		3
Myers, Abraham (S)	1848	Wise—sld				
Farmer; 39		Grayson	Tenn.	Tenn.		
Myers, David (M)	1848	Dallas				
Farmer; 53		Dallas	Ky.	Ill.		6
Myers, Elias T. (M)	1848	Collin & Dallas				
Blacksmith; 29		Dallas	Tenn.	Mo.		2
Myers, Jesse (M)	1845	Denton—sld, Grayson				
Farmer; 27		Grayson	Ohio	Ohio		1
Myers, John M. (M)	1848	Collin & Dallas				
Bapt. Minister; 26		Dallas	Ky.	Ill.		4
Myers, Meredith (S)	1848	Ellis—sld				
Surveyor; 21		Dallas	Ky.	Ky.		
Myers, William (M)	1848	Dallas				
Farmer; 49		Dallas	Ky.	Ky.		3
Nanney, Andrew T. (M)	1847	Dallas				
Farmer; 27		Dallas	Tenn.	Ill.		3
Narboe, John J. (S)	1843	Dallas				
Narboe, John P. (M)	1843	Dallas				
Farmer; 28		Dallas	Norway	Norway ?		
Narboe, Peter (W)	1843	Dallas				
Farmer; 82		Dallas	Norway	Norway		4
Narboe, Paul M. (S)	1843	Dallas				
Farmer; 25		Dallas	Norway	Norway		
Naugle, Benj. J. (S)	1848	Collin			X	
Farmer; 19		Collin	Penn.	Penn.		
Naugle, Jacob J. (M)	1848	Collin—sld				
Farmer; 47		Collin	Penn.	Penn.		2
Neace, Ireneous (M)	1848	Tarrant				
Neely, Charles (M)	1848	Dallas				
Laborer; 30		Dallas	Tenn.	Tenn.		2 ?
Newsom, Phineas (S)	1848	Collin				
Newton, Anderson (M)	1848	Tarrant—sld				
Farmer; 45		Ellis	Ky.	Mo.		6
Newton, Charles C. (M)	1847	Dallas				
Carriage maker; 32		Dallas	Conn.	Ark.		4
Newton, Elbert C. (M)	1848	Ellis				
Farmer; 35		Ellis	Tenn.	Mo.		4
Newton, James R. (S)	1848	Tarrant				
Newton, John L. (S)	1845	Tarrant—sld				
Newton, Larkin (M)	1848	Ellis				
Farmer; 56		Ellis	S.C.	Ark. to Mo.		9

117

Name (Marital Status) Occupation; Age	Yr/Mig	County County	Birth	Removal	Illit.	Chld.
Newton, Samuel G. (S) Lawyer; 25	1847	Young? Dallas	Ky.	Ky.		
Newton, Asa R. (M) Farmer; 26	1844	Ellis Ellis	Ark.	Ark.		2
Newton, Wm. A. (M) Farmer; 50	1846	Dallas—sld Dallas	Va.	Mo.		5
Newton, Wm. H. (S) Farmer; 25	1847	Dallas Dallas	Mo.	Mo.		
Newton, Thomas D. (S)	1848	Tarrant				
Nix, David H. (S) Farmer; 24	1848	Dallas & Collin Dallas	Ill.	Ill.		
Nix, John (M) Farmer; 45	1848	Dallas—sld. pt. Dallas	Ky.	Ill.		8
Noblit, Samuel T. (M) Farmer; 38	1848	Collin Collin	Penn.	Mo.		2
Nolan, Christopher (M)	1848	Collin & Grayson				
Noling, Samuel (M) Farmer; 32	1848	Denton—sld Denton	Ar.	Mo.	X	3
Noris, Wm. (M) Wheelwright; 62	1848	Tarrant Dallas	N.C.	Mo.		7
Norton, Daniel E. (M) Farmer; 26	1848	Tarrant—sld. pt. Tarrant	S.C.	Ill.		1
Noyer, Peter (M) Farmer; 42	1848	Dallas—sld Dallas	Penn.	Ohio to Ill.		7
Nugent, John (M) Farmer; 26	1848	Ellis Ellis	Ireland	Ire.		1
O'Neil, Martin (S) Farmer; 36	1848	Denton Dallas	Ireland	Ire.		
O'Neal, Wm. (M) Farmer; 35	1848	Tarrant Ellis	Ill.	Ill.	X	1
Onstott, Abraham H. (S)	1848	Johnson—sld				
O'Quin, Leonidas (S) Farmer; 21	1848	Dallas Dallas	Tenn.	Tenn.		
O'Quin, Stephen C. (S)	1848	Dallas				
O'Quin, Wm. (M) Farmer; 52	1848	Dallas Dallas	N.C.	Tenn.		6
Overton, Aaron (M) Farmer; 61	1845	Dallas Dallas	N.C.	Mo.	X	
Overton, Caswell C. (M) Farmer; 34	1845	Dallas—sld Dallas	Mo.	Mo.		4
Overton, Jesse (S) Laborer; 20	1848	Tarrant Dallas	Mo.	Mo.	X	
Overton, John W. (M) Millwright; 47	1848	Dallas—sld Dallas	N.C.	Mo.		5
Overton, Wm. P. (S) Farmer; 27	1845	Dallas—sld Dallas	Mo.	Mo.		
Owen, Matthew J. (S) Farmer; 30	1845	Denton—sld Denton	Ky.	Ky.		

Name (Marital Status) Occupation; Age	Yr/Mig	County County	Birth	Removal	Illit.	Chld.
Owen, Robert (S) Farmer; 26	1848	Denton Denton	Ky.	Ky.		
Paine, Wm. (M) Farmer; 30	1848	Ellis—sld Ellis	Va.	Mo.	X	3
Pancoast, Josiah (S) Farmer; 33	1845	Dallas—sld Dallas	N.C.	N.C.		
Parks, Alfred S. (S) Farmer; 22	1848	Ellis Ellis	Ind.	Ind.		
Parks, Curtis (M) Farmer; 40	1848	Dallas Dallas	N.C.	Ind.		9
Parks, Elias R. (S) Farmer; 24	1848	Dallas Dallas	Ind.	Ind.		
Parks, George C. (M) Farmer; 29	1848	Ellis Ellis	Ind.	Ind.		2
Parks, Maraday (M)	1848	Dallas				
Parks, Robert (M)	1848	Dallas & Ellis				
Park, Isiah (M) Stonemason; 44	1848	Dallas Dallas	Ky.	Mo.		5
Park, Simeon E. (S)	1848	Denton				
Parsons, James W. (S-M) Farmer; 37	1848	Collin Collin	Penn.	Ky.		
Patterson, James M. (S) Merchant; 34	1846	Dallas Dallas	Ky.	Ky.		
Patterson, Wm. (M) Wheelwright; 45	1848	Collin Collin	N.C.	N.C.		4
Patton, James E. (M) Surveyor; 57	1845	Ellis Ellis	N.C.	Mo.		3
Patton, John Sr. (S)	1845	Ellis				
Patton, Wm. T. (S) Farmer; 27	1845	Ellis Ellis	Tenn.	Tenn.		
Paxton, Edwin H. (S)	1848	Dallas—sld				
Paxton, John C. (S)	1848	Ellis—sold			X	
Paxton, Thomas J. (M)	1848	Grayson				
Payton, Samuel (W) Farmer; 48	1848	Denton Denton	Ky.	Mo.		3
Pearce, Francis (M) Farmer; 75	1844	Denton Denton	Va.	Ark.	X	
Pearce, Wm. Poston (S) Farmer; 20	1848	Denton Denton	Ark.	Ark.	X	
Pearson, Dudley F. (S) Farmer; 27	1845	Dallas Dallas	Ky.	Ky.		
Pearson, Wm. (W)	1845	Dallas				
Pegues, Geo. H. (M) Farmer; 49	1848	Collin Collin	S.C.	Ill.		3
Pegues, Leonidas R. (S)	1848	Collin				
Pellham, Thomas E. (S)	1848	Collin				
Pemberton, Gideon (M) Wagonmaker; 39	1848	Dallas Dallas	Ky.	Ill.		5

Name (Marital Status) Occupation; Age	Yr/Mig	County County	Birth	Removal	Illit.	Chld.
Perrin, Abner B. (S)	1845	Collin				
Farmer; 25		Collin	Ky.	Ky.		
Perrin, Charles (S)	1848	?				
Farmer; 28		Collin	Ky.	Ky.		
Perrin, Geo. (S)	1845	Collin—sld				
Farmer; 27		Collin	Ky.	Ky.		
Perrin, Wm. (S-M)	1845	Collin				
Farmer; 50		Collin	Ky.	Ky.		5
Perry, Alex. W. (M)	1845	Dallas				
Farmer; 30		Dallas	Ill.	Ill.		5
Perry, Franklin S. (S)	1848	Tarrant				
Farmer; 18		Dallas	Ill.	Ill.		
Perry, Middleton (M)	1845	Dallas				
Farmer; 35		Dallas	Ind.	Ind.		3
Perry, Sally (W)	1845	Dallas				
51		Dallas	Ky.	Ill.		3
Perry, Weston (M)	1848	Dallas				
Farmer; 42		Dallas	Ky.	Ill.		9
Phalen, Richard (M)	1844	Collin?				
?Farmer; 37		Dallas	Ohio	Ark.		6
Phelps, Josiah S. (S-M)	1843	Dallas				
Philips, Geo. (S)	1848	Collin				
Farmer; 23		Collin	Tenn.	Tenn.		
Philips, John (S)	1848	Collin			X	
Philips, Jonathon (M)	1848	Collin				
United B. Preacher; 55		Collin	N.C.	Tenn.		5
Philips, Josiah (S)	1848	Denton				
—; 19		Denton	Ohio	Ohio ?		
Philips, Thomas (S)	1848	Collin—sld				
Farmer; 30		Collin	Tenn.	Tenn.		
Philips, Thomas A. (M)	1848	Dallas				
Farmer; 31		Dallas	Ky.	Ky.		3
Philips, Wm. (M)	1845	Denton				
Phipps, Charles (S)	1848	Tarrant—sld, Ellis—sld			X	
Farmer; 19		Ellis	Ky.	Mo.		
Phipps, Wm. (M)	1848	Johnson—sld				
Farmer; 40		Ellis	Tenn.	Ky. to Mo.		5
Pickett, Elisha (S-M)	1844	Denton—sld				
Farmer; 26		Denton	Tenn.	Tenn.		3
Pierce, Nathan P. (M)	1848	Dallas—sld, Grayson				
Farmer; 29		Grayson	Tenn.	Tenn.		3
Pierce, Thomas M. (M)	1848	Grayson				
Farmer; 31		Grayson	Tenn.	Mo.		4
Pierce, Wm. G. (S)	1848	Grayson			X	
Laborer; 21		Grayson	Ill.	Ill.		
Pinnell, Horace R. (S)	1848	Collin				
Farmer; 23		Collin	Mo.	Mo.		
Pogue, Westly (S)	1848	Denton				

Name (Marital Status) Occupation; Age	Yr/Mig	County County	Birth	Removal	Illit.	Chld.
Popplewell, Simcoe (M)	1846	Dallas & Tarrant				
Farmer; 32		Dallas	Ky.	Mo.		3
Porter, Geo. F. (S)	1848	Dallas				
Farmer; 21		Tarrant	Ala.	Ala.		
Porter, James (M)	1848	Dallas				
Porter, Hohm F. (M)	1848	Dallas				
Farmer; 58		Tarrant	S.C.	Tenn.		7
Powell, Wm. (S)	1848	Denton—sld				
Farmer; 28		Collin	Tenn.	Tenn.		
Powers, Ambrose (M)	1848	Dallas—sld, Johnson			X	
Farmer; 26		Ellis	N.C.	Mo.		4
Powers, Jourdan (S)	1848	Ellis			X	
Farmer; 26		Ellis	N.C.	N.C. ?		
Powers, Mary (W)	1848	Ellis—sld				
56		Ellis	N.C.	N.C.		4
Powers, Shadrick (S)	1848	Ellis			X	
Farmer; 26		Ellis	N.C.	N.C.		
Prigmore, Benj. J. (S)	1848	Dallas				
Farmer; 19		Dallas	Mo.	Mo.		
Prigmore, Joseph (M)	1845	Dallas				
Farmer; 43		Dallas	Ky.	Mo.		8
Pringle, Jonathon (M)	1845	Ellis				
Farmer; 36		Ellis	**Tenn.**	Ark.		4
Pritchitt, Edley (M)	1848	Denton				
Pritchitt, Samuel A. (M)	1848	Denton				
Farmer; 25		Denton	N.C.	N.C.		4
Pruitt, Albert S. (M)	1848	Ellis				
Farmer; 32		Dallas	N.C.	Ark.		6
Pruitt, Martin (S)	1848	Dallas				
Farmer; 34		Navarro	**Ill.**	Ill.		
Pruitt, Samuel (M)	1848	Collin—sld Grayson				
Farmer; 26		Grayson	Ky.	Ky.		2
Pruitt, Wm. (M)	1845	Dallas				
Farmer; 49		Dallas	Tenn.	Ill.		6
Pruitt, Wm. A. (S)	1848	Dallas				
Pryor, Samuel B. (M)	1846	Dallas				
Physician; 30		Dallas	Va.	Va.		2
Pulliam, John L. (S)	1843	Dallas				
Farmer; 40		Dallas	**Tenn.**	Tenn.		
Pulliam, Marshal S. (S)	1848	Dallas				
Farmer; 31		Collin	Tenn.	Tenn.		
Pulliam, Samson (S)	1848	Collin—sld. pt.				
Farmer; 45		Collin	**Tenn.**	Tenn.		
Pulse, Elisha (S)	1848	Ellis			X	
Queen, Jeremiah (S)	1848	Collin			X	
Queen, Samuel (M)	1848	Collin—sld pt.			X	
Farmer; 30		Collin	Tenn.	Tenn.		1
Ragan, Geo. W. (S)	1848	Tarrant			X	

121

Name (Marital Status) Occupation; Age	Yr/Mig	County County	Birth	Removal	Illit.	Chld.
Ragland, John W. (M)	1848	Denton—sld pt.				
Farmer; 39		Denton	Tenn.	Tenn.		3
Ramsey, John (M)	1845	Denton				
Wheelwright; 52		Navarro	N.C.	Ky. to Ill.		9
Ramsay, Isaac (M)	1848	Dallas				
Blacksmith; 34		Dallas	Ky.	Iowa		2
Ramsay, Samuel (M)	1848	Dallas				
Farmer; 37		Dallas	Tenn.	Mo.		6
Ramsay, Wm. G. (S)	1845	Denton				
Farmer; 23		Navarro	Ky.	Ky.		
Ramsower, Michael (M)	1845	Denton—sld, Collin				
Farmer; 36		Denton	N.C.	N.C.		2
Randolph, James M. (M)	1845	Cooke				
Ratton, Thomas (M)	1845	Collin—sld				
Farmer; 59		Collin	S.C.	Ill.		1
Ratton, Wm. S. (S)	1845	Collin				
Rawlins, Hubbard M. (M)	1848	Dallas				
Rawlins, James A. (S)	1848	Ellis				
Farmer; 16		Dallas	Ill.	Ill.		
Rawlins, John M. (S)	1846	Dallas				
Farmer; 24		Dallas	Ill.	Ill.		
Rawlins, Roderick (M)	1845	Dallas				

(b. Mass. 1776, to N.C., to Tenn., to Ky., to Ind., to Ill.; m. Milly Parks, Bedford Co., Tenn., 1816.)—*Lancaster Herald* June, 1888; April 5, 1951.)

Name (Marital Status) Occupation; Age	Yr/Mig	County County	Birth	Removal	Illit.	Chld.
Rawlins, Wm. (M)	1848	Dallas				
Blacksmith; 55		Dallas	Ky.	Ill.		3
Rawlins, Wm. Sr. (M)	1846	Dallas				
Farmer; 50		Dallas	Ky.	Ind.		6
Ray, James (S)	1847	Dallas—sld				
Ray, Robert (M)	1847	Dallas & Tarrant				
Blacksmith; 45		Dallas	S.C.	Ill.		6
Ray, Wm. (S)	1847	Tarrant—sld			X	
Laborer; 25		Dallas	Ill.	Ill.		
Reagon, Jacob (M)	1848	Dallas				
Farmer; 34		Dallas	Tenn.	Miss.		7
Rearn, Sarah (W)	1848	Dallas			X	4
Reid, Benj. S. (S-M)	1848	Dallas—sld				
Reid, Edwin (S)	1848	Dallas—sld				
Reid, James B. (S)	1848	Denton—sld				
Reid, James L. (S)	1845	Collin—sld				
Teamster; 23		Collin	Tenn.	Tenn.		
Reid, Leonard (M)	1848	Grayson—sld				
Farmer; 45		Grayson	Mo.	Mo.		4
Reid, Nathan R. (M)	1848	Cooke—sld				
Farmer; 30		Denton	Mo.	Mo.		3
Reeves, Geo. R. (M)	1848	Grayson—sld pt.				
Clerk; 25		Grayson	N.Y.	Ark.		2
Reeves, Thomas M. (S)	1848	Grayson				

Name (Marital Status) Occupation; Age	Yr/Mig	County County	Birth	Removal	Illit.	Chld.
Reeves, Wm. J. (S)	1848	Grayson				
Laborer; 20		Grayson	Tenn.	Ark.		
Reeves, Wm. S. (M)	1848	Grayson				
Farmer; 36		Grayson	S.C.	Tenn. to Ark.		6
Reynolds, Micajah R. (M)	1848	Dallas—sld,	Ellis—sld.			
Blacksmith; 43		Grayson	N.C.	Mo.		3
Rhodes, Frederick S. (M)	1848	Dallas				
Farmer; 47		Dallas	N.C.	Tenn. to Mo.		6
Rhodes, Elisha S. (W)	1848	Dallas			X	
Cabinet maker; 43		Dallas	N.C.	Tenn.		2
Rhodes, Thomas S. (S)	1848	Dallas				
Farmer; 20		Dallas	Tenn.	Tenn.		
Rice, Charles P. (S)	1848	Collin				
Rice, Joseph R. (S)	1844	Collin				
Rice, Pascal H. (S)	1844	Dallas—sld			X	
Farmer; 24		Navarro	Mo.	Mo.		
Rice, Wm. (M)	1844	Collin				
Farmer; 49		Collin	Va.	Tenn. to Ark.		9
Richardson, Jonathon (S)	1845	Ellis-sld				
Farmer; 23		Navarro	Tenn.	Tenn.		
Rickett, David M. (S)	1848	Dallas				
Laborer; 22		Dallas	Ky.	Ky.		
Ricketts, Samuel D. (S)	1848	Dallas				
Ricketts, Wm. S. (S)	1847	Tarrant-sld				
Laborer; 26		Dallas	Ky.	Ky.		
Ricketts, Zedekiah (M)	1848	Dallas			X	
Farmer; 60		Dallas	Va.	Ky.		4
Riggs, Stephen (M)	1844	Denton-sld				
Ritter, Columbus (S)	1848	Denton				
Farmer; 35		Denton	Ill.	Ill.		
Ritter, John (M)	1845	Denton				
Farmer; 35		Denton	Unk.	Ill.		6
Ritter, Wm. (S)	1845	Denton				
Ritter, Wm. (S)	1848	Denton				
Farmer; 30		Denton	Ind.	Ill.		
Roark, Wm. M. (M)	1848	Denton				
Sheriff; 35		Denton	Tenn.	Mo.		5
Roberts, James A. (S)	1845	Tarrant				
Roberts, James T. (M)	1845	Collin				
Farmer; 45		Collin	Ky.	Mo.		6
Roberts, Joel (M)	1848	Dallas				
Farmer; 21		Dallas	Tenn.	Tenn.		1
Roberts, John (S)	1845	Tarrant				
Farmer; 23		Denton	Tenn.	Tenn.		
Roberts, Joseph B. (S)	1848	Grayson				
Roberts, Rezin (M)	1848	Denton				
Farmer; 45		Denton	S.C.	Tenn.		7

Name (Marital Status) Occupation; Age	Yr/Mig	County County	Birth	Removal	Illit.	Chld.
Roberts, Zachariah (M)	1845	Collin				
Blacksmith; 39		Collin	Tenn.	Ala.		5
Robinson, Archibald (M)	1848	Tarrant-sld.pt.				
Farmer; 40		Tarrant	Ky.	Mo. to Ark.		6
Robinson, Hugh (W)	1848	Dallas				
Farmer; 64		Ellis	N.C.	Ill.		2
Robinson, Joseph M. (S-M)	1846	Denton-sld, Dallas				
Farmer; 22		Dallas	Mo.	Mo.		1
Robinson, John B. (S)	1846	Dallas				
Farmer; 35		Dallas	Ind.	Ind.		
Robinson, Wm. M. (S-M)	1845	Tarrant				
Farmer; 24		Tarrant	Ill.	Ill.		1
Robinson, Wm. S. (S)	1845	Dallas-sld				
Rogers, Clayton (M)	1848	Collin-sld				
Farmer; 30		Collin	Tenn.	Tenn.		3
Rogers, Elijah (S-M)	1848	Tarrant-sld.pt.				
Farmer; 26		Tarrant	Ky.	Ky.		1
Rogers, John (M)	1848	Denton				
Farmer; 50		Denton	S.C.	Tenn. to Ind.		17 ?
Rogers, Matthew (S)	1848	Denton				
Rogers, Wm. (M)	1848	Collin				
Farmer; 35		Collin	Tenn.	Ill.		5
Rountree, Jesse B. (S)	1848	Collin			X	
Routh, Hugh C. (M)	1848	Collin				
Farmer; 37		Collin	Tenn.	Mo.		3
Routh, Levin (M)	1848	Collin				
Farmer; 35		Collin	Tenn.	Mo.		3
Row, Wm. B. (M)	1848	Dallas				
Farmer; 51		Dallas	N.C.	Tenn.		5
Rulon, Morrison (M)	1848	Grayson-sld				
Lawyer; 42		Grayson	Ky.	Ind.		3
Runyon, Silas B. (M)	1848	Dallas				
Farmer; 42		Dallas	Ky.	Ky.		
Runyon, Jefferson B. (S)	1848	Dallas-sld, Cooke				
Russell, James (S)	1848	Dallas-sld				
Russell, Joseph (M)	1848	Collin				
Farmer; 49		Collin	N.C.	N.C.		1
Russell, Louis (M)	1845	Johnson			X	
Rutledge, David (S)	1848	Cooke			X	
Farmer; 20		Grayson	Ill.	Ill.		
Rutledge, James (S)	1844	Cooke				
Rutledge, Mary Jane (W)	1844	Cooke & Clay				
Rutledge, Thomas (S)	1844	Cooke				
Rylie, James R. (M)	1848	Dallas				
Sackse, Wm. C. (M)	1845	Collin				
Farmer; 29		Collin	Prussia	Tenn. to Mo.		3
Sackett, David (W)	1848	Cooke				4

Name (Marital Status) Occupation; Age	Yr/Mig	County County	Birth	Removal	Illit.	Chld.
Sagers, Carle (M)	1848	Cooke				
Farmer; 20		Denton	Germany	Ger.		
Salmons, John M. (M)	1848	Collin				
Farmer; 25		Collin	Ill.	Ill.		2
Sargent, Hugh F. (M)	1848	?				
Farmer; 30		Dallas	N.C.	Tenn.		2
Saunders, Isaac (M)	1848	Cooke				
Savage, James R. (M)	1848	Collin				
Schoonover, Isaac (S)	1848	Tarrant-sld			X	
Farmer; 22		Tarrant	Ind.	Ill. to Mo.		
Schoonover, Peter (S)	1848	Tarrant-sld				
Farmer; 20		Tarrant	Ind.	Ill. to Mo.		
Scott, Robert J. (S-M)	1848	Cooke				
Farmer; 23		Cooke	Ind.	Ind.		1
Scott, Thomas (M)	1848	Dallas				
Screech, Joseph (W)	1848	Tarrant				
Screech, Nathan (S)	1845	Dallas-sld			X	
Screech, William (S)	1845	Tarrant			X	
Scroggins, Wm. (S)	1848	Dallas-sld			X	
Scurlock, John (M)	1845	Dallas				
Chairmaker; 33		Dallas	Ind.	Ark.		5
Searcy, Christopher (S)	1845	Collin			X	
Farmer; 36		Collin	Ky.	Ky.		
Searcy, Gallatin (S)	1845	Collin				
Farmer; 43		Collin	Ky.	Ky.		
Searcy, Langdon (M)	1845	Collin				
Farmer; 34		Collin	Ky.	Ky.		2
Searcy, Leonard (M)	1845	Collin				
Farmer; 69		Collin	N.C.	Ky.		
Searcy, Strashley (S)	1845	Collin				
Searcy, Thomas H. (S)	1845	Collin			X	
Farmer; 23		Collin	Mo.	Mo.		
Self, Charnock (S)	1848	Ellis-sld			X	
Farmer; 18		Dallas	Ky.	Ky.		
Selbey, Thomas (M)	1848	Ellis				
Selvidge, Michael K. (S)	1848	Tarrant				
Farmer; 33		Dallas	Tenn.	Mo.		
Severe, James (M)	1848	Denton				
Shahan, Benj. C. (S)	1848	Denton				
Shahan, David (M)	1844	Dallas				
Farmer; 45		Dallas	Va.	Mo.		3
Shahan, Elizabeth A. (W)	1848	Denton				
Shahan, Wm. P. (S)	1844	Dallas				
Shannon, Andrew J. (S)	1848	Cooke				
Laborer; 20		Grayson	Ohio	Mo.		
Shannon, Robert E. (M)	1848	Cooke			X	
Farmer; 49		Grayson	Va.	Ohio to Mo.		6

Name (Marital Status) Occupation; Age	Yr/Mig	County County	Birth	Removal	Illit.	Chld.
Sharrock, Everard Sr. (M)	1848	Dallas-sld				
Farmer; 56		Dallas	Ky.	Ohio		
Sharrock, Everard Jr. (S-M)	1848	Dallas-sld.pt.				
Farmer; 23		Dallas	Ohio	Ohio		2
Sharrock, Geo. W. (S)	1848	Dallas			X	
Farmer; 19		Dallas	Ohio	Ohio		
Sharrock, James (M)	1845	Dallas				
Farmer; 33		Dallas	Ohio	Ill.		4
Shaver, John (S)	1848	Ellis-sld				
Shelby, Ezra (S)	1848	?				
Farmer; 39		Collin	Penn.	Penn.		
Shelby, James (S)	1844	Collin-sld				
Farmer; 24		Collin	Ill.	Ill.		
Shelby, James S. (M)	1844	Dallas				
Farmer; 35		Dallas	Tenn.	Tenn.		2
Shelton, Jesse J. (M)	1845	Grayson-sld				
Farmer; 33		Grayson	Ind.	Ind.		2
Shelton, Willis H. C. (S)	1848	Dallas			X	
Farmer; 25		Dallas	Mo.	Mo.		
Shelton, Wm. C. (S-M)	1848	Dallas				
Shelton, Wm. H. (M)	1848	Dallas & Ellis			X	
Farmer; 73		Dallas	Va.	Va.		
Shepperd, Elijah (S)	1844	Dallas-sld				
Shields, Geo. (M)	1848	Tarrant-sld			X	
Farmer; 25		Grayson	Tenn.	Mo.		3
Shields, John (S)	1848	Grayson-sld			X	
Shirley, Edmund (M)	1844	Ellis-sld				
Silkwood, Solomon (S)	1843	Dallas				
Simmons, James A. (M)	1848	Dallas				
Simmons, John W. (M)	1848	Denton				
Farmer; 35		Denton	Tenn.	Ark.		3
Simmons, Joseph (S)	1848	Dallas				
Simpson, Lionel (S)	1848	Dallas				
Farmer; 25		Dallas	Eng.	Eng.		
Skaggs, Robert (M)	1848	Collin			X	
50		Collin	Ky.	Ill.		4
Slack, Henry (M)	1848	Collin-sld				
Farmer; 24		Grayson	Ky.	Ill.		3
Slayback, Anderson (M)	1848	Dallas			X	
Farmer; 37		Dallas	Ohio	Ohio		1
Sloane, James (M)	1843	Dallas				
Sloane, William E. (S)	1844	Dallas				
None; 26		Ellis	Ind.	Ind.		
Smith, Absalom (M)	1848	Dallas & Tarrant				
Smith, Chilton (W)	1848	Dallas				
Farmer; 55		Dallas	Unk.	Ill.		4
Smith, Elisha (M)	1845	Denton				
Farmer; 35		Navarro	Tenn.	Tenn.		2

Name (Marital Status) Occupation; Age	Yr/Mig	County County	Birth	Removal	Illit.	Chld.
Smith, Francis M. (S)	1845	Johnson				
Smith, George W. (S) Farmer; 22	1848	Ellis Tarrant	Mo.	Mo.		
Smith, Hans (M) Farmer; 50	1848	Ellis Tarrant	Pa.	Mo.		6
Smith, Henry (M) Farmer; 35	1848	Collin-sld Collin	Tenn.	Mo.		4
Smith, James A. (M) Farmer; 30	1847	Dallas Collin	Tenn.	Tenn.		
Smith, John W. (S) Merchant; 44	1848	Dallas Dallas	N.C.	N.C.		2
Smith, John W. (S) Farmer; 23	1848	Dallas Dallas	Ala.	Ala.		
Smith, Patrick P. (S) Farmer; 23	1848	Dallas Dallas	Ark.	Ark.		
Smith, Pleasant M. (S) Farmer; 22	1848	Dallas-sld Dallas	Tenn.	Tenn.	X	
Smith, Robert (S) Farmer; 22	1848	Ellis Tarrant	Mo.	Mo.		
Smith, Robert A. (M) Saddler; 30	1848	Denton Tarrant	Tenn.	Mo.		3
Smith, Samuel K. (S) School teacher; 25	1845	Tarrant Collin	Tenn.	Tenn.		
Smith, Wm. B. (M) Farmer; 39	1845	Collin-sld Grayson-sld Grayson	Tenn.	Tenn.	X	2
Smith, Wm. (S)	1845	Tarrant				
Snider, John (S) Farmer; 22	1848	Collin Collin	Ky.	Ky.		
Snider, John D. (S)	1848	Parker				
Snider, Wm. (M) Wagon maker; 43	1844	Collin Collin	Ky.	Ill.		
Snow, Wm. J. (S-M) Farmer; 27	1848	Dallas Dallas	Tenn.	Tenn.		
Snyder, James M. (S)	1848	Collin-sld			X	
Snyder, John (S)	1847	?				
South, Elijah (M)	1848	?				
Sparks, Benjamin (M)	1848	Collin			X	
Sparks, Moses (M)	1848	Collin-sld				
Sparks, Richard (S)	1848	Collin			X	
Spearman, John M. (S) School teacher; 23	1848	? Dallas	Tenn.	Tenn.		
Spencer, Major W. (M) Farmer; 33	1848	Dallas-sld.pt. Dallas	Ind. 9	Ill.		3
Spencer, William (M) Farmer; 32	1845	Dallas-sld Dallas	Ill.	Ill.	X	2
Spoon, John (M)	1844	Dallas-sld				
Springer, Edward F. (M) Farmer; 33	1845	Denton-sld Collin	Ky.	Ky.		2

Name (Marital Status) Occupation; Age	Yr/Mig	County County	Birth	Removal	Illit.	Chld.
Spruce, John H. (M)	1847	Dallas-sld			X	
Squires, Clarinda (W)	1843	Dallas				3
Staddin, John (M)	1846	Dallas				
Farmer; 31		Dallas	Ohio	Ill.		3
Stallcup, Thomas (M)	1848	Collin				
Farmer; 34		Collin	Tenn.	Ark.		6
Stamps, George W. (S)	1848	Grayson-sld				
Farmer; 23		Grayson	Tenn.	Tenn.		
Stamps, John (S)	1848	Grayson-sld				
Farmer; 27		Grayson	Tenn.	Tenn.		
Stamps, Polly (W)	1848	Grayson			X	
56		Grayson	Va.	Tenn.		2
Standifer, Mary (W)	1844	Collin				2
Stang, David (M)	1848	?				
Stang, John S. (S)	1848	Dallas-sld				
Stanley, Harris (M)	1845	Grayson-sld			X	
Farmer; 30		Grayson	Mo.	Mo.		
Stanley, Jeremiah (S)	1845	Grayson-sld			X	
Stanley, Mynyard G. (S)	1845	Grayson-sld			X	
Farmer; 23		Grayson	Mo.	Mo.		
Stanley, Page (M)	1845	Grayson-sld				
Farmer; 49		Grayson	Tenn.	Mo.		3
Stapp, Andrew (M)	1848	Collins-sld				
Farmer; 45		Collin	Ky.	Mo.		8
Stapp, Abner Golson (S)	1848	Collin-sld				
Stapp, Benjamin (S)	1848	Collin-sld pt.				
Farmer; 22		Collin	Mo.	Mo.	X	
Stapp, Wm. J. (S)	1848	Collin-sld			X	
Farmer; 21		Collin	Mo.	Mo.		
Steel, John P. (M)	1844	Cooke-sld				
Steel, Joseph (S)	1848	Ellis-sld				
Stephens, Thomas (S)	1848	Johnson			X	
Stewart, Jeremiah T. (M)	1848	Denton				
Farmer; 40		Denton	Ky.	Mo.		5
Stewart, Joel F. (M)	1848	Collin				
Clerk; 48		Collin	Ky.	Mo.		3
Stewart, Samuel (M)	1848	Dallas				
Farmer; 35		Dallas	Ill.	Ill.		2
Stewart, Wm. T. (S-M)	1848	Dallas				
Farmer; 25		Dallas	Mo.	Mo.		4
Stockton, Samuel C. (M)	1844	Dallas & Tarrant				
Stokes, Thomas (S)	1844	Dallas				
Stone, James (S)	1848	Collin-sld				
Stout, Peter (M)	1848	Ellis				
Farmer; 38		Tarrant	N.C.	Mo.		4
Stout, Peter B. (M)	1848	Dallas & Ellis				
Farmer; 32		Dallas	Ohio	Ohio		2
Stover, John (M)	1844	Dallas-sld			X	

Name (Marital Status) Occupation; Age	Yr/Mig	County County	Birth	Removal	Illit.	Chld.
Straly, Elizabeth (W)	1845	Dallas			X	2
Straughan, Gordon A. (M)	1848	Collin-sld				
Strickland, Daniel (S-M)	1848	Denton				
Justice of Peace; 27		Grayson	Mo.	Mo.		
Strickland, John (M)	1844	Denton				
Farmer; 37		Denton	Mo.	Mo.		3
Strong, Hiram (M)	1848	Cooke				
Suggs, Henry (M)	1848	Tarrant-sld pt.				
Farmer; 30		Tarrant	Tenn.	Tenn.		
Sutton, Edward (M)	1848	Denton				
Sutton, James (M)	1848	Denton				
Sutton, Jesse (M)	1848	Denton-sld				
Farmer; 37		Denton	Ill.	Ill.		4
Sutton, Vincent R. (S-M)	1848	Denton-sld				
Farmer; 24		Denton	Ill.	Ill.		
Sykes, Joel (S)	1848	Dallas-sld				
Syms, George (S)	1848	Dallas-sld pt.				
Shoemaker; 48		Dallas	Eng.	Eng.		
Tannahill, David (M)	1848	Tarrant			X	
Farmer; 27		Tarrant	Ala.	Ark.		2
Tannahill, James M. (S)	1848	Denton				
Tansy, Lewis (M)	1848	Dallas-sld				
Tansy, Wm. A. (M)	1848	Denton				
Taylor, John A. (M)	1848	Collin				
Farmer; 31		Collin	Ala.	Ark.		3
Taylor, Pleasant (M)	1845	Dallas				
Farmer; 34		Dallas	Tenn.	Ill.		5
Teal, Wm. (S)	1848	Cooke			X	
Farmer; 25		Cooke	Tenn.	Tenn.		
Terry, John L. (M)	1848	Collin-sld				
Thomas, Alexander A. (S)	1844	Dallas-sld				
Farmer; 25		Dallas	Tenn.	Tenn.		
Thomas, David G. (M)	1845	?				
Thomas, Ellis C. (S-M)	1844	Dallas				
Farmer; 27		Dallas	Tenn.	Mo.		2
Thomas, Isaac T. (M)	1844	Tarrant				
Thomas, Jesse F. (S)	1848	Grayson				
Farmer; 25		Grayson	Tenn.	Tenn.		
Thomas, John (M)	1844	Dallas				
Farmer; 56		Dallas	Tenn.	Mo.		2
Thomas, John C. (M)	1845	Grayson-sld				
Farmer; 21		Collin	Ill.	Ill.		
Thomas, John P. (S)	1848	Tarrant				
Thomas, John W. (S)	1848	Dallas-sld				
Thompson, Alexander (S)	1848	Tarrant				
Thompson, James G. (M)	1844	Grayson				
Farmer; 45		Grayson	S.C.	Ark.		3
Thompson, Pleasant (S)	1848	Grayson-sld			X	

Name (Marital Status) Occupation; Age	Yr/Mig	County County	Birth	Removal	Illit.	Chld.
Thompson, Wm. M. (S)	1848	Grayson				
Throop, Charles M. (M)	1848	Tarrant				
Throop, Francis (M)	1848	Tarrant				
Tilly, Jefferson (S-M)	1844	Dallas				
Farmer; 34		Dallas	Tenn.	Tenn.		1
Tinsley, Lewis G. (M)	1848	Tarrant				
Traughber, Wm. (M)	1848	Collin & Dallas				
Treese, Crawford (S-M)	1845	Dallas & Johnson			X	
Farmer; 24		Dallas	Ill.	Ill.		1
Trimble, Allen S. (M)	1848	Tarrant				
Farmer; 31		Dallas	Ky.	Ky.		
Trimble, Wm. A. (S)	1848	Tarrant				
Farmer; 23		Dallas	Ill.	Ill.		
Trimble, Wm. C. (M)	1848	Dallas & Tarrant				
Farmer; 46		Dallas	Tenn.	Tenn.		
Tucker, Andrew J. (S)	1845	Collin				
Farmer; 24		Collin	Mo.	Mo.		
Tucker, David Martin (S)	1848	Collin-sld			X	
Tucker, Henry H. (M)	1845	Grayson-sld Collin				
Farmer; 39		Collin	Ky.	Mo.		6
Tucker, Henry (M)	1845	Denton			X	
Farmer; 63		Denton	N.C.	Mo.		7
Tucker, John S. (M)	1848	Dallas			X	
Farmer; 45		Dallas	N.C.	Mo.		4
Tucker, Malachi (S)	1845	Collin			X	
Tucker, Robert R. (S-M)	1845	Dallas-sld Ellis-sld				
Meth. Minister; 47		Dallas	N.C.	Ill.		3
Tucker, Samuel (S)	1844	Tarrant				
None; 25		Dallas	Ohio	Ohio		
Tucker, Wm. B. (S)	1845	Collin-sld pt.				
Farmer; 25		Collin	Mo.	Mo.		1
Tuggle, Henry P. (M)	1848	Tarrant				
Blacksmith; 30		Dallas	Va.	Va.		
Tuney, John (S)	1844	Collin-sld				
Carpenter; 31		Grayson	Ky.	Ill.		
Tunnell, Wm. C. (S)	1848	Ellis-sld				
Laborer; 30		Dallas	Tenn.	Tenn.		
Turner, John B. (S)	1845	Cooke ?				
Turner, Levi (M)	1848	Dallas			X	
Turner, Richard D. (M)	1848	Cooke				
Farmer; 42		Cooke	Ky.	Mo.		9
Turner, Wm. R. (M)	1845	Dallas				
Farmer; 46		Dallas	Va.	Mo.		2
Underwood, Syrus	1844	Cooke				
Underwood, Edward (M)	1848	Grayson				
Farmer; 27		Cooke	N.Y.	N.Y.		1
Underwood, Norman (M)	1844	Tarrant				

130

Name (Marital Status) Occupation; Age	Yr/Mig	County County	Birth	Removal	Illit.	Chld.
Vaden, James H. (M)	1848	Grayson				
Saddler; 43		Grayson	Tenn.	Tenn.		8
Vail, Hiram (S-M)	1844	Dallas			X	
Farmer; 30		Dallas	Ky.	Ky.		1
Vance, Charles K. (M)	1848	Collin-sld				
Carpenter; 27		Collin	Ill.	Ill.		6
Vance, David (S-M) ⌐	1845	Grayson-sld			X	
Farmer; 34		Grayson	Tenn.	Ind. to Mo.		4
Vance, Fountain J. (S)	1848	Collin				
Surveyor; 25		Collin	Mo.	Mo.		
Vance, James G. (S)	1848	Collin				
Farmer; 21		Collin	Mo.	Mo.		
Vance, John N. (M)	1848	Collin-sld				
Preacher; 39		Collin	Ky.	Mo. to Ill.		9
Vance, Thomas (M)	1848	Collin				
Carpenter; 65		Collin	Ga.	Mo.		3
Van Slyke, Andrew (M)	1848	Cooke				
Farmer; 53		Cooke	N.Y.	Mo. to Ark.		4
Van Slyke, Andrew H. (S)	1848	Cooke				
Vaughan, Lucy (W)	1848	Ellis			X	
36		Ellis	Mo.	Mo.		4
Venters, Stephen A. (S)	1848	Denton-sld pt.				
Trading horses; 25		Denton	N.C.	N.C.		
Vernooy, Thomas (S)	1846	Dallas				
Farmer; 27		Dallas	N.Y.	N.Y.		
Waggoner, John (M)	1844	Denton				
Wagner, Jeremiah (W)	1845	Collin				4
Walker, Albert G. (M)	1846	Tarrant				
Farmer; 41		Dallas	Va.	Va.		1
Walker, Isaac B. (M)	1848	Grayson				
Farmer; 38		Grayson	Tenn.	Ill.		6
Walker, Joel (M)	1848	Dallas & Tarrant			X	
Farmer; 54		Dallas	Tenn.	Tenn.		
Walker, Thomas E. (S)	1848	Cooke-sld				
Walker, Wm. J. (M)	1848	Dallas				
Farmer; 52		Dallas	Tenn.	Tenn.		
Wampler, Austin C. (S)	1847	Dallas				
Farmer; 22		Dallas	Ind.	Ind.		

(To Be Concluded in the Next Issue)

KENTUCKY COLONIZATION IN TEXAS

A HISTORY OF THE PETERS COLONY

SEYMOUR V. CONNOR

LIST OF COLONISTS

Name (Marital Status) Occupation; Age	Yr/Mig	County County	Birth	Removal	Illit.	Chld.
Wampler, Thomas J. (M)	1847	Dallas				
Farmer; 43		Dallas	Va.	Ind.		9
Wampler, Martin J. S. (S)	1848	Dallas				
Wampler, Valentine (M)	1845	Dallas—sld pt.				
Farmer; 49		Dallas	Va.	Ill.		2
Wampler, Wm. R. (S)	1847	Dallas				
Farmer; 23		Collin	Mo.	Mo.		
Ward, Henry (M)	1845	Dallas				
Mason; 32		Ellis	Eng.	Ark.		3
Ward, John F. (M)	1845	Grayson—sld				
Carpenter; 40		Grayson	Ohio	Ohio		2
Warden, John (M)	1848	Grayson—sld			X	
Farmer; 26		Collin	Mo.	Mo.		5
Warden, Williams (M)	1848	Collin—sld			X	
Farmer; 75		Grayson	N. C.	N. C.		
Wash, Sally Ann (W)	1848	Young—sld				
47		Collin		Ky.		4
Watkins, Wm. A. (M)	1848	Grayson—sld Cooke				
Grocer; 39		Grayson	N. C.	Mo.		3
Watkins, Wm. B. (M)	1848	Collins—sld				
Watson, James R. (S)	1848	Ellis				
Farmer;		Ellis	Ill.	Ill.		
Watson, Joab (M)	1848	Johnson—sld Tarrant				
Farmer; 46		Ellis	Md.	Ill.		6
Watson, Morton (S)	1848	Tarrant—sld			X	
Farmer; 26		Grayson	Ky.	Ky.		
Weatherford, Jefferson (M)	1846	Dallas				
Farmer; 29		Dallas	Tenn.	Ill.		6
Weaver, Daniel (M)	1848	Ellis				
Farmer; 58		Ellis	Tenn.	Ala.		4
Webb, Isaac B. (M)	1844	Dallas				
Farmer; 49		Dallas	Tenn.	Tenn.		6
Webster, Elisur D. (M)	1848	Grayson & Cooke				
Carpenter; 51		Grayson	Mass.	Mo.		4
Weldon, Wm. B. (S)	1844	Denton—sld			X	
Farmer; 32		Denton	Ark.	Ark.		

Name (Marital Status) Occupation; Age	Yr/Mig	County County	Birth	Removal	Illit.	Chld.
West, Aaron (M)	1845	Collin—sld pt.				
Farmer; 36		Collin	Ill.	Ark.		4
West, James (M)	1845	Dallas				
Farmer; 32		Dallas	Ohio	Ohio		1
West, Joshua (S-M)	1845	Grayson				
Sheriff; 31		Grayson	Ill.	Ill.		1
West, Michael (W)	1848	Grayson			X	
Farmer; 57		Grayson	Ky.	Ky.?		
West, Michael T. (S)	1848	Grayson				
Farmer; 23		Grayson	Ohio	Ohio		
West, Robert J. (M)	1848	Dallas				
Farmer; 37		Dallas	Tenn.	Tenn.		6
West, Thomas A. (M)	1848	Denton				
Farmer; 46		Denton	N. C.	Ill.		6
Wetherly, Abner (W)	1848	Denton				
Wetherspoon, Joseph H. (S)	1848	Ellis				
Farmer; 26		Ellis	Tenn.	Mo.		4
Wetsel, David (S)	1848	Collin				
Carpenter; 25		Collin	Ohio	Ohio		
Wetsel, Henry (M)	1848	Collin—sld				
Carpenter; 58		Collin	Pa.	Ohio to Ill.		3
Wetsel, James (S)	1848	Dallas			X	
Teamster; 20		Collin	Ill.	Ill.		
Wetsel, Lewis (S)	1848	Collin			X	
Cabinetmaker; 23		Collin	Ill.	Ill		
Wetsel, Peter (M)	1848	Collin—sld pt.				
Carpenter; 31		Collin	Pa.	Ark.		3
Wheeler, James N. (S)	1848	Grayson—sld Cooke—sld				
Wheeler, Thomas (M)	1848	Grayson				
Farmer; 44		Grayson	Ky.	Ill.		7
Wheelock, Charles	1844	Cooke				
Wheelock, Robert (S)	1848	Cooke				
Farmer; 25		Cooke	Ky.	Ky.		
Whisenaunt, Robert C. (M)	1844	Collin				
Farmer; 39		Collin	Ga.	Ark. to Mo.		7
Whitaker, Jonas (M)	1848	Collin—sld			X	
Farmer; 24		Collin	Tenn.	Mo.		3
Whitaker, Samuel (M)	1848	Collin				
Farmer; 45		Grayson	Ky.	Mo.		2
White, George (S)	1848	Collin				
Surveyor; 29		Collin	Mass.	Mass.		
White, John (M)	1848	Denton			X	
Farmer; 29		Denton	Germ.	?		2
White, Thomas (S)	1848	Dallas			X	
Farmer; 22		Tarrant	Mo.	Mo.		
White, Wm. O. (M)	1845	Cooke				
Whitly, Ethelred (M)	1848	Collin				
Farmer; 34		Collin	Tenn.	Ark.		6

133

Name (Marital Status) Occupation; Age	Yr/Mig	County County	Birth	Removal	Illit.	Chld.
Wiggins, Coonrod (M)	1848	Cooke				
Wilburn, Edward (M)	1845	Tarrant			X	
Wilburn, Edward (M)	1845	Dallas				
Farmer; 45		Dallas	Ky.	Mo.		8
Wilburn, Hiram (M)	1844	Dallas			X	
Laborer; 25		Dallas	Mo.	Mo.		
Wilburn, Hiram Jr. (S)	1845	Dallas			X	
Wilburn, Robert (M)	1844	Dallas			X	
Farmer; 49		Dallas	Ky.	Mo.		8
Wilcox, George (S)	1844	Collin				
Wiley, Jacob (S)	1848	Dallas				
Farmer; 26		Dallas	Tenn.	Tenn.		
Wilhite, McKinsie (S)	1848	Collin				
Wilhite, Wm. (S)	1845	Collin				
Williams, Frederick (M)	1845	Ellis				
Farmer; 29		Ellis	Tenn.	Mo.		5
Williams, Grafton (M)	1844	Collin			X	
Williams, P. W. (M)	1844	Collins—sld				
Williams, Thomas C. (M)	1848	Dallas				
Farmer; 31		Dallas	Tenn.	Tenn.		2
Wilmeth, Francis C. (M)	1848	Collin—sld pt.				
Farmer; 44		Collin	N. C.	Tenn. to Ark.		5
Wilmeth, Joseph B. (M)	1848	Collin				
Farmer; 42		Collin	N. C.	Tenn. to Ark.		11
Wilmeth, Mansel W. (S)	1848	Tarrant				
Farmer; 20		Collin	Tenn.	Ark.		
Wilson, Aaron B. (M)	1845	Dallas—sld				
Farmer; 27		Dallas	Tenn.	Tenn.		
Wilson, Alexander (S)	1848	Grayson			X	
Wilson, Andrew J. (S)	1848	Dallas				
Wilson, David C. (M)	1848	Grayson				
Farmer; 31		Grayson	Tenn.	Tenn.		5
Wilson, David (M)	1848	Grayson				
Farmer; 65		Grayson	N. C.	Tenn.		
Wilson, George A. (S)	1848	Collin				
Farmer; 20		Collin	Tenn.	Tenn.		
Wilson, Gulaver, (S)	1848	Tarrant			X	
Wilson, Harvey G. (S)	1848	Dallas			X	
Wilson, Henry R. (M)	1848	Cooke				
Farmer; 48		Cooke	Va.	Va.		
Wilson, James (M)	1845	Collin				
Farmer; 36		Collin	Tenn.	Tenn.		3
Wilson, Jeremiah H. (M)	1845	Collin				
Farmer; 33		Collin	Tenn.	Mo.		5
Wilson, Joseph (M)	1848	Tarrant				
Farmer; 55		Ellis	Va.	Mo.		3
Wilson, Leonidas (S)	1848	Collin				
Farmer; 24		Collin	Tenn.	Tenn.		

Name (Marital Status) Occupation; Age	Yr/Mig	County County	Birth	Removal	Illit.	Chld.
Wilson, Richard (M)	1848	Dallas—sld				
Farmer; 37		Dallas	Ky.	Mo.		3
Wilson, Samuel S. (M)	1848	Ellis & Johnson				
Blacksmith; 35		Ellis	N. Y.	Ill.		1
Wilson, Thomas C. (M)	1848	Denton—sld				
Blacksmith; 44		Denton	N. C.	Ala. to La.		3
Wilson, Whitson W. (S)	1848	Denton			X	
Farmer; 22		Denton	N. C.	N. C.		
Wilson, Wm. B. (S)	1845	Collin—sld				
Blacksmith; 28		Dallas	Ind.	Mo.		
Wilson, Wm. C. (M)	1848	Grayson				
Farmer; 40		Grayson	Tenn.	Tenn.		5
Wilson, Wm. S. (S)	1848	Dallas				
Farmer; 34		Dallas	Ind.	Ind.		
Wingfield, John J. (M)	1848	Tarrant				
Farmer; 32		Ellis	Ky.	Ark.		2
Winn, Francis A. (M)	1848	Dallas				
Farmer; 35		Dallas	Tenn.	Ala.		4
Wise, Carlos (S-M)	1845	Dallas—sld				
Farmer; 31		Dallas	Ill.	Ill.		2
Wiswell, John (M)	1844	Denton—sld				
Wiswell, John (S)	1848	Denton—sld				
Farmer; 19		Denton	Ill.	Ill.		
Withers, James W. (M)	1845	Denton				
Witt, Eli W. (S)	1845	Collin				
Farmer; 24		Collin	Tenn.	Tenn.		
Witt, Hogan (S)	1845	Collin				
Farmer; 26		Collin	Tenn.	Tenn.		
Witt, John (S)	1844	Dallas-slid			X	
None; 70		Dallas	Va.	Va.?		
Witt, Preston (M)	1843	Tarrant—sld Dallas				
Farmer; 30		Dallas	Ill.	Ill.		3
Witt, Wade H. (M)	1846	Collin				
Farmer; 27		Dallas	Ill.	Ill.		3
Womack, Elizabeth M. (W)	1845	Collin			X	6
Woodruff, Robert W. (S)	1848	Dallas—sld				
Farmer; 29		Denton	Tenn.	Tenn.		
Woolsey, Josiah P. (M)	1844	Ellis				
Farmer; 34		Ellis	Ill.	Mo.		4
Worley, Briah (S)	1848	Collin				
Farmer; 21		Cooke	Ind.	Ind.		
Worley, Joseph (M)	1848	Cooke			X	
Farmer; 49		Cooke	Va.	Ind.		7
Worthington, Richard (S)	1848	Tarrant				
Farmer; 31		Tarrant	Eng.	Eng.		
Wright, John W. (M)	1844	Dallas				
Farmer; 30		Dallas	Tenn.	Tenn.		2
Yager, Thomas L. (S)	1848	Collin—sld				

135

Name (Marital Status) Occupation; Age	Yr/Mig	County County	Birth	Removal	Illit.	Chld.
Yoacham, John (S)	1848	Denton—sld			X	
Farmer; 24		Denton	Mo.	Mo.		
Yoacham, Michael (M)	1848	Denton				
Yoacham, Solomon Jr. (S)	1848	Denton			X	
Farmer; 25		Denton	Mo.	Mo.		
Yoacham, Solomon Sr. (M)	1848	Denton			X	
Farmer; 47		Denton	Va.	Mo.		8
York, John B. (M)	1848	Tarrant				
Farmer; 25		Ellis	Tenn.	Tenn.		
Young, John (M)	1844	Dallas				
Farmer; 55		Dallas	Tenn.	Mo.		4
Young, Samuel (M)	1845	Collin—sld pt.				
Farmer; 33		Collin	Va.	Va.		1
Younger, Alexander (M)	1848	Ellis				
Farmer; 63		Navarro	N. C.	N. C.		3
Younger, Geo. W. (M)	1848	Ellis				
Farmer; 29		Ellis	Tenn.	Tenn.		2
Younger, Richard H. (S)	1848					
Zachary, Sarah (W)	1848	Dallas			X	
39		Dallas	Va.	Va.		3

2. Colonists who moved away before receiving land

Name (Marital Status) Occupation; Age	Yr/Mig	County County	Birth	Removal	Illit.	Chld.
Allan, George (S)	1844					
Allison, Edward (S)	1845					
Anderson, Rufus (S)	1845					
Applegate, P. W. (S)	1845					
Asbury, Richard (M)	1844					
Archer, Wm. P.	1845					
Augusta, Holly (M)	1844					
Avantz, Isham (M)	1845				X	
Avantz, James L. (S)	1845					
Bailey, John (S)	1844					
Baker, Larkin (M)	1844					
Bankhead, George W. (M)	1845					
Bankhead, R. M. (S)	1845	? Johnson—sld				
Bankhead, Wm. C. (S)	1845					
Barr, John (S)	1844					
Bartlett, John (S)	1845					
Bartlett, Joseph (M)	1845					
Farmer; 35		Navarro	Tenn.	Tenn.		4
Bartlett, Joseph (S)	1845					
*Bean, Robert (M)	1845					
Farmer; 30		Grayson	Ark.	Ark.		3
Benton, Peter S. (M)	1845					
Bethel, Wm. B. (S)	1844					

Name (Marital Status) Occupation; Age	Yr/Mig	County County	Birth	Removal	Illit.	Chld.
Black, Wm. (S)	1844					
Blalock, Joseph ( )	1844					
Blanchard, Ira (S)	1845				X	
Bledsoe, Levi (S)	1845					
Bledsoe, Smith (S)	1845				X	
Boiles, Daniel (M)	1844					6
Boiles, John G. (S)	1844					
Stock Keeper; 21		Navarro	Ark.	Ark.		
Braley, Hugh (S)	1844					
Braley, Wm. T. (S)	1844					
Browning, John (M)	1844					
Burgess, John (S)	1844					
Burris, Hudson (S)	1844					
Butler, J. (S)	1844					
Byrd, Pleasant (S)	1844					
Caldwell, Hezakiah (M)	1844	? Parker				
Caldwell, John (S)	1844	? Parker				
Caldwell, Kincaid (M)	1844					
Callahan, Stephen W. ( )	1845					
Carr, John (M)	1844					
Case, Elmore W. (S)	1844					
Case, Richard N. (S)	1844					
Case, Samuel (M)	1844					
Casey, Thomas (M)	1844					
Casey, Timothy (S)	1844					
Chalfield, Hormon (M)	1844					
Chandler, Samuel (S)	1845					
Clark, Benjamin F. (S)	1844					
Clark, Franklin (S)	1844					
Clark, Isaac (M)	1844					
Clark, John (M)	1845					
Clevenger, Braxton (S)	1845					
Clevenger, James (M)	1845					
Clevenger, M. C. (M)	1845					
Clevenger, Reubin (M)	1845					
Copeland, Wiley (S)	1845					
Corbin, George (S)	1845					
Costin, Josiah (S)	1845					
Cotton, M. G. (M)	1845					
(? First Clerk of Grayson County, 1846—*Sherman Democrat*. Sept 19, 1948)						
Coween, Lawrence (S)	1845					
Cowsen, Wm. R. (S)	1845					
Cowsen, David P. (S)	1845					
Cox, Benjamin (M)	1845					
Cox, George M. (S)	1844					
Farmer; 26		Dallas	Ill.	Ill.		3
Cox, Wm. (S)	1845					
Cox, Wm. B. (M)	1844					

Name (Marital Status) Occupation; Age	Yr/Mig	County County	Birth	Removal	Illit. Chld.
Crager, John	1844				
Cunbrough, James T. (M)	1844				
Darbry, Dathon (S)	1845				
Davidson, H. M.	1845				
Davidson, R. B. T. (S)	1845				
Davidson, S. W. (S)	1845				
Davidson, W. E. (S)	1845				
Davis, Aaron (S)	1845				
Dean, Powel	1844				
Decker, John B. (S)	1845				
Dick, S. P. (S)	1845				
Diven, (Dixon?) A. (S)	1844				
Doss, B. P. (S)	1845				
Dotton, Joseph (S)	1844				
Durill, Abner (S)	1844				
Durill, Duran (S)	1844				
Durill, John (M)	1844				
Earp, Calvin (M)	1844				
Edwards, James B. (M)	1845				
Edwards, John B. (M)	1844				
Elkins, Abial (S)	1844				
Ellis, Asa (M)	1844				
Embree, G. W. (S)	1845				
Ethridge, Thomas (M)	1844				
Evans, Ephraim L. (S)	1845				
Evans, Lemuel D. (S)	1844				
Evans, Silas (S)	1845				
Falkner, Franklin (M)	1844				
Falon, B. H. (S)	1845				
Fletcher, Syrus (S)	1845				
Fletcher, Wm. (S)	1845				
Fogg, L. F. (S)	1845				
Fowler, Daniel (M)	1845				
Fowler, John (S)	1845				
Fowler, Joseph (M)	1845				X
Fowler, Josiah (M)	1845				X
Frazier, Eli (M)	1845				
Frazier, John S. (S)	1845				
Frazier, Samuel G. (M)	1845				
Frazier, Thomas M. (S)	1845				
Frazier, Wm. H. G. (S)	1845				
*French, Leffard (M)	1844				
Fryer, James (S)	1844				
Fulgham, Thomas (M)	1845				
Funk, Thomas (S)	1845				
Garrout (?), James D. (S)	1844				
Garrout, Jeremiah (S)	1844				
Gilliam, Henry (S)	1844				

Name (Marital Status) Occupation; Age	Yr/Mig	County County	Birth	Removal	Illit.	Chld.
Glover, Richard L. (S)	1844					
Gookin, T. M. (S)	1845					
Glover, John H. (M)	1844					
Graham, Wm. M. (S)	1844					
Green, James (M)	1845					
Green, Wm. (M)	1845				X	
Grier, Robert (S)	1844					
Griswold, Fayette (M)	1845					
Gunter, C. D.	1844					
Haggard, James (M)	1845					
*Haggard, Wm. (S)	1845					
Halsey, Elizah (M)	1845					
Hamers, James (M)	1845					
Hanvey, Wm. R. (S)	1844					
Hardaway, A. (M)	1845					
Hart, Wm. J. (M)	1844					
Head, E. T. (M)	1845					
Headstream, J. G. (S)	1844					
Lleighten (?), Levi (M)	1845					3
Helms, Isaac	1845					
Hensley, Joseph (S)	1844					
Herrold, Robert (S)	1844					
Hewz, (Hughes?), Dinton (S)	1844					
Hews, John (M)	1844					
Hews, Wm. R. (S)	1844					
Hebert, Charles (S)	1845					
Higgins, Wm. (M)	1844	? Wise				
Hodge, John (M)	1845	? Johnson				
Hodges, Joshua (M)	1845	? Cooke				
Hoffman, Nathan (M)	1845					
Holden, Wm. (S)	1844					
Holt, Littleton M. S. (M)	1844					
Hooper, John (M)	1845					
Hooper, Jonathon (S)	1845					
House, Mathew W. (S)	1845				X	
House, Susan Jane (W)	1845					
? 25		Collin	Tenn.	Tenn.		2
Houston, Archibald (S)	1844					
Howard, Wm. C. (S)	1845	? Tarrant				
Howe, Andrew J. (S)	1844					
Howel, Andrew (S)	1844					
Huddlesboro (?), J. H. (S)	1845					
Hudsley, Charles S.	1845					
Huntsiecker, James (S)	1845					
Hutchins, Zachariah (M)	1845					
Jackson, Joseph (S)	1845	? Grayson				
Jacobs, John (M)	1845					
Jenkins, James (M)	1845	? Parker				

Name (Marital Status) Occupation; Age	Yr/Mig	County County	Birth	Removal	Illit. Chld.
Jenkins, Wm. (S)	1845				
Jenning, Benjamin (S)	1844				
Johnson, Asa (S)	1844				
Jones, Wm. R. (S)	1845				
Joy, George (M)	1845	? Collin			
Kean, Barry (S)	1844				
Kennedy, Calvin W. (S)	1844				
Kennedy, Samuel (S)	1844				
Kerrigan, Arthur (M)	1845				
Key, Joseph (M)	1845	? Tarrant			
Keys, Wm. (S)	1845				
King, Dixon P. (S)	1844				
Kinsey, Kenneth (M)	1845				X
Lair, Peter (M)	1845				
Lake, Jacques (S)	1845				
Lake, Thomas (M)	1845				
Late, Wm. (S)	1845				
Langsten, Henry (M)	1845				
Laramox, John (M)	1845				
Larew, Isam (M)	1844				
Ledley, Joseph (S)	1845				
Lee, Henry (M)	1845				
Lennox, Samuel (M)	1845				
Lucas, Abram (S)	1845				
Lucas, Solomon R. (S)	1845				
Luster, Lloyd (M)	1844				
Luttrell, Benjamin (S)	1845				
Luttrell, Nathaniel, S. L.	1844				
Lyon, Sydney (S)	1844				
McAfee, Thomas (M)	1845				
McCarty, Wm. Jr. (M)	1845				
McClain, Thomas (S)	1845				
McClelland, John G. (M)	1844				
McClelland, John J. (S)	1844				
McDaniel, Robert W. (S)	1845				
McDavid, George W. (S)	1844				
McDuffer, John (M)	1844				
McGravey, Elijah (S)	1844				
McKean, James (M)	1844				
McKellar, Robert (M)	1844				
McManus, Joab	1845				
Manihan, Charles (M)	1844				
Marley, Harvey (S)	1845				
Marshall, Francis (M)	1845				
Martin, Anthony (S)	1844	? Hood			
Matthews, Polly (W)	1844				
Matthewson, Robert Campbell (S)	1845				
Maxfield, Jenkins (S)	1845				

140

Name (Marital Status) Occupation; Age	Yr/Mig	County County	Birth	Removal	Illit. Chld.
Maxfield, Madison (S)	1845				
Maxfield, Thomas (S)	1845				
May, David (M)	1845				
Maybury, Russell (M)	1844				
Meadbury, Hall (M)	1844				
Meadbury, Ownn (M)	1844				
Means, James (S)	1845				
Medlock, Thomas (M)	1845				
Meneer, Wm. (M)	1844				
Meupin, James (S)	1844				
Miller, Nicholas (S)	1845				
Minter, T. J. (S)	1845				
Moon, Benjamin (S)	1844				
Morgan, Lewis W. (M)	1844				
Morris, Hamrod B. (S)	1844				
Mudget, Miram (M)	1844				
Nail, Nicholas (S)	1844				
Nash, R. W. (S)	1844				
Navon (?), James (S)	1845				
Navon (?), Wm. (M)	1845				
Odle, John (S)	1844				
O'Harra, John (S)	1844				
Onstrott, Joshua (M)	1845				
Ottis, Peter (S)	1845				
Pair, Thomas J. (S)	1845				
Pallet, Wm. (S)	1845				
Palmer, Wm. A. (S)	1845				
Pannell, Victor (M)	1844				
Parks, Willis E. (M)	1844				
Pattan, Isaac (S)	1845				
Peaveyhouse, John (S)	1844				
Perrin, James M. (M) (Physician)	1845				
Perrin, Isaac N. (S)	1845				
Peters, John (?) (S)	1845				
Phayer, Benjamin (M)	1845				
Pick, Samuel	1844				
Polk, Thomas (S)	1844				
Pool, Joseph M. (S)	1845				
Prince, Daniel (M)	1844				
Prince, Glihen (M)	1844				
Pruitt, Milas (S)	1844				
Rainey, Joseph	1844				
Rall, Preston (S)	1845				
Reeder, Bluford (S)	1845				
Rice, John (S)	1845				
Richardson, D. M. (S)	1845				
Richardson, John Jr. (S)	1845				

Name (Marital Status) Occupation; Age	Yr/Mig	County County	Birth	Removal	Illit.	Chld.
Richardson, John Sr. (M)	1845					
Richardson, Jonathon Sr. (M)	1845					
Richardson, Joshua Jr. (M)	1845					
Richardson, Joshua Sr. (M)	1845					
Richardson, Lewis (M)	1845					
Richardson, Paul (S)	1845					
Richardson, Thomas (M)	1845					
Rightman, Edwin (M)	1845					
Rictor, Nelson (M)	1844					
Rippetor, Adney (S)	1844					
Rippetor, Elam (S)	1844					
Rippetor, Mary (W)	1844					
Rippetor, Wm. (S)	1844					
Ritchey, Crawford (M)	1845					
Ritchey, James (S)	1845					
Roberson, Ezekiel (S)	1844					
Robbins, Wm. (M)	1845				X	
Rossin, Wm. (S)	1845					
Routh, John (M)	1845					
Rullidge, Bennet (M)	1844					
Rullidge, James (M)	1844					
Russell, Absalon C. (M)	1845					
Russell, Lydia (W)	1845				X	
Russell, Wm. (M)	1845	? Dallas				
Scaggs, Aaron (M)	1844					
Scott, Andrew D. (S)	1845					
Seymour, Anderson (S)	1845					
Shelby, David (M)	1844					
Simpkins, Thomas C. (S)	1844					
Sinclair, James (M)	1845					
Skinner, James (M)	1845					
Sloane, Fortinatus (S)	1844					
Smith, Bartlett S. (M)	1844					
Smith, John	1845	? Montague				
Smith, Wm. (S)	1844					
Sorrell, Alexander (M)	1845					
Sorrell, Thomas (S)	1844					
Southward, John (S)	1845					
Stanley, Joseph (S)	1845					
Stephenson, John P. (S)	1845					
Stephenson, Josiah (S)	1845					
Stephenson, P. M. (S)	1845					
Stephenson, Wm. B. (S)	1845					
Stinnett, George (S)	1844					
Stinnett, John (M)	1844					
Stocks, J. D. (M)	1845					
Storey, Elisha (S)	1845					
Stotts, Sims (M)	1844					

Name (Marital Status) Occupation; Age	Yr/Mig	County County	Birth	Removal	Illit.	Chld.
Stover, Isaac (S)	1845					
Stubblefield, Robert (S)	1845					
Tackitt, Hillyard (M)	1845					
Thomas, Jonathon G. (M)	1844					
Thornton, Fillimicus (S)	1845					
Truner, Wm. (S)	1844					
Turner, Elias T. (S)	1845					
Usher, Moses H. (M)	1845					
Valentine, Wm. L. (S)	1844				X	
Venters, Jesse (S)	1844					
Vivian, James (S)	1844					
Vivian, John (S)	1844					
Vivian, Thacker (S)	1844					
Wall, Samuel (S)	1845					
Warren, Wm. H. (M)	1845					
Weaver, Andras J. (S)	1844					
Weaver, Samuel (M)	1844					
Webb, George (S)	1844					
Weldon, James A. (M) Farmer; 33	1844	(Ward's Cert. in Collin) Denton	Ark.	Ark.		1
West, Vinson (M)	1845					
Wheelock, Napoleon (S)	1844					
Wilcox, Danny (M)	1845					
Willete, Robert (S)	1844					
Williams, Rodderick Y. (S)	1845				X	
Wilson, Jackson (M)	1845					
Witt, Pleasant (S) Farmer; 31	1844	Collin	Ill.	Ill.		2 ?
Worth, Abraham (S)	1844					
Young, Henry (M)	1844					
Young, Wesley (S)	1844					
Young, Wm. (S)	1844					

3. **Persons issued county court certificates as colonists who received land: Probable colonists**

Name (Marital Status) Occupation; Age	Yr/Mig	County County	Birth	Removal	Illit.	Chld.
Adey, Edmund (S)	1844	Denton—sld				
Allen, Edwin (M)	1848	Collin				
•Allen, Moses (M)	1848	Jack—sld—pt.				
Allen, Wm. P. (M)	1848	Collin				
Atkinson, Henry (M)	1848	Tarrant—sld				
Baker, Wm. S. (S)	1848	Tarrant—sld				
Baracus, John (M)	1848	Clay				
Barroux, Etine (S)	1848	Dallas				
Bean, John R. (M) Merchant; 34	1848	Grayson—sld Grayson	Cooke—sld Tenn.	Tenn.		1

143

Name (Marital Status) Occupation; Age	Yr/Mig	County County	Birth	Removal	Illit. Chld.
Billingsley, Jesse (S)	1848	Johnson			
Farmer; 20		Ellis	Ark.	Ark.	
Billingsly, John (S)	1848	Ellis			
Farmer; 20		Ellis	Ark.	Mo.	
•Blackwell, Upton O. (S)	1848	Johnson—sld			X
Farmer; 16		Collin	Tenn.	Tenn.	
Bound, J. B. (M)	1848	Ellis—sld			
Wagoner; 23		Collin	Mo.	Mo.	
Bradley, Wesley W. (S)	1848	Grayson			
Laborer; 20		Grayson	Ala.	Ala.	
Brown, Crawford (S)	1844	Tarrant—sld			
Brown, Edward (S)	1844	Denton			
Brown, J. P. (S)	1845	Grayson			
Clerk; 28		Navarro	Tenn.	Tenn.	
Bledsoe, Abram (M)	1848	Dallas—sld			
Farmer; 38		Grayson	Mo.	Mo.	6
Bonds, George W. (M)	1848	Cooke ?			
Brogden, Wm. S. (M)	1848	Grayson			
Farmer; 46		Grayson	N. C.	Tenn.	6
Browning, Elias P. (S)	1848	Johnson—sld			
Laborer; 21		Grayson	Tenn.	Tenn.	
Browning, James (M)	1848	Grayson			
Burnett, R. H. (S)	1848	Tarrant—sld			
Burns, John A. (S)	1848	Grayson—sld			
Farmer; 27		Grayson	Mo.	Mo.	
Barslley, John (S)	1848	Tarrant—sld			
Butler, Jesse (M)	1844	Grayson—sld			
Butler, Joab (M)	1848	Collin—sld			
Farmer; 33		Grayson	Mo.	Mo.	7
Cabrell, Simon (M)	1848	Tarrant—sld pt.			
•Cantrell, W. C. (S)	1848	Denton—sld			
•Cockrum, Henry (M)	1848	? Denton—sld			
•Criner, G. A. (S)	1848	Tarrant—sld			
Crittendon, Wm. H. (M)	1844	Dallas			
Crockett, George (S)	1844	Ellis—sld			
•Crocker, Alfored (S)	1848	Ellis—sld Collin Cooke			
Farmer; 50		Collin	Mass.	Ill.	6
Crutchfield, Albertus (S)	1848	Wise—sld Dallas			
Carpenter; 25		Navarro	Ky.	Ky.	1
Darbry, Denton (S)	1845	Collin—sld			
Darbry, Denton Sr. (M)	1845	Johnson			
Dixon, John (M)	1848	Johnson			
Farmer; 18		Dallas	Mo.	Mo.	
Earhart, Joseph B. (M)	1845	Dallas—sld			
Evans, John (S)	1848	Dallas—sld			
———; 24		Dallas	Tenn.	Tenn.	
Everett, J. N. (S)	1848	Dallas			
Farmer; 23		Dallas	Tenn.	Tenn.	

Name (Marital Status) Occupation; Age	Yr/Mig	County County	Birth	Removal	Illit.	Chld.
Fitch, John A. (S)	1848	Tarrant—sld				
Farmer; 26		Grayson	Ala.	Ala.		
Fletcher, Wm. (M)	1845	Dallas—sld				
Farmer; 23		Navarro	Mo.	Mo.		1
Foreman, Josephus (S)	1848	Dallas—sld				
Foreman, Wm. (M)	1848	Dallas—sld				
Gardner, Wm. S. (S)	1845	Ellis				
Garrison, Mitchell (M)	1848	Tarrant—sld				
Goodwin, J. W. (S)	1848	Tarrant—sld				
Graham, John L. (M)	1844	? Montague				
? Farmer; 57		Dallas	Va.	Mo. to Ark.		5
Guerin, —— (S)	1848	Tarrant				
? Tailor; 60		Grayson	France	France		
*Haning, Henry (S)	1848	Grayson—sld				
Farmer; 19		Grayson				
Hanna, Archibald (M)	1848	Collin				
Harbott, James (M)	1844	Cooke—sld				
Farmer; 27		Grayson	Pa.	Pa.	X	1
Hardaway, Thomas E. (M)	1845	Grayson & Cooke				
Harding, John (M)	1845	Dallas				
Farmer; 36		Dallas	Ky.	Ill. to Mo.		7
Harris, Mahulda (W)	1848	Tarrant—sld				
52		Grayson	Ky.	Tenn. to Ill.		6
Harris, Wm. (S)	1845	Dallas				
*Hartzog, Geo. W. (S)	1848	Tarrant—sld				
Laborer; 18		Grayson	Tenn.	Tenn.		
Hays, Hiram E. (S)	1845	Collin—sld				
Farmer; 31		Collin	Ala.	Ala.		
? Hedgcoxe, Henry O. (S)	1848	Denton				
Helms, John T. (M)	1848	Dallas				
Henry, Anderson (S)	1845	Denton—sld				
Henry, Josiah (S-M)	1845	Denton				
Herron, John M. (S)	1848	Collin				
Farmer; 32		Collin	N. C.	N. C.		
Hews, Cleborne (S)	1844	Young—sld				
Hickman, William S. (M)	1845	Ellis				
Higgins, John (S)	1844	Denton & Hood				
*Hill, Thomas D. (S)	1848	Cooke				
Laborer; 18		Grayson	Ala.	Miss.		
Hood, Alexander (S)	1845	Tarrant—sld pt.				
Hood, Morgan (M)	1845	Tarrant				
Jackson, Calvin (S)	1848	Parker				
*Jennings, James (M)	1848	Johnson				
Farmer; 62		Grayson	S. C.	Mo.		3
*Jennings, James W. (S)	1848	Grayson—sld				
Farmer; 23		Grayson	Mo.	Mo.		
Johnson, Jonathon (M)	1848	Ellis—sld				
Farmer; 42		Grayson	Ky.	Ark.		5

Name (Marital Status) Occupation; Age	Yr/Mig	County County	Birth	Illit. Removal	Chld.
Joy, James A. (S)	1845	Ellis			
Keefer, Benjamin (S)	1845	Dallas			
Keen, Wm. W. (M)	1848	Dallas			
Farmer; 54		Dallas	Va.	Ind.	4
Kendall, Allison D. (M)	1848	Cooke—sld			
Farmer; 29		Grayson	N. Y.	N. Y.	1
Langley, James (S)	1848	Grayson—sld			
Laborer; 20		Grayson	Mo.	Mo.	
Langley, Joseph (S)	1848	Collin—sld			
Laborer; 18		Grayson	Mo.	Mo.	
Langley, Thomas (M)	1848	Dallas—sld			
Farmer; 40		Grayson	Ga.	Mo.	8
Langston, James J. (S)	1848	Grayson—sld			
Farmer; 20		Denton	Mo.	Mo.	
Lavender, Archibald M. (M)	1848	Ellis			
Farmer; 35		Ellis	S. C.	Ala.	9
Ledbetter, Arthur (M)	1848	Dallas (See Gammel, *Laws of Texas* IV.)			
Farmer; 51		Dallas	Tenn.	Tenn.	6
Ledbetter, Lewis B. (S)	1848	Tarrant—sld Ellis—sld			
Farmer; 19		Dallas	Tenn.	Tenn.	
Leeper, Peter F. (S)	1848	Grayson—sld			
None; 19		Collin	Mo.	Mo.	
Lewis, Hiram (M)	1848	Johnson—sld			
Farmer; 32		Ellis	Ky.	Ill.	8
Lewis, Wm. J. (S)	1848	Dallas			
Farmer; 37		Dallas	N. Y.	N. Y.	
*Littlepage, Ellis (M)	1845	Tarrant—sld			
Littlepage, J. B. (S)	1848	Ellis—sld Johnson—sld			
Luttrell, Colbert (S)	1848	Collin—sld Parker—sld			
McBrayer, A. W. (M)	1848	Johnson—sld			
McCan, James (S)	1845	?			
McKinney, Marcus S. (S)	1848	Grayson—sld			
Farmer; 26		Grayson	Ky.	Ky.	
McMillan, J. (S)	1848	Grayson—sld			
M.E.C.S. Preacher; 25		Grayson	Tenn.	Tenn.	
McNamara, J. (M)	1844	Ellis			
McQueen, Donald (S)	1848	Tarrant—sld			
Mackey, James (M)	1848	Johnson—sld pt.			
Nothing; 27		Navarro	Ind.	Ind.	2
Martin, James (M)	1848	Cooke			
Farmer; 40		Cooke	Tenn.	Ill. to Wis.	10
Martin, Silas (S)	1848	Cooke—sld			
Laborer; 24		Grayson	Ill.	Ill.	X
Menifee, J. B. (M)	1848	Dallas—sld Collin			
*Miller, Stephen H. (S)	1848	Dallas			
Mitchell, John R. (S)	1848	Dallas—sld			
Mitchum, Joseph (S)	1848	Collin—sld			
Laborer; 20		Grayson	Ill.	Ill.	

Name (Marital Status) Occupation; Age	Yr/Mig	County County	Birth	Removal	Illit. Chld.
Mounts, Geo. W. (S)	1848	Jack			
Murphy Eli (S)	1845	Collin—sld			
Myers, Benjamin C. (S)	1848	Collin—sld Dallas			
Orr, John B. (S)	1848	Dallas—sld Ellis sld			
Painter, Wm. C. (M)	1845	Cooke—sld			
*Parris, E. P. (M)	1848	Tarrant—sld			
Carpenter; 45		Grayson	Mass.	Ill.	2
Parrish, James (S-M)	1844	Dallas			
Farmer; 32		Dallas	Ohio	Ohio	
Pegues, E. E. (M)	1848	Palo Pinto—sld			
Pegues, Wm. S. (S)	1848	Dallas—sld			
Quillin, Charles C. (S)	1848	Grayson—sld			
Farmer; 24		Grayson	Unk.	Unk.	
Reed, Harrison (M)	1845	Dallas—sld			
Reed, Joseph (S)	1844	Ellis			
Farmer; 24		Denton	Unk.	Unk.	
Reed, Wm. D. (M)	1845	Dallas—sld			
Redding, James F. (S)	1844	Tarrant			
Roberson, Elizabeth (W)	1844	Dallas			
Russel, Robert (M)	1845	Ellis			
Sanders, R. H. (S)	1848	Wise—sld			
Scott, Solomon J. (M)	1848	Grayson—sld			
Farmer; 26		Grayson	Ky.	Mo.	3
*Size, John (M)	1848	Tarrant—sld			
Smith, Jesse (M)	1844	Tarrant—sld			
Farmer; 26		Grayson	Tenn.	Tenn.	
Southward, Elijah (S)	1848	Cooke—sld			
Southward, Henry (S)	1845	Grayson—sld			
Southward, Irawell (M)	1845	Grayson—sld			
Southward, Wm. (M)	1845	Grayson—sld			
*Spencer, Elizabeth W. (W)	1848	Cooke—sld Denton			
*Spray, Elias (M)	1848	Montague			
Sprowls, Wm. (M)	1848	Dallas—sld pt.			
Carpenter; 31		Dallas	Ky.	Ky.	
Starrett, James (M)	1844	Johnson & Ellis			
Stephens, John (M)	1848	Tarrant—sld			
Farmer; 53		Navarro	Va.	Mo.	7
*Stephens, Wm. H. (M)	1848	Tarrant—sld			
Farmer; 28		Navarro	Ind.	Mo. to Ark.	2
Stinson, Alfred (S)	1848	Tarrant—sld			
Farmer; 23		Grayson	Ind.	Ind.	
*Sullivan, James (M)	1848	Baylor—sld			
Sutherland, Elijah (M)	1848	Cooke—sld Tarrant—sld			
Sutherland, George (M)	1848	? Hood			
Sutton, Joseph (M)	1845	Denton—sld			
Terrell, Edward S. (M)	1848	Tarrant			
Farmer; 29		Tarrant	Ky.	Ky.	2
Thomas, Joseph A. (S)	1845	Dallas—sld			

Name (Marital Status) Occupation; Age	Yr/Mig	County County	Birth	Removal	Illit.	Chld.
Thompson, Wm. (M)	1848	Grayson				
•Travis, Conrad (M)	1845	Ellis—sld				
•Travis, James G. (M)	1845	?				
•Travis, Wm. A. (M)	1845	Dallas—sld				
Truitt, J. M. (S)	1848	Tarrant—sld				
Turner, Henry B. (M)	1845	Denton				
Turner, Joseph T. (M)	1844	Tarrant—sld Denton—sld				
Vestell, Allen (S-M)	1844	Denton				
Farmer; 25		Collin	N. C.	Tex. to Mo.		2
Waggoner, Peter (M)	1844	Denton—sld				
Walker, Henderson C. (S)	1844	Dallas—sld				
Walker, Landon C. (M)	1844	Tarrant—sld				
Warren, Alexander C. (S)	1848	Tarrant—sld				
Welch, Wm. (M)	1844	Tarrant—sld				
West, Samuel (S)	1844	Tarrant				
•Wharton, Wm. C. (M)	1848	? Cooke				
Farmer; 28		Collin	**Tenn.**	Ark.		4
White, Archibald (M)	1844	Young—sld				
Farmer; 25		Collin	**Tenn.**	Mo.	X	3
White, Coleman (S)	1848	Collin—sld Denton—sld				
•Wilburn, J. S. (S)	1848	Tarrant				
Wilson, John H. (M)	1848	Collin—sld				
Physician; 27		Grayson	Tenn.	Tenn.		
Wilson, Pleasant (W)	1841	Collin				
Farmer; 45		Collin	Tenn.	Tenn.		3
Woolsey, Gilbert (M)	1844	Denton				
Woolsey, James (M)	1844	Johnson				
•Worthington, W. P. (S)	1848	Johnson				
Allen, Jonathon (S)	1848	Collin				
Barnes, Wm. (S)	1848	Tarrant				
Benefield, R. (M)	1848	Collin				
Benson, James (S)	1848	Ellis				
Berry, Edward T. (S)	1848	Collin				
Bess, Lemuel (S)		Dallas—sld				
•Blevin, Wm. (S)		Dallas				
Boissonet, John Louis (S)		Ellis				
Bone, Azuriah (M)		Johnson				
Bone, Grigsby (S)		Grayson—sld				
Bone, John W. (S)		Cooke—sld				
Bone, Marcus (S)		Grayson—sld				
Boydstone, Wm. (S)		Denton—sld				
Bradford, Adam (S)		Tarrant—sld				
Bradford, James E. (M)		Tarrant—sld				
Britton, N. (M)		Denton				
•Brown, Allen W. (M)		Ellis—sld				
•Brown, Bryant (M)		Wichita—sld				
Burke, Evan H. (M)		Tarrant				
Casey, Harvey (S)		Dallas				

Name (Marital Status)	Yr/Mig	County			Illit.
Occupation; Age		County	Birth	Removal	Chld.
Casey, John (S)		Tarrant–sld			
Clark, Edward W. (S)		Tarrant–sld			
Clay, John (M)		Collin			
Collet, John (S)		Ellis			
Collins, Thomas (M)		Dallas			
Combs, Stephen (S)		Collin			
Coner, A. B. (M)		Tarrant–sld			
*Cooper, John H. (M)		Johnson–sld			
Crookes, Wm. E. (S)		Tarrant			
Dalton, J. N. (M)		Trockmorton–sld			
Deaver, Reuben H. (S)		Grayson–sld pt.			
Delaney, Dan (M)		Tarrant–sld			
Dooley, James (M)		Denton–sld			
Dooley, Wm. (S)		Tarrant–sld			
Edwards, Wm. (S)		Tarrant–sld			
Evans, Jonathon (M)		Denton			
Glaize, Ira (M)		Johnson–sld			
Guillot, P. Guilaume (S)		Palo Pinto			
Harris, James W. (S)		Johnson			
Hopkins, James A. (S)		Young & Archer			
Hopkins, John (M)		Palo Pinto			
Hopkins, Samuel B. (S)		Tarrant–sld			
Farmer; 40		Dallas	Tenn.	Mo.	
Horn, Mary (W)		Tarrant			
Horton, Robert (S)		Ellis			
Hunter, George (S)		Denton			
Jackson, W. J. (S)		Tarrant–sld			
Johnson, Mary (W)		Tarant			
Johnson, Wm. (M)		Dallas			
King, Edmund M. (S)		Tarrant–sld pt.			
King, John H. (S)		Denton			
*Kirk, John W. (S)		Dallas–sld			
Larremore, John (M)		Collin–sld			
Lee, A. J. (S)		Tarrant			
*Logsden, H. H. (M)		Ellis–sld			
*Logsden, Joseph (S)		Cooke–sld			
Lovejoy, John (S)		Grayson–sld			
Ludwick, George (S)		Dallas			
McClary, Patrick (M)		Dallas–sld			
McKinney, James A. (S)		Grayson–sld			
Marshall, Lewis M. (M)		Collin			
Martin, Joseph (S)		Tarrant			
Matson, Naoma Elizabeth (W)		Cooke–sld pt.			
May, Wm. C. (M)		Dallas–sld			
Medlin, Hall (M)		Tarrant–sld			
Medlin, Owen (M)		Tarrant–sld			
Medlin, Rachel (W)		Tarrant			
Montgomery, Stephen P. (M)		Dallas			

Name (Marital Status) Occupation; Age	Yr/Mig County	County	Birth	Removal	Illit. Chld.
Montgomery, Thomas (S)		Dallas—sld			
Moore, Benjamin L. (S)		Dallas			
Moutry, Garland F. (S)		Wise			
Newton, Harvey H. (M)		Dallas—sld			
Parker, Joseph R. (S)		Tarrant			
Patton, Andrew J. (S)		Johnson			
Prather, Ranson (S)		Denton			
Quillin, Wm. H. (S)		Cooke			
Reeves, Robert O. (M)		Cooke—sld Tarrant			
Richards, Frank (S)		Tarrant—sld			
Merchant; 21		Grayson	Tenn.	Tenn.	
*Richards, John (M)		Dallas—sld			
Riggs, James M. (M)		Ellis			
Roberts, Nancy (W)		Tarrant—sld			
Romine, Wm. (S)		Dallas			
Rovira, Juan (S)		Dallas			
Sackett, Thompson D. (S)		Dallas			
Salmons, James (M)		Palo Pinto			
Farmer; 63		Collin	Va. ?		
Sampson, Jonathon (M)		Dallas			
Self, Harbin (S)		Ellis			
Shacklett, Wm. (S)		Tarrant			
Slack, Harvey (S)		Grayson—sld			
Slayback, Ashton (M)		Ellis & Johnson			
Smith, Alfred M. (S)		Tarrant			
Smith, Joshua (S)		Parker			
Snow, Jeremiah (M)		Dallas & Parker—sld			
Stamps, Jason (M)		Grayson			
Stapp, Isaac Newton (S)		Tarrant—sld			
Stephens, Absalem (S)		Tarrant—sld			
Stephens, Andrew J. (S)		Tarrant—sld			
Strickland, D. C. (S)		Tarrant			
Thomas, James M. (M)		Grayson—sld Tarrant—sld			
Thomason, Wm. H. (S)		Collin—sld			
*Thompson, Thomas A. (S)		Tarrant			
*Thornhill, John (M)		Tarrant			
Throckmorton, James W. (M)		Young			
Physician; 28		Collin	Tenn.	Ill.	1
Throckmorton, Robert W. (S)		Tarrant—sld Parker—sld			
*Tucker, Wm. L. (S)		Tarrant—sld			
Vance, Mary (W)		Cooke—sld			
Wales, Francis M. (S)		Tarrant			
Wampler, David J. (S)		Ellis—sld			
*Warden, Hezekiah (M)		Ellis—sld			
Farmer; 45		Grayson	Ky.	Mo.	6
Warwick, Lydia Jane (W)		Tarrant—sld			
*Watson, Paul (M)		Dallas—sld			

Name (Marital Status) Occupation; Age	Yr/Mig	County County	Birth	Removal	Illit.	Chld.
Weatherford, Hardin (S)		Tarrant—sld				
Farmer; 16		Dallas	Ill.	Ill.		
Welch, Peter T. (S)		Tarrant—sld				
Wells, Philip T. (M)		Cooke—sld				
•Wheat, Wm. W. (M)		Tarrant—sld				
Farmer; 30		Grayson	Ala.	Ark.		5
Wilson, Robert (M)		Wise—sld Montague—sld				
Winniford, David (S)		Ellis				
Winniford, Wm. (S)		Dallas				
Zachary, T. G. (S)		Tarrant				

5. Persons issued county court certificates as colonist who did not receive land:

Name (Marital Status) Occupation; Age	Yr/Mig	County County	Birth	Removal	Illit.	Chld.
Aikman, A. A. (S)						
•Alexander, A. M. (M)						
Merchant; 30		Grayson	Ky.	Ky.		1
•Alexander, L. C. (S)						
Ayres, B. P. (S)						
Farmer; 49		Ellis	Ky.	Tenn.		5
Baird, James H. (M)						
Barnett, George W. (S)						
Merchant; 29		Collin	Ky.	Ky.		
•Beaty, Robert R. (M)						
Farmer; 40		Grayson	Tenn.	Tenn.		
•Beatty, Wm. C. (M)						
Benge, Wm. (S)						
Merchant; 30		Grayson	Tenn.	Tenn.		
•Blevins, C. N. (M)						
•Blevins, Duke (M)						
•Blevins, Esquire (M)						
•Blevins, Hough L. D. (M)						
Bryant, C. P. O. (S)						
Butridge, Riley E. (S)						
Canin, Lowrey (S)						
Capps, Jemima (S)						
•Capps, Wm. S. (S)						
Chambers, James (M)						
Chambers, Rebecca (W)						
Chapman, J. W. (M)						
Charvin, James (S)						
•Clark, Joseph (S)						
•Cockran, Edward (S)						
•Cockran, Wm. (S)						
•Coffey, Wm. (M)						
Farmer; 25		Collin	Ky.	Mo.	X	2
Collins, Thomas (S)						

Name (Marital Status) Occupation; Age	Yr/Mig County County	Birth	Removal	Illit. Chld.
*Cooper, N. B. (S)				
Crunshaw, Wm. (M)				
*Dye, Jacob (M)				
*Evans, B. J. (M)				
*Evans, John W. (S)				
Everard, T. (M)				
Fauset, James H. (M)				
Farmer; 30	Grayson	Ind.	Mo.	2
*Finch, W. A. J. (M)				
*Fletcher, J. R. (S)				
Flinchum, George W. (S)				
*Freeman, Wm. M. (S)				
French, Michael (M)				
Farmer; 20	Denton	Ohio	Ohio	
*Garrison, Wm. A. (S)				
Hackett, Wm. (S)				
Hambright, G. W. (S)				
Hardwicke, Richard (M)				
*Hartzog, Richard N. [M] (S)				
Hawood, Jonathon (S)				
Hawse, John H. (S)				
Farmer; 23	Denton	N. C.	N. C.	
Hearn, Wm. A. (S)				
*Helms, C. C. (S)				
*Helms, John A. (M)				
Hocklin, Wm. J. (M)				
Hoger, Benj. (M)				
Irby, D. H. (S)				
*Kirk, Isaac (S)				
*Kirk, Jacob (S)				
*Kirk, James (S)				
*Kirk, Lewis (S)				
*Kirk, Peter (M)				
*Kirk, Willis (S)				
Langley, James H. (S)				
Leake, Samuel (S)				
Levy, Henry (S)	? Ellis			
*Lovejoy, James H. (S)				
Farmer; 18	Collin	Ark.	Ark.	
McCary, P. T. (S)				
*McGlothlin, Wm. (M)				
Farmer; 36	Grayson	Ind.	Mo.	5
Martin, A. R. (S)				
Martin, Patrick P. (S)				
*Martin, Wm. N. (S)				
Moss, Joseph (M)				
Farmer; 29	Grayson	Ark.	Ark.	
Moutry, Wm. (M)				

Occupation; Age Name (Marital Status)	Yr/Mig	County County	Birth	Removal	Illit.	Chld.
Neely, Elcany (M)						
Pogard, Perry (M)						
Porter, W. W. (S)						
Trader; 32		Grayson	Tenn.	Tenn.		
Ralton, Thomas (M)						
*Reasonover, Early T. (M)						
*Reasonover, John (M)						
*Rutledge, Jamison (S)						
Sauge, Henri (S)						
*Savage, Hiram (M)						
R.P.M. Preacher; 44		Grayson	Ky.	Mo.		7
*Shipman, Jacob (S)						
Shultz, Valentine (S)						
*Shultz, Wade H. (S)						
Southward, James (S)						
*Steel, A. P. (S)						
Stutts, John (M)						
Farmer; 45		Grayson	N. C.	N. C.		4
*Thornhill, Achillis (M)						
*Tucker, Amos B. (S)						
*Watson, Josiah (S)						
Farmer; 30		Grayson	Ky.			
*Weever, S. C. (S)						
Webb, Henry T. (S)						
Welch, John						
*Wells, Nelson (M)						
Wooten, W. R. (S)				END		